FOR *the* RIGHT REASONS

FOR *the* RIGHT REASONS

America's Favorite Bachelor
on Faith, Love, Marriage,
and Why Nice Guys Finish First

SEAN LOWE

WITH NANCY FRENCH

NELSON
BOOKS

An Imprint of Thomas Nelson

Published in Nashville, Tennessee, by Nelson Books, an imprint of Thomas Nelson. Nelson Books and Thomas Nelson are registered trademarks of HarperCollins Christian Publishing, Inc.

Published in association with Stéphanie Abou, Foundry Literary+Media, 33 West 17th Street, PH, New York, NY 10011.

Interior designed by Mallory Perkins.

Thomas Nelson, Inc., titles may be purchased in bulk for educational, business, fundraising, or sales promotional use. For information, please e-mail SpecialMarkets@ ThomasNelson.com.

Unless otherwise noted, Scripture quotations are taken from the *Holy Bible*, New Living Translation, copyright © 1996, 2004, 2007 by Tyndale House Foundation. Used by permission of Tyndale House Publishers, Inc., Carol Stream, IL 60188. All rights reserved.

Scripture quotations marked ESV are taken from THE ENGLISH STANDARD VERSION. © 2001 by Crossway Bibles, a division of Good News Publishers.

The names and identifying characteristics of some individuals have been changed to protect their privacy.

Library of Congress Cataloging-in-Publication Data

Lowe, Sean, 1983-
  For the right reasons : America's favorite bachelor on faith, love, marriage, and why nice guys finish first / Sean Lowe with Nancy French.
      pages cm
  Includes bibliographical references and index.
  1. Lowe, Sean, 1983- 2. Bachelor (Television program) 3. Television personalities--United States--Biography. I. French, Nancy. II. Title.
  PN1992.4.L72A3 2014
  791.4502'8092--dc23
  [B]

2014023723

Printed in the United States of America

15 16 17 18 19 RRD 6 5 4 3

To my beautiful wife, Catherine:
Your love, encouragement, and friendship
inspire me to be better than I am.

CONTENTS

PROLOGUE

I'd been kidnapped.

I was stuck in the back of the Suburban, and my heart was about to pound out of my chest. Several emotions swirled inside me—anger, embarrassment, hurt. But mostly, I felt shock.

I'd just been dumped.

Of course, everyone experiences heartbreak in life. If I had been back home in Texas, I would've gone to the gym, grabbed some weights, and worked my way through it. When I get angry or upset, I need some space.

But I was hardly alone.

I was in a vehicle with a driver, cameramen, and two producers—all of them watching my every move. And they weren't going to let me out of there without talking.

To make matters worse, this moment would soon be broadcast to millions of viewers across the nation as they tuned in for season 8 of *The Bachelorette*. The show is a spin-off of ABC's dating game show, *The Bachelor*, which debuted in 2002. It goes like this: one pretty, available woman dates twenty-five eligible bachelors—sometimes on group dates, sometimes on one-on-one dates, and sometimes on the dreaded two-on-one dates. Will her future husband be in that group? The people at home watch eagerly as she gets to know the men and sends them home, one by one. As the weeks progress, the choices get harder. Eventually, she meets the parents of the remaining few bachelors on hometown dates, chooses whether to get even more acquainted with them on overnight dates, and—if all goes as planned—gets engaged on the show.

My sister and brother-in-law were the ones who encouraged me to get in to all this. They submitted my name to the show, helped me make my audition video, and even bought me a tailored suit. (The guys on *The Bachelorette* have to buy their own clothes, and I definitely didn't have the funds to splurge on an expensive suit.)

People come from all walks of life, and it's interesting to see how everybody gets along in the house. Of course, the ultimate criticism of contestants is that they didn't come on the show "for the right reasons." For example, in season 5 of *The Bachelorette*, the "singing cowboy" Wes Hayden made it to the final four even though it was said he had a girlfriend back home. Apparently, it took Jillian Harris awhile to figure out he was there to promote his music career. In season 6, there was the infamous wrestler who had a girlfriend back home. In fact, it was rumored he had two! Then, in season 7, episode 3, a guy named Bentley admitted to the camera he fantasized about a different bachelorette and then called his season's potential wife an "ugly duckling."

Presumably the only "right reason" for going on *The Bachelorette* is to find true love. As terrible as the lies and deception in the above examples are, I guess I might as well admit it now: I didn't go on the show "for the right reasons" either.

I went on the show to meet fun people, travel to interesting places, and then get on with my life back in Dallas with a few good stories to tell. And, in fact, I did travel. I proclaimed my love for Emily Maynard in London's Hyde Park, I ran through the streets of Prague to get a few extra minutes with her, and I ended up on the island of Curaçao, located in the southern Caribbean Sea just off the coast of Venezuela.

No, I didn't go on the show to get married.

But before you judge me, wouldn't it be a little crazy to think your path to the altar might go through a reality TV show?

I was as surprised as anyone that I fell so hard for Emily and made it all the way to the last rose ceremony. It came down to me and two other guys:

bad-boy, racecar driver Arie Luyendyk and entrepreneurial do-gooder Jef Holm. Even though I had stiff competition, I was convinced Emily would choose me.

There was something about the show's atmosphere that fostered romance: candlelight, exotic locales, and producers telling me there was an obvious connection between us. Plus, I wasn't able to communicate with friends and family back home after the producers made us give up our cell phones, tablets, and laptops. (I heard on set that former bachelor Brad Womack somehow got a phone toward the end of filming his season, contacted his old girlfriend, and convinced her to give him another chance. That season ended up without a proposal for either of the final contestants.) Because I had no contact with the outside world, I was either *with* Emily or *thinking about* Emily. I had already considered what I'd say when I was down on one knee. I would think about my life with her and wonder what it would be like to become an instant dad to her daughter. Never, in all my daydreaming, did it cross my mind she'd send me home.

But on that night, in a picturesque Caribbean locale, she did just that. I was riding away from Emily for a final time.

<hr />

It's sometimes called "the limo ride of shame," but I was in a black Suburban. This is the time after every rose ceremony when the rejected bachelor gets to react to the news of his elimination. It's usually a desperate moment, with crying and blame. But this felt different from every other ride I'd witnessed from the comfort of home, and not just because it was happening to me.

First, I wasn't the only person who thought Emily and I would end up together. The producer assigned to me, Scott Westerman, was supposed to ask me probing questions on the ride. But he was completely choked up. So was another producer with whom I'd grown close, Jonah Quinn. He may have had a glass of wine too many, but he was also bawling.

Second, the ride was unusually long. Getting to my hotel should've taken about ten minutes, but we were still rolling after half an hour. That's when I realized the producers intended to drive until they got good footage. After all, we were making a reality television show. It might have felt like a breakup to me, but my heartbreak was ratings gold.

"Sure is a long way to the hotel," I joked when I realized they had effectively kidnapped me. In spite of it all, everyone laughed. I definitely wasn't mad at them. They had made my time on *The Bachelorette* a real pleasure. I was touched everyone seemed to be taking it so hard. It sort of made my heartache seem justified. I hadn't imagined the connection between Emily and me, had I? No, I could tell by my cameraman's face that we'd all gotten blindsided.

In our conversations, Emily always flattered me. She'd said I was a "nice guy" and that I was "good." Even more, she frequently used the word *perfect* to describe me. She said I was perfect in every way—that I possessed the qualities any woman would want in a husband. When she went on my hometown date, she met my two dogs, who are admittedly very well behaved, and said, "Even your dogs are perfect."

That was just one of the not-so-subtle hints that made me think we were destined for each other. Another was that—in spite of what the viewing public saw at home—I did see the inside of Emily's "fantasy suite," but more on that later. What I'm trying to say is that I was shocked when Emily called out Arie's name instead of mine.

The producers had taken out the Suburban's middle row to accommodate the cameramen and staff who would take this final trip with me. The cameras were positioned about three feet from my face. This production team had been together for ten weeks, and I had grown very close to them all. But the last thing I wanted to do was spill my heart to the cameras.

I put my hand on my face and didn't speak. As the Suburban wound through the island, I went through the evening in my head. *What did I do wrong? Didn't Emily give me every indication that we'd spend the rest of our lives together?*

"Sean," one of the producers gently said. "What's going through your mind?"

There I was, in a moment that would be televised to millions, in the unenviable position of explaining one of the worst moments of my life.

"It hurts," I said. "A lot." I could tell they needed more for the cameras, for the viewing audience at home, so I went on. "A lot more than I can probably describe. I've had all week to think about this. Never did I think I'd go home. All week, my thoughts were consumed with being a father, being a husband."

"Why do you think it hurts so much, Sean?" the producer prompted. I could tell he didn't want to be asking me these questions almost as much as I didn't want to answer. Almost.

"I want to love someone with every ounce of my being," I said sadly before looking out the window.

At the time, considering Emily had kept bad-boy Arie, I couldn't help but shake the feeling that nice guys finish last. Somehow my image of being "good" and "perfect" seemed to hurt my chances for true love.

Of course, that ride of shame was not the end of the story.

If you watch *The Bachelor* or *The Bachelorette*, you know everyone is on a *journey*. That word is thrown around on the show a great deal, even more than the phrase *the right reasons*. But this book is about the very real journeys we all have to take. More times than not, our personal journeys are big disappointments. If you've lived long enough, you've learned the hard lessons of life: being good is right, but it's not enough; betrayal is so commonplace it's almost expected; and that thing called perfection is a cruel myth.

But I've learned a few things from my two seasons on the hottest romance shows on television. I've learned that good does eventually win, that lies will be discovered, and that nice guys do ultimately finish first.

So, together, let's take a trip toward life, joy, and—yes—love.

one

THE GUY
WITH POTENTIAL

"What if we transferred you to Lamar?"

My spoon filled with Cinnamon Toast Crunch paused, halfway between my bowl and my mouth, and I looked at him. It was a Sunday morning, I was a junior in high school, and I was scarfing down a breakfast of champions. My mom and sister were getting ready for church.

I should've been surprised that my dad had suggested such a thing. He is so stable that we'd lived in the same house on Woodenrail Lane since I was two, we'd never changed phone numbers, and we'd sat in the same pew at the same church my entire life.

But there were two things my dad loved more than stability.

Me and football. Almost always in that order.

When I was seven years old, he signed me up in a community peewee league. I'll never forget walking onto the field that first day, knowing nothing about the game. My coach taught us how to throw the ball and how to run for a touchdown. It was basic stuff, but I thought it was fun to hang out with my friends, and I grew to love the sport. Some of my fondest memories happened while tossing the ball with a neighbor before my mom called me to dinner. On Friday nights when my sister was in high school, we'd go to the football games, and I'd stand behind the end zone imagining what it'd be like to play under those lights. I dreamed of being in the players' cleats and wondered if I'd be tough enough to withstand my own bumps and bruises.

As much as I enjoyed playing football, my dad loved me being on the team and was thrilled I had a knack for it.

By the time I got to Irving High School, a Class 5A school with two thousand students, I'd gotten pretty good. When I was in tenth grade, I was one of two sophomores to start on varsity. I loved being a Tiger, going to the pep rallies, and helping my team win games in front of a loud home crowd. When I was a junior, colleges began actively recruiting me. Then my coach moved me to defensive end, and it threw me off-kilter. Defensive ends are usually big, sometimes 275 or 280 pounds. I was only 180 pounds, and maintaining that weight was full-time work. I'd take two sandwiches to school every day, along with protein shakes. I ate constantly and drank weight-gain shakes every chance I could. My frame just couldn't maintain enough weight to make me a good defensive end.

After every game, I was frustrated. "If I want to get a scholarship to a good school," I told my dad, "I need to be a linebacker. It's what I know . . . what I'm good at doing."

It was halfway through the year, and I'd been wearing Irving's black and gold for my entire high school career. I had a schedule, friends, and—honestly—a lot of fun at Irving High School. However, I couldn't shake the feeling that my new field position was going to limit my college choices.

That's why my dad brought up the far-fetched idea of transferring schools. Irving was the only home I'd ever known. More than just a Dallas suburb, we were a community in our own right, a community that loved football. In fact, our town hosted the Dallas Cowboys in our notable Texas Stadium with its iconic hole in the roof. Originally the roof was supposed to be retractable, but the engineers had misjudged how much weight it could bear. Instead, they left it open, which caused all kinds of problems—and jokes. People said the hole existed so God could watch his favorite team.

We lived about three miles away from that landmark, in a modest neighborhood. Mom never let me sit inside playing video games like some of my friends. "Go outside and play," she'd say. My friends and I played basketball, football, and anything else every day until dinner. My sister, Shay, had graduated from Irving High in 2000 and was living with us as she attended college. Dad operated his State Farm office on MacArthur Boulevard. And we attended Plymouth Park Baptist Church every time the doors were open.

I had a strong lineage of Christian believers. My grandfather, a pastor, had the entire New Testament memorized. He baptized me when I was eight years old.

"I take Jesus into my heart," I said before my grandfather plunged me into the cool water. Looking back, I'm not sure I really understood those words. I knew I shouldn't lie, cheat, or steal, but I'm not sure I was quite old enough to understand fully what it meant to be a Christian. It didn't hit me until a few years later, when I was at Latham Springs Camp and Retreat Center. We had scheduled events during the day—recreational time when we played softball and kickball, followed by group activities.

One night, the camp brought in a guest speaker who stood at the front of what was probably a pretty smelly group of kids. His message cut through the excitement of camp and washed all over me. It's hard to recall the details of that night, but I vividly remember I cried at the thought of Jesus and his sacrifice for me. The gospel wasn't about the fact that my parents were churchgoers or that I could—sometimes—make it through the day without lying or being mean to my sister. This is what sank in that day: I messed up all the time, but Jesus lived a perfect life. He loved me so much that he was willing to pay the penalty for the things I'd done wrong. He did that by dying on the cross. That meant I was forgiven. The cost had been paid. I was saved.

As he spoke, I felt forgiveness—and joy—wash over me. At the end of his talk, the guest speaker gave an invitation for us to come forward to commit our lives to God. As a sixth grader, I made my way out of my metal folding chair and went forward. Tears streamed down my face.

So I've known God pretty much all my life. Even when some of my friends veered off course during high school, I still believed. It's interesting that Dad posed the question about switching high schools on a Sunday morning.

Sometimes you forget God is always there, nudging you in certain directions and planning good things for your future.

———

If I did transfer to Lamar, it would be a big change for my whole family. Lamar had a thousand more students than Irving. We'd have to move into a different school district, which would affect my dad's commute to work and my sister's drive to college. But mostly it would affect my mother. An interior designer, my mom had made our house into her little kingdom, and she made sure it was as beautiful and comfortable as possible. Did it make sense to uproot my family because of high school football? I looked at my dad standing in the door, and he seemed serious.

"Really?" I asked.

Dad nodded.

"Sure," I said before stuffing the cereal into my mouth and taking a gulp of orange juice.

And that was that. Looking back, I'm not sure why I didn't question this decision more. People sometimes pray more for parking spaces than I prayed about leaving my school a year and a half before graduation.

My parents put the house on the market. I was excited about the future and eager to get established in Lamar's football program. Of course, that didn't stop me from being a little choked up as I stuffed my clothes into a cardboard box and took down my Michael Jordan poster and my mini hoop. We found a new place to live within the school district—a temporary townhouse about fifteen minutes away from Lamar. Mom, I now realize, must've hated trading our home for a townhouse, but she never let on that she had been inconvenienced.

———

I remember walking through the front doors on my first day that spring semester and wondering, *How will I ever feel comfortable here?* People teemed through the hallways wearing the navy and gold of their Viking mascot, chatting at their lockers, and laughing in the halls. I ducked my head, studied the printout of my new schedule, struggled to find my classes, and couldn't figure out the lock on my locker. But even worse was the looming noon hour.

Lunch is the worst part of high school. I had to make some immediate decisions: *Who am I going to sit with? Where should I sit?* I had to think fast on the walk from class to the cafeteria, and even faster once I walked through the double doors and checked out the scene. I needed to have a plan or else I'd end up sitting in the wrong spot and be forever isolated, drinking milk out of a carton by myself all year. Since I'd missed an entire semester, students had already settled in to their groups. Would there be a place for me?

Then I realized something awesome. Lamar students could leave campus for lunch.

"Hey, Mimi," I said into my cell phone on the way to class. Mimi and Papa, my dad's parents, live near the school. "Want some company for lunch today?"

She was thrilled that I stopped by, and I—avoiding the lunchroom as much as possible—went there every single day. Eventually, I made friends at school, and Mimi welcomed them all with a smile and big plates of fried chicken and fried okra. She also made sure they never saw the bottom of their glasses of sweet tea. Those were the perfect meals, because I was trying to get bigger. On days Mimi didn't cook, Papa bought me two foot-long steak subs from Subway and asked me to step on his scale to see how much weight I'd gained. Everyone loved Mimi and Papa, and they loved my group of friends.

◆———◆

One of the advantages of spending more time with my grandparents was that I got to be around a marriage that has lasted more than sixty years.

Papa, a World War II veteran, married Mimi when she was only nineteen years old and he was twenty-one. Now Mimi has white hair, and Papa has lost most of his. However, it's wonderful to see them interact after all these years of matrimony.

"Papa," I once asked him, "do you believe Mimi is your soul mate?"

He looked at me a little funny. To him, the phrase *soul mate* was hippie language. "Well, I'll tell you this. I think men have the ability to be good husbands or not. I don't think there's this one magical person out there for you. Proverbs 18:22 tells us, 'The man who finds a wife finds a treasure, and he receives favor from the LORD.' Note that the Word doesn't say, 'the man who finds that certain someone.' It's less specific than that. You find a wife, you get favor from God. It's not all that complicated."

"Well, you found Mimi."

"There were other women before Mimi."

At this, I almost laughed. My grandparents had been together so long, it was hard for me to imagine Papa existing before Mimi.

"And I think I could've made it work with one of them too," Papa said. "So, no. I don't believe in that soul-mate stuff."

I wasn't sure about the idea of love anyway. In high school, I had lots of friends, went on plenty of dates, and was the type of guy girls' parents loved. Of course, my dating in high school consisted of walking together between classes and driving girls to the movies in my first truck, a '97 Ford F-150. Though I was just getting familiar with the idea of girls and dating, I knew I had excellent role models in my own family for lifelong love.

———

I fit right in with the new Viking team at Lamar. My coach, Eddy Peach, had been the football coach since the school opened, and so had his offensive coordinator, Coach Jones, and defensive coordinator, Coach Ward. They were the coaching team during the 1970s, when my dad was a player. Lamar had a legendary football program and a playoff streak that had lasted four-teen consecutive years. (Oddly enough, the year I played we missed the playoffs.) The coaches were godly men and were quite a contrast to the screaming, yelling, and cussing coaches I'd left. As the first Texas coach to win three hundred games at the Class 5A level, Coach Peach knew the game. He put me as the school's starting linebacker, where I thrived for the rest of my high school career.

By the time I graduated, I was ranked fifty-second among inside line-backers across the entire nation by Rivals.com, was a member of the *Dallas Morning News* All-Area Team, was listed in the *Fort Worth Star-Telegram*'s top seventy-five prospects, and was Lamar's most valuable defensive player. In my senior year, I had ninety-six tackles and four sacks. As a "three-star athlete," several colleges were interested in me, but I narrowed it down to Oklahoma State, University of Arkansas, and Kansas State. In the spring of 2002, I accepted a scholarship to Kansas State.

My family's decision to transfer me to Lamar was a big risk. I'm glad my parents had the guts to do it. In fact, it was a moment that shaped the person I was to become. Before then, risk taking was not a common Lowe activity—still isn't, to be honest.

But something changed in me while I was eating Cinnamon Toast Crunch that Sunday. My dad, by asking a simple question, taught me an important lesson. He'd already instilled in me the virtue of being even-tempered and steady. But that morning, he showed me what it looks like to put aside fear, to risk comfort, and to dive in headfirst to a new adventure.

It was a lesson I'd use later in life: sometimes the right path might seem like a really crazy move.

And in the fall, I had another move to make.

—⁂—

"How many towels does a guy need?" I asked my mom, pointing to a stack Dad was loading into the back of our car.

"You can't blame me for wanting you to be clean, can you?" Mom asked.

"No, but we might need a third car just to bring all this stuff," I said, looking at the bags and boxes we had to load. "Or an extra dorm room."

"Okay, I think I've got just enough space for the mini fridge here," Dad said, making room in the Tahoe before slamming down the hatch. Mom had apparently been preparing for this moment all summer—physically, if not emotionally.

"Do I really need these?" I asked, holding up a pair of flip-flops.

"You never know how filthy the shower might be," she said.

"Maybe I should explain to Sean what this is." Shay held up a bottle of laundry detergent.

"How would you know?" I asked.

The worried expression on my mom's face indicated that she doubted I could handle the pressures and demands of college, but I knew I was ready.

"I guess that's it," Dad said as he stuffed the last bag into the vehicle and wiped his hands on his pants.

I took one last look at our home—the place where I shot many basketball hoops and tossed many footballs with friends—grabbed my keys, and jumped into the driver's seat toward a new life. Mom and Shay rode together in the car behind Dad and me. For the next eight hours, we drove—through the city of Dallas, the lowlands of Oklahoma, and the Flint Hills of Kansas. You know that song "Home on the Range"? Whoever wrote it was probably imagining buffalo roaming in an area like the gently rolling acres of Kansas tallgrass prairie.

As the miles passed, I wondered what it would be like to be a part of the Kansas State team. In my experience, football teams had been, in a way, like a family. At least that's what I'd felt at Irving High and then Lamar. Would a Big 12 college program have the same kind of vibe? Would I be able to hang with the other guys? I'd been recruited as a strongside linebacker. K-State's previous three were drafted into the NFL. Would I be next?

Dad and I talked about football much of the way, and I assumed Mom and Shay were talking about my sister's recent heartbreak. She had broken up with a guy she had dated for years, but she seemed to be in good spirits that day. I was proud of her. She took at least eighteen credit hours each semester, sold insurance while working another job, and studied all the time. Ever since she and her long-term boyfriend split up, Shay had been more serious than usual. I hoped things would look up for her soon, but our family wasn't the type that sat around and talked about the details of our romantic lives.

"Sean," Dad said as we neared the school. His voice cracked just a tad. "When you're in college, things will be different." Dad might've been driving me to college, but he wasn't finished being my dad. "Remember . . . you're going to be *in* the world, but you don't have to be *of* the world."

I looked through my windshield at Manhattan—a small city tucked away in the northeastern part of Kansas, known as the Little Apple.

Just a couple of months earlier, I'd gone to the bigger version of Manhattan—the one in New York—where my team was doing preseason training and conditioning. Immediately, I noticed my new teammates were huge, a reality check for someone who'd always been the big man on campus. There's a major difference between an eighteen-year-old kid just arriving from high school and a twenty-two-year-old man who has been in the university weight program for a few years.

K-State's training program was more intense than anything I'd ever seen. In New York, the summer workouts were led by the strength and conditioning team, and we'd run 7-on-7 in the evenings. It gave me a chance to learn the fundamentals of their defense and get to know the team. The upperclassmen had known one another for a long time and had a casual comfort with each other. They loved to make sure the freshmen always knew our place as the new guys: sit down and shut up! But one guy—Andrew, who was the captain of the team and probably six foot five—was kind to us when we showed up to train for our abbreviated two-week period. He was a senior, an All-American defensive end, and he treated even the lowly freshmen with respect.

"What are you doing for the Fourth of July?" I asked him one afternoon as I was preparing to go home.

"More of this," Andrew said, motioning to the downtown gym designated for our training.

"Why don't you come with me to Dallas?" I asked. "My family always gets together for holidays." I wasn't exaggerating. We get together with aunts, uncles, grandparents, cousins, you-name-it for almost every imaginable holiday.

To my surprise, he took me up on it. He threw some stuff in a bag and drove all the way to my hometown.

"I was bored," he told me as he got out of his car and unloaded his bags onto our driveway.

This, to me, was what was cool about being a part of a collegiate football team—spontaneous friendships, new adventures. One of my buddies threw a Fourth of July party at his ranch, so I took Andrew to show him a good Texas time. We shot fireworks and basically acted like teenagers. It was a great weekend.

———————

Kansas State University is located east of the junction of the Kansas River and the Big Blue River, and we were getting close.

"This is about as far away from New York City as you can get," I said, noticing the town's laid-back, Western feel. A young couple slowly walked their dog in front of us at a red light, and Dad consulted the map. The closer we got to the university, the more things began looking purple. Grocery stores advertised back-to-school deals for K-State students, gigantic purple balloons flew high above car dealerships, and some of the old cars on the road were seemingly held together with purple pride bumper stickers.

When we finally drove up on the campus, I found the dorm I'd be living in for the next few weeks. It was August, and the football team was arriving three weeks before the regular students. As much as I hated giving up my summer, I was relieved to get settled before everyone else. Being part of a team made the transition to college a little easier. By the time all the other nervous freshmen arrived, hopefully I'd already feel like I belonged.

"Mom, you really outdid yourself," I said, my arms full of Target bags.

"Gotta take care of my baby boy."

I groaned at those two words. "I'm *eighteen*, Mom."

She smiled and shoved a bag in my chest. "Well, make yourself useful, then, and carry this up to your new room."

After a long day of moving, we said a tearful good-bye. As I watched my family drive away, I was glad to have some breathing room—five hundred miles of it, to be precise. I was the youngest in the family, so it's natural Mom doted on me. By the time I was towering over her, I resented that she treated me like a kid.

I was responsible enough to earn a free ride to college, after all. And not to just any college. I was a Kansas State University athlete, which meant I had the honor of playing under one of the best college football coaches of all time, Bill Snyder. When he came to Kansas State in 1988, he inherited a program that easily had the most losses of any team in Division I-A at the time. *Sports Illustrated* called K-State "America's most hapless team."[1] In ten years under Coach Snyder's leadership, Kansas State had an undefeated regular 1998 season and earned its first-ever number one ranking in the national polls.

That's why the entire community was so supportive of the Wildcats. After years of having an abysmal program, they didn't take Coach Snyder's success for granted. Most of the locals were somehow connected to the university—either through employment or attendance—so it was hard to go anywhere in town without being reminded of our team. Wildcat gear could be found everywhere. Preachers wore Wildcat ties, girls wore purple bows, guys wore K-State jackets, and I even saw a baby wearing a onesie that read "I Drool Purple." Plus, as a part of the Big 12 Conference, the games would be broadcast nationally every week.

Every time I felt this excitement, I remembered: I was a part of the team. It was a little heady.

———

The players were required to stay together as a team before school started, even the upperclassmen who had the privilege of living off campus during the school year. Before we put on the pads, before we started training, and before we could take one step onto the gridiron, we met together in the dorms. Everyone laughed and joked about their misadventures in New York that summer. It was great to see everyone—including Andrew.

"If you need any help finding anything on campus," he offered, "just let me know."

The next day, the team's intense practices began. These would help determine who'd start and in what position. I was redshirted my first year, which meant I practiced, lifted weights, and watched films with the team, but I didn't play in games. That gave me a year to grow without losing a year of eligibility. The coaches hoped I'd eventually be a starting linebacker, so they were willing to wait to let me become more seasoned.

The summer training session was the first time I got to see Coach Snyder in action. During the season, he ate one meal a day to save time, slept only four or five hours per night, and always wore Nike Cortez tennis shoes. (He wore the same type of tennis shoes for two decades and hoarded dozens of pairs when Nike stopped making them.) That meant his shoes—as well as his work ethic—were a blast from the past. He made us wipe our feet before we walked into the athletic complex, wouldn't tolerate earrings, made sure everyone's facial hair was neatly trimmed, and always had a mug of hot coffee during our intensely long practices. They lasted three hours—Monday through Wednesday—and we did them in full pads.

Old school.

Every morning, my alarm went off at five thirty to lift weights at six. (Pretty soon, I was as strong as an ox and no longer intimidated by my teammates.) My business classes started at eight o'clock, but it was sometimes hard to pay attention to my professor after such an intense morning workout. In high school, I made all As and was in the National Honor Society. But in college, I could tell I'd really have to buckle down and study. At two thirty in the afternoon, I'd head back to the football complex and work out until four. That's when Coach Snyder would walk in, pop in the tape of our most recent game, and settle in to his chair with remote control in hand. He'd evaluate a single toss from our previous game for five minutes. After we watched ourselves and learned from our mistakes, we moved on to watching films of our upcoming opponents.

Then we ate at the training table until seven o'clock. Because the university had so much invested in us eating the right balance of carbs and protein, they provided us with a smorgasbord of options. They told us what we ate was as important as how much we could lift. But that didn't stop me from eating just about everything in sight. I'm not built to be a huge guy, so I had to eat all the time to bulk up for the season. My teammates with big frames were naturally formidable on the field. Since I was smaller, I set my goal weight at 240 pounds. Our coaches didn't monitor our diets, so I'd pile my plate full of chicken fried steak and pizza. Sometimes I'd eat pasta five times a day. After dinner, we had a mandatory study hall from eight to ten. Every second of my life was scheduled from five thirty in the morning until ten o'clock at night.

I loved football and everything that came with it. Anytime I was introduced by people, they'd say, "This is Sean. He plays football at K-State." It was flattering, but I wanted to be more than a jock. I always envisioned myself as a businessman or some sort of entrepreneur.

The only problem was that I couldn't quite make myself go to bed after my mandatory study halls. There were so many fun things to do. If guys weren't knocking on my door or blaring music in the rooms next to mine, I'd come up with other distractions. Frequently I'd flip on the television and get interested in whatever was on. *Seinfeld* reruns were always good, but it didn't even have to be interesting to seem better than sleep. Something like a PBS program about African wildebeests would ensnare me until late into the night. What would happen when the wildebeest got locked in an epic battle against the lions? I had to find out.

I rolled out of bed for my six o'clock weightlifting session after going to sleep at three. With Coach Synder, skipping anything football related was not an option. But after an intense lifting session on so little sleep, it was hard to prioritize that eight o'clock class.

Thankfully, Andrew was always a great influence on me. The guy was really competitive on the football field, and one of the most disciplined people I've ever met. He was a great example of taking advantage of every opportunity that came his way, doing well on the field and in the classroom.

———————

Even though I was redshirted and wouldn't be playing my freshman year, my family drove the eight hours to see the first game of my college career—K-State versus Western Kentucky. I loved that my big sister was excited that her little brother was a part of something as big as KSU football.

At about the sixth hour on the road, though, I think she lost her enthusiasm. Apparently, that's when she leaned up from the backseat and told our parents, "I'm just letting you know this now: the odds of me going back for any of Sean's other games are slim to none!"

That was before she bumped into Andrew after the game. They'd met earlier when he spontaneously came to visit us in Texas over the summer, and I could tell she was happy to see him again.

"Andrew seems like a nice guy," my mom, the matchmaker, said to me on the phone a few days later. "What do you think of getting him to ask out Shay?"

Andrew *was* great. He was outspoken about his faith, treated people with respect, and was one of the only guys who reached out to help me adjust to college life. He created a sense of brotherhood on the team by pulling pranks and giving nicknames. He also rode on a tiny yellow scooter all over campus because he wanted to save his energy for practices. I always laughed when I saw the big six-foot-five guy on that microscopic scooter.

Come to think of it, he was exactly the type of guy I'd want my sister to date. And evidently, Shay was just the type of girl he wanted to date.

He proposed to Shay five months later. I was thrilled for both of them. Shay is awesome—even though I've spent most of my life aggravating her—and I knew they'd be happy together. Plus, I'd always get credit for introducing them.

———————

My second year, while still technically a freshman, I tried to make my presence known on the team. I'd had a year to grow and get stronger from the university's weight program and our infamous practices. Playing for Coach Snyder helped me learn the true meaning of self-discipline, leadership, and hard work. Those things didn't come naturally, but I was ready to see what I could do.

Our co-defensive coordinator at the time was Coach Brett Bielema. As our linebacker coach, he seemed to like me and recognize my potential. I played quite a bit as a freshman, which is fairly rare at that level. I even started a game against Baylor because the guy in front of me had gotten hurt. It was a big opportunity for me.

Also, I played on all the special teams, which included kickoff, kickoff return, punt, and punt return. That was also rare for a freshman.

✦——————✦

When my alarm jarred me awake before the sun rose, I should've bounded out of bed, grabbed a shower, and told myself this: "Okay, I'm gonna embrace the day. This is gonna be really hard, but I'll get better today."

That's what Coach Snyder would've said. That's what my dad would've said.

Instead, I pressed the snooze button.

I rarely went to class. Before test days, I'd stay up all night and try to memorize as much information from the textbook—since I had no notes—as I possibly could. Then, during the actual exams—regrettably—I sat next to my friends, and we'd share answers while the professors weren't looking. I was still a Christian, of course, but I admit I failed to live out some of my principles during college. Because I was raised a strict Baptist, I didn't drink alcohol or sleep around. My girl-crazy teammates made fun of me for being a virgin, and I'm sure I was a walking contradiction. I was a guy who didn't drink or sleep around but was perfectly fine skipping classes and cheating on tests.

I rationalized it. Football was my passion, and it was a full-time job.

Through cramming and cheating, I figured I could get decent enough grades to keep my focus on sports. My days were so long and physically exhausting, I figured I had nothing left over for studying. Plus, how could I go to class and do homework when we were on the road?

For the first time in my life, I did as little as possible to get by. This attitude seeped in to other areas of life. During practice, I went through the motions so I could go back to my apartment to watch more television. I had never before been characterized by laziness. Looking back, I might have just been immature. As much as I had wanted Mom to treat me like a man, I realized being on my own was a bit overrated. Now that I was trying to balance this tough schedule, I understood how much my parents' presence had really grounded me.

So I was hovering on the edge. If I leaned in one direction, I could get a lot of rest, go out at night, have a great time in college, and blow the chance of a lifetime. If I leaned in the other, I could be the starting linebacker for a Division I, Big 12 school and possibly have a career in the NFL.

I knew which way I had to go, and my coaches did everything to help.

"You've got potential," Coach Bielema encouraged me one day during practice at the beginning of my sophomore year. "Just keep working and this could be your year!"

Okay, so maybe he said that a little more harshly and with a lot more profanity. But that was the sentiment, and it was just what I needed to hear. As a kid, I dreamed of making it all the way to the college level in football, and this was my chance. I set my eyes on the goal and was pleased when I got some good playing time.

⊢———⧫———⊣

Then Coach Bielema made an announcement that he was leaving Kansas State for Wisconsin. (He'd later move to Arkansas, where he is currently the head coach of the Razorbacks.) His replacement was a defensive coach named Chris Cosh, who came from South Carolina. As soon as he started coaching us, he was always on me. I'm not sure whether he missed the potential Coach Bielema saw in me, or whether he was the only one who could see my lack of effort clearly.

During the first game of the season, I played miserably. Just awful. Coach Cosh yanked me out of the game at halftime, and I never started again.

In fact, I didn't play much at all that year.

I really wanted to play football. Not only had I dreamed about this opportunity my whole life but it also meant a lot to my family. I can't tell you how many conversations with my dad related to football as a kid. Though my parents didn't push me in athletics, they gave up sleeping in on Saturdays to take me to Pop Warner youth football, drove thousands of miles across the state to watch me play high school football, and flew across America to see my college games. Dad somehow managed to mention I played for K-State in his daily conversations. He'd talk about me to his friends and even brag to complete strangers. "These grapes are a gorgeous color," he might tell an unsuspecting cashier. "Know what else is purple? Kansas State. My son plays football up there, ya know."

I couldn't imagine a worse feeling than not being able to play.

Pretty soon, I wouldn't have to imagine.

During Christmas break, I was home relaxing when my mom handed me a huge stack of mail she'd collected while I'd been gone.

"Here's some pleasant reading," she said. The pile was a mixture of Christmas cards and junk mail, but I paused when I saw a letter from the Kansas State School of Business.

"Dear Sean Lowe," it read. I almost put it in the junk-mail pile because it looked like a form letter. "I regret to inform you that . . ."

I grabbed the letter with both hands and quickly looked over the document. I couldn't believe my eyes. Apparently, my GPA had fallen below the required 2.5 minimum for the program.

How could that be? I wondered. *I'm not the type of guy who gets bad grades. I'm an all-A student, right?*

As I held the letter, shame came over me.

I wasn't good enough at academics. I wasn't good enough at football. Apparently, I wasn't even good enough at cheating!

I had to force my eyes to read all the way to the bottom of the letter, which was from the dean of Kansas State University's Business School.

K-State had asked me to leave the business program.

Embarrassed, I decided to try to salvage what was left of my football career. After all, I'd given up on my classes so I could play football. Now I wasn't even playing. Even though I hadn't been putting forth the effort, I still felt like I should be on the field. But Coach Cosh wouldn't put me in. That's when I decided to appeal to a higher power.

"Coach Snyder," I said one day after walking down the narrow hall to his office in the Vanier Football Complex, "do you have a moment?"

Normally, I wouldn't plead my case, but I'd gotten desperate.

"I just want to get in," I said. "What if you played me as tight end?"

Tight ends are usually about my size or a little bigger—around 250 pounds and at least six foot four. They block, they give good solid hits, and they catch the ball if the quarterback can't find an open receiver.

"Have you ever played that position before?" Coach Snyder asked, incredulous.

"I can do it," I assured him, but I knew it was crazy even as I said it. At that level of college athletics, it's hard to compete in a new position. My competitors would've been playing tight end since Pop Warner. But Coach Snyder understood my frustration. Maybe he sensed my desperation and hoped it would spur me to greatness.

"Give it a try," he said.

So I switched positions. I imagined a scenario where I went out there and, through grit and determination, became the best tight end in the history of Kansas State.

Of course, it didn't turn out that way.

I wasn't really playing tight end. I was playing catch-up.

My biggest regret in life is that I wasted my college opportunities—academically, athletically, and spiritually. In my fourth year of college football, because of my redshirt year, I had one more year of eligibility. Even though I'd dreamed of playing college football, I'd had enough. I just wanted to get into the real world. I wanted to have a career, maybe become an entrepreneur. So I decided to take eighteen hours of classes that fall semester so I could graduate after my fourth year.

I had turned twenty-two, and I'd had just about enough of football and college. That's when I decided to break a little from the Baptist prohibition against alcohol. Though I might be the only person in American history who waited until after he or she was twenty-one, I decided it was time for a drink.

Guess what? It wasn't so bad.

My last semester of my fourth year was the only semester I didn't have to worry about being in shape for football or getting up at the crack of dawn for weightlifting. Instead, I started going out with my friends to bars and drinking. Oh, and I met a few girls.

Lots of girls.

Finally, I saw the appeal of college life.

Though I made it through college without compromising my conviction against premarital sex, I'm not proud of how I acted with the girls I met at the bars during college. If I had a good time with a girl one night and I decided she wasn't for me, I'd disappear. I wouldn't call or even text her with an explanation. It wasn't that I was callous; I was just immature. It was easier to avoid all uncomfortable conversations with women, so I did.

I graduated after four years with a bachelor's degree in social science—the best degree I could piece together after I was kicked out of business. That's how I ended up giving up my fifth year of eligibility. I just took my degree and went home.

I had a lot of memories. Some were fun; some were shameful. But my main regret was that I'd always been the guy "with a lot of potential."

Now I had to get used to the idea that I didn't live up to it.

two

ANSWERING THE CALL

When quarterback Tom Brady was drafted by the New England Patriots, he tearfully exclaimed, "I don't have to be an insurance salesman!"[2]

This didn't go over too well with insurance salesmen across America, but I understood where Brady was coming from. He had played at the University of Michigan. Of course he'd be disappointed if he ended up on the phone talking about risks rather than on the field taking risks he'd never recommend for his clients. Andrew—who, by this time, was my brother-in-law—had been signed by the Detroit Lions as a free agent after he graduated.

But after giving up my last year of eligibility at Kansas State, I had to face it: my football career was over.

It was a little disorienting. After all, I'd played football since I could read books without pictures. Come to think of it, a large part of my identity growing up was found in football.

Who was I now?

The advice I have always heard is "do what you know" and "do what you love." I definitely knew two things. First, I didn't want to be an insurance agent. Though the business had served my grandfather and father well, I didn't want to spend all day in an office. Second, I felt at home when I was at the gym. I loved the gigantic exercise balls, the hum of the treadmills, the clank of weights dropping on the padded ground, the climate-controlled air, the rows of televisions all tuned to different channels, the yoga mats rolled tightly on the shelves.

So after college, I became a sports performance trainer who helped athletes increase their speed and power through customized personal training sessions. I quickly developed a pretty good clientele—athletes from junior high to the NFL.

+ —···— +

One day, I was training a group of high school basketball players, a mouthy bunch. I loved trash-talking them as I absolutely wore them out. I started them out jogging for about fifteen minutes, then worked their abdominals and lower backs. We were doing medicine-ball drills when one of the Dallas Cowboys cheerleaders walked by. The gym gave free memberships to the cheerleaders, a deal that worked both ways: the cheerleaders got a free place to work out, and the gym magically ended up with a higher male membership.

Needless to say, I completely lost my group's attention when the cheerleader walked by. "Okay, guys," I said. "You gotta concentrate on *your* glutes—not hers."

"Sean," said one of the guys who'd just taken a swig of water from his bottle, "a few minutes ago she told me she thought you were cute."

"Lying won't get you out of squats," I said.

"I'm not making it up," he said. "She wanted me to give you that message."

The guys laughed as I looked in her direction. Was I imagining it, or did she smile at me? I had a hard time concentrating on the rest of the workout.

After class, I made my way over to her group of friends, who were finishing up on the ellipticals.

"Hey," I said. "I'm Sean."

"So you got my message?" She smiled.

I started training—and dating—Brooke almost immediately. I loved everything about her: how she would spend hours watching Shark Week on the Discovery Channel, how she went out of her way to do things for me, and how silly she was. She got along with my family really well, and they loved her back. We had an absolute blast.

I trained her—and other athletes in the gym—and my practice grew. However, I always had an itch to do something more.

———

That "something more" presented itself mainly as a fluke of geography. In certain parts of Texas, pump jacks dot the landscape, bobbing rhythmically for the black gold lurking beneath the surface. The oil and gas industry is big in Texas and creates some of the wealthiest people in the world. I wanted to be a part of it.

After taking a few months off from my athletic training job, I was hired to solicit investors for oil and gas ventures. That meant I'd approach wealthy individuals and talk to them about why they should put their money into drilling, mineral leases, or fracking. These investments are notoriously risky—boom or bust—but they have proven over and over to be great long-term investments. After all, the whole world operates on oil.

Brooke was always supportive of me—not only of every new business idea I concocted, but in life. Her encouragement and affection made me also want to support her in her endeavors.

When she came to me and told me she wanted to get a puppy, I went with her to find the right one.

"Look at this one," I said, instinctively reaching for the velvet head of an adorable brown-eyed boxer.

"Oh," Brooke purred. "She's beautiful. What should I name her?"

"What about . . . Lola?" I offered. It seemed to fit.

"Lola?" Brooke said the word and thought about it for a few seconds. "Perfect!"

We watched as the newly named Lola scampered across the floor, her tail wagging so hard it moved half her body.

Normally, dogs are wary of newcomers, but Lola took to Brooke and me within seconds. This, incidentally, was about how much time it took me to fall in love with this silly, sweet, and mischievous puppy.

"I've got to get me one of these," I said as Lola ran around.

"You should do it!" Brooke said. "Get Lola a best friend."

It wasn't hard to convince me. When I saw an ad in the paper for Labrador retriever puppies, I went to see the litter full of yellow labs. Right there in the middle was a single chocolate one.

I had to have her.

"Look at her paws!" Brooke said, gently picking up the puppy and admiring her features. "They're gigantic!"

"It helps them swim," said the breeder.

"We have to take her to the beach!" she exclaimed. Brooke was originally from Florida, and I suspected sand ran through her veins instead of blood.

"What are you going to name her?" she asked as she nuzzled the dog's neck.

Lola walked over to the puppy so they could do the dog equivalent of a handshake—they sniffed each other out.

"What about Ellie?"

Immediately, Ellie and Lola became inseparable. Anytime we went to the dog park, they would run and play together—no matter how many other dogs were there. If I needed to know where Ellie was, all I had to do was find Lola, and vice versa. We would take turns having both dogs sleep at each other's house. We even crate-trained them together, so they slept in the same space as puppies. They were so close.

Ellie's intelligence and eagerness to please made her very easy to train. Within three weeks, she was housebroken because she couldn't bear to disappoint me. Over the months, she became strong, agile, enthusiastic, and—best of all—glued to my hip.

Lola and Ellie became "our dogs," and having them made us feel—just a little—like a family.

⊹⸺ꞏꞏꞏ⸺⊹

Things were very comfortable with Brooke, except when it came to one thing.

Marriage.

Whenever the subject came up, things got awkward really fast for me. I loved her. Brooke was funny, playful, compassionate, and always going out of her way to surprise me or to help me out in some way. She was my best friend, and I could definitely see marrying her. However, I was far, far away from wanting to walk down the aisle.

"You tensed up when I brought up our future," Brooke said one night. "I just don't get it."

There comes a time when honesty is the only policy left.

"It's just that I'm doing all kinds of different things right now," I said, taking her hand in mine. "I'm pursuing different career options and trying to figure out where life will take me."

"Where it will take *us*, you mean?" she said softly.

I grew quiet.

She cleared her throat, pushing back emotion, and said, "We've been together for three years, Sean. Three! That's a long time for you not to know how you feel about me."

"Don't you know I love you?" I asked.

There's something that happens when one half of the couple is ready to tie the knot and the other isn't. My unwillingness to make a lifelong commitment made me treat Brooke differently, maybe a little more distantly. Of course, she picked up on that. I looked into her green eyes, which now had tears streaming from them.

"You're my best friend," I said. "We're as close as family."

I definitely didn't want her out of my life. Even though I knew it was the right thing to do, it seemed so final. Instead of breaking up, I suggested a less-final version.

"I think we need some time apart," I said.

She started crying. For the past three years, she had assumed we were on the path to marriage. However, I just couldn't get there at that time in my life.

"No, no," I said. I loved her so much that I couldn't bear the sound of her crying. My strongest desire at that moment was to console her. "Let's just see how it goes and reexamine it in a few weeks."

We sat next to each other on the couch, a million miles of expectations separating us.

For the next few weeks, we were technically on a break.

She went out of town to sort through her feelings about our relationship and called me one afternoon.

"Are you okay?" I asked when I picked up the phone.

"I'm great, actually," she said. The tremor in her voice I heard during our last conversation was completely gone. "I just wanted you to know that I understand where you're coming from about our breakup."

"You do?"

"Yeah," she said quietly. "Sean, I'll always love you, but I think you're right. We *should* break up."

I knew in my head this was good, but this turnaround—and her confidence—surprised me.

"Really?" I said. "Oh, okay. Great. I'm glad. Really." I wanted what was best for Brooke, but I wasn't ready to let her go. "Well, I hope everything goes well for you."

And so a new phase of life began.

—————

After work, I'd go out with my guy friends. Or, even better, I'd go out on dates with women I met at the gym, at church, or through friends. After three years of seriously dating the same woman, it was pretty exhilarating. Honestly, I didn't give Brooke much thought, except when I saw her to let the dogs visit. Even though we'd broken up, we couldn't simply yank the dogs from each other. Ellie, the sensitive chocolate lab, was technically mine, and Lola, the happy-go-lucky boxer, was technically hers.

"We've gotta figure out what to do," Brooke said. "We can't just keep going back and forth like this."

"But we can't separate them forever," I said. "It's not fair."

"I know," she said thoughtfully, biting her lip. "But what can we do?"

Absent an obvious solution, we'd take them back and forth, from my place to hers. I'd have the dogs for several days, and then we'd switch, like divorced parents trying to juggle custody of children.

One night when she came over to get Ellie and Lola, she noticed I was dressed up to go out. "You're not going on a date, are you?" She looked away from me and down at Lola.

"No," I lied. Brooke was the nicest girl in the world, and there was no way I wanted to hurt her. I gave her a hug good-bye and then went on a date with whomever it was that week. I loved the freedom of going wherever I wanted, whenever I wanted. Life was good.

Three months later, I got the wind knocked out of me.

"Did you hear Brooke is dating a professional baseball player?" someone at the gym mentioned to me.

I hadn't.

At that moment—standing next to the weights—it finally hit me. I'd lost my best friend, and she was never coming back.

Immediately, I went to her apartment. "I think I may have made the biggest mistake of my life," I told her. "I don't want to lose you."

"You're telling me this now?"

"It just hit me," I said. "I've made a mistake!"

"If we were meant to be together," she said sweetly, putting her hand on my shoulder, "you wouldn't have gone this long without telling me this. I want to be with someone who can't live a day without me, much less a few months."

In hindsight she was right, but I didn't believe her at the time. I was heartbroken.

"If things work out with the ball player," she said, "we're going to have to move around a lot and travel."

"What about Lola?" I asked. "How can you keep her if you're traveling everywhere?"

"I know it'll be complicated," she said. "But she's my dog and I'll figure it out."

"It's not a matter of figuring it out," I said. "She's not small enough to take her with you."

"Well, I can't give her up," she said. "Worst-case scenario? I'll give her to my mom to keep while we're gone."

"Your mom? That's not fair!" I said, though it *was* perfectly fair. I had no claim on Lola. I was just incredibly emotional because I'd already lost Brooke. I didn't want to lose Lola too.

"You're acting like she's your dog!"

"Well, I love her like she's mine."

"Sorry, Sean," Brooke said gently. "It's *all* over."

When I went home to my apartment, I think Ellie was almost as depressed as I was. I sat on the couch with her, buried my head in the fur on her neck, and sighed. "What have I done?"

<hr />

I plunged myself into my somewhat boring work. One day, however, something happened that would potentially change the course of my life.

I was talking to an investor on the phone when my coworker Josh Brown walked in. I lifted my index finger to him as I wrapped up the conversation. "And there are permanent tax benefits."

I finished up my call and jotted down notes on the potential investor. By this time, another guy—Donald Wallman—had popped into my office as well.

"To what do I owe this pleasure?" I asked. Though we had a very friendly office, our workload was so heavy we had little time to socialize.

"We have an offer for you," Don said.

"Lay it on me," I said. I always was interested in new ways to make money.

"You know how to raise money," said Josh. He had blond, floppy hair and the casual air of being born into wealth. He took a sip of coffee and spread out several pieces of paper on my desk like a fan. "Check this out."

I picked up the paper and realized they were spreadsheets.

"What am I looking at?" I asked.

"This is your future," Don said.

"I don't see anything about mineral leases."

"Because it's not about oil or gas. It's called debt settlement, and it's the hottest way to make money now. People are making some crazy cash from this," Don said.

"So are you going to make me guess what it is?" I asked.

"It's simple," Josh jumped in. "Someone with a lot of debt calls us up and tells us about their situation. It's usually someone on the verge of bankruptcy, someone with medical issues that make it hard to pay their bills, someone who doesn't have insurance or whatever."

"They get calls from people they owe every day," Don said. "And they're desperate to make that phone stop ringing."

"That's where we come in," said Josh.

"So they give us names of their creditors and the amount they owe. We then give them an estimate for reducing their debt, along with a new, lower monthly payment. They stop paying their creditors and instead send payments to us as their new debt settler."

"So they pay us first?" I asked.

"You got it," Josh said. "Then their other payments go into a trust that's for their debt."

"And then we pay the creditors?"

"We negotiate the amounts and time frame with the creditors," Don said. "We deal directly with the people they owe, and it gives our client a little breathing room."

I picked up a sheet of paper that had the data on the number of people in bad financial situations. *Poor guys*, I thought. I didn't want to say so immediately, but it seemed like a great way to help people and make a lot of money.

"Will you consider it?" Don asked. "We can handle all the back-end aspects of the business, but we need you out there talking to the people."

For the next few weeks, I mulled over the numbers, which seemed to paint a positive picture. Though no business is ever guaranteed, it seemed as though Josh and Don were right. There was money right there for the taking.

A lot of money.

One morning, I walked down the hall and found them both near the coffeemaker.

"Hey, guys." I smiled. "I think we're going to be partners."

◆——◆

"What *is* social science?" Andrew asked one day when I stopped by his office—his insurance office—that he'd set up after he got out of the NFL.

"You know," I said, maybe a little defensively. "It's about understanding the workings of . . . human society."

"And that qualifies you to . . . ?" he asked, waiting for me to elaborate. "Ask rich guys to invest in fracking? Why don't you get a normal job?"

"I don't *want* a normal job," I said before looking around at his surroundings. "No offense."

"You think this is bad?" He knocked on his mahogany desk, which was neatly arranged—a stack of papers on his left, a wedding photo of Shay and him on the corner. "I make my own hours, my income is up to me, and I answer to myself."

I'd heard this make-your-own-hours argument from my grandfather, who had been an insurance salesman, and from my dad, who had followed in his footsteps. The business had served our family well, but I didn't want to hear it from Andrew. I'd always known the family business wasn't for me. I thought of myself as more of a risk taker, and insurance felt safe. Boring. I felt destined to do something big. Something interesting. Something that didn't require slacks or a tie.

"I'm a bit more entrepreneurial," I said. "A couple of guys from work asked me to check out this thing called debt settlement."

"You're in debt?" he asked, his eyebrows arched in concern.

"*I* don't have debt," I said hurriedly. That was mostly true, if you didn't count the Visa bill I'd run up during college. "They want me to be a part of a new company that helps other people who have debt. Like, a lot of debt. It's super profitable right now, and people are making a ton of money."

"Like debt consolidation?" he asked.

"No," I said. "We don't lump it all into one big sum of debt. We help negotiate down people's debts with their debtors."

"Sounds like a scam." Andrew laughed and tossed a wadded piece of paper. He banked the paper wad off the wall, and it fell into the trash can in the corner. "Haven't you heard of those guys taking advantage of poor people?"

"Yeah, but that's not what we do, obviously. Anyway," I said, getting up from his uncomfortable office chair, "let's continue this riveting conversation over dinner." I stood up, took one look around his office, and sighed. Though some people can look at an office space and feel at home, to me it felt like a prison.

"Wanna grab something to eat?" I glanced at the clock on the wall. "It's getting late."

"Tonight's Monday," Andrew said.

"You don't eat on Mondays?"

"Yes, but it's always in front of the television."

"Oh, so you're a couch potato now?" I asked.

"Shay and I watch television that night."

"Is there a good game on?" I asked. "I'll grab a bite to eat and come over too."

"It's not athletic," he said sheepishly. "It's . . . *The Bachelor.*"

I looked at him silently for a moment.

"Sorry," I said, walking to the door, turning around, and looking back at him. "I was under the mistaken impression that you were a guy."

"I'm a *married* guy," he said. "There's a big difference." Apparently, this All-American, former NFL player had let my sister convince him to watch girly television.

Every week.

I walked out of his office, glad I wasn't an insurance salesman *and* glad I wasn't married.

"Twenty-five thousand dollars," I said to myself after I turned my phone off and took a deep breath. I'd just gotten another investor signed on to our new business venture, which we'd named Beller Financial Services.

I wrote down this figure on a piece of paper, along with the other investments, and put them all in one—rather long—column. Just like grade school.

Being in charge of getting investment money for our new debt settlement company, I knew our chances of success sat squarely on my shoulders. At least initially.

I practiced my long addition, then added up the numbers one more time to check my math. Then I grabbed my phone and texted Josh and Don the same, simple message: *Five hundred thousand dollars.*

Within seconds, they were both at my door.

"You did it?"

"Five hundred thousand!" I said. "I just got this last bit."

"Who?" Don asked.

"A guy I know named Jim Perryman."

"Is he one of your oil and gas guys?"

"No," I said with a little bit of pride. I was happy that I'd been able to find investors outside of my oil and gas contacts. I knew Jim from a mutual friend. "He just retired from IBM and wants to make some money for his daughter's wedding."

"You're good," said Don, pointing at me. "This guy is *good*!"

"I couldn't do it without you guys," I said. This wasn't false modesty. I was the guy who sold people on our idea. Josh and Don were the ones who would make it work on the business side. Because so much money was being made in this industry, it was an easier sale than the long-term oil and gas investments.

"I have to admit," I said, "half a million dollars is a lot of money for a bunch of guys in their midtwenties."

We high-fived, laughed, and talked about what we were going to do when this made us rich. But first we had to get everything in order. Our business had grown so big there was no way we could keep operating it in our spare time.

A few weeks later, I got to see our future up close.

"*This* is ours?" I asked, walking through the carpeted hallways of our new office building in the Dallas financial district.

"Well, it's not *ours* ours," said Josh. "We're just renting."

"Can we afford it?" I asked.

"It's all thanks to you," Don said.

"Do I dare ask how much the rent is?" I asked. Though I wasn't involved in the business aspects of our new venture, I knew how much money was coming in. I think the financial term for it was *a lot*! This new space was going to be the hub of our ever-growing practice.

"Come check out the break room," Josh said. "And I'll show you the conference room along the way."

We walked through the spacious, empty office space. There was one huge room with floor-to-ceiling windows on one wall. We were on the fifth floor, and our view was amazing. It overlooked the Ritz-Carlton pool across the street.

"The cubicles are arriving this week," Don said. "I splurged and got the kind with glass panels at the top. Like windows."

"I want an office." I laughed. "Corner, preferably."

"Yes, I'll show you your space," Don said. "But we've got twenty-five employees ready to move in as soon as we set up."

I took a deep breath and smelled the aroma of success. It smelled like new carpet and the bleach used on the beautiful, sparkling bathrooms.

An office is great, if you aren't the guy punching the clock.

I'd finally figured out the right direction for my life. Entrepreneurship, like football, required guts. I was certain I was going to be a millionaire before I was thirty, and I couldn't have done it with two better friends.

＋———ｕｅｅ———＋

"Sagi," I said into the phone, tightly holding the piece of paper I had with his phone number scrawled on it. "I've heard you're the guy who can transform any body."

Sagi Kalev was a legend among the fitness crowd. He became a body-builder when he was sixteen, and then had a four-year tour of duty in the Israeli Army, where he learned the discipline and training techniques he later used to start his bodybuilding business. I'd heard he'd been shot and stabbed while in the military—it added to his mystique.

It had taken me months to get up the nerve to call him. However, after Brooke and I broke up, I wanted to change things around. Getting serious about fitness seemed like a good next move.

"Are you interested in training?" he asked in his Tel Aviv accent. "If you become my client, you can transform your body from the inside out. You can be the person you've always wanted to be."

"How is your program different than all the others?" I asked him. I knew a great deal about fitness, after all. Was this guy really worth his $150 fee?

"I'll take all the guessing out," Sagi said. "I'll make you gain muscle and lose body fat at the same time. It'll be hard, but you can do it if you follow my instructions."

As he began rattling off his services and the costs, I interrupted.

"Actually, I can't afford one-fifty," I said. It was true. I was stretched thin. I'd made plenty of money in oil and gas, but it quickly evaporated when I didn't take a paycheck for several months getting the start-up off the ground. Was an exercise regimen worth the sacrifice?

"If you truly want the transformation you say," Sagi said, "you'll find a way to pay for it."

The man was like an Israeli Yoda. Even though I had only a few hundred bucks in my bank account, he was right. I worked, saved money, and—finally—was able to afford it. When I met him in person, I noticed he was about five foot ten but absolutely solid. I don't normally notice whether guys are attractive, but Sagi had been "Mr. Israel"—twice—with eyes that seemed to see right through me. Immediately, I could tell he was the real deal. He wasn't just some big guy telling me how to bench-press more weight. This was a very well-respected man with an amazing, holistic understanding of the body and how it works. The first thing he asked me to do was to have blood work done, then a saliva test, and even a hair analysis.

He wasn't interested in just building bulk. He looked at every aspect of my health as a detective looks for clues.

As he pored over my medical results, he grew quiet.

"Did I pass?" I laughed. Even though I was strong and had a lot of muscle, I didn't have great symmetry yet, and I wanted to be absolutely ripped.

"If you follow my book—take your supplements, say lots of prayers, and eat right—you'll be a new man in no time at all," Sagi assured me. "You ready to do whatever it takes?"

Josh and I were talking one morning over a cup of coffee in our office with the sounds of a company waking up in the background of our conversation—phones were ringing, people were exchanging morning pleasantries, a fax machine was emitting its high-pitched ring. The sound of money.

Don burst into the room with a splotchy, red face. "You're not going to believe this," he said, plopping a copy of the newspaper on my desk.

The headline caused my throat to tighten: "Debt Relief Companies Prohibited from Collecting Advance Fees under FTC Rule."

Don shook his head vigorously. "Read it and weep."

"The Federal Trade Commission has created a new regulation that protects consumers trying to settle their debts," I read. "They will now be protected by a rule that stops debt settlement companies from charging fees before settling or reducing a customer's credit card debt."[3]

I stopped and swallowed hard. "Does this mean what I think it means?"

Josh was already tapping away on his phone, trying to find more information about the new FTC rule. "The government wouldn't just come in and tell us our way of doing business is illegal. We're not doing anything wrong."

We all got quiet. Debt-relief companies had sprung up overnight, and there was definite abuse. We'd heard heartbreaking stories about how some unscrupulous firms told people to quit paying their creditors and send their monthly payments to them. Of course, the firms simply stole their money—including "referral fees" and "cancellation fees." We'd heard about these guys, but we were definitely not these guys.

"So," I said, taking a deep breath, "this means we can't charge our clients until after we settle their debts?"

Josh, who had found several articles on the subject, read from his phone. "If you charge consumers before actually helping them, the FTC and state enforcers will knock at your door to enforce the rule."

I popped my knuckles as I looked out the window. There were cars stopped at a red light below while people walked through the intersection. It sometimes took a year to eighteen months to start showing results for our clients.

"How can we survive this?" I asked. "We can't just float all this money—people depend on us."

There was only one answer and we all knew it. We needed more money. It was hard for me to accept since I was the one on the phone asking people to hand over their hard-earned savings, but I knew my co-founders were right. We needed money to make money. Because the new government regulation prohibited us from taking money, we had to come up with it some other way. That's how I found myself on the phone with Jim Perryman once again.

"How are the kids?" I asked him.

"Sean," he said, skipping the small talk, "I told you already. I don't have it."

There's one thing I've learned from all my time with investors. When they say they don't have any more money, they always do.

"You know I wouldn't come to you if I didn't need it."

"I heard about the new FTC regs," he said. "Do you have a plan to combat it?"

"Yeah, we've got it covered. We've switched to loan modifications instead of settlement. That means we'll work with attorneys to modify people's interest fees. Which is exactly why I'm calling. With the changes, we'll need more operating money."

Faced with the possibility of losing his initial investment, Jim's voice—finally—started to soften.

"How much more do you need?"

Within the week, I had the thirty thousand dollars we needed to pay our twenty-five employees and our exorbitant rent.

At least for the time being.

My phone rang and my heart stopped.

"Jim Perryman," read my caller ID.

"This is Sean," I answered with a forced casual tone.

"Hey, thanks for picking up," he said. "I tried to call Josh and Don, but it went straight to voice mail. I guess they're already gone for the weekend. Hey, I guess it's five o'clock somewhere."

I knew why they didn't answer. For the same reason I didn't want to answer. Our business, which had been going so well, had gone belly up. We tried to realign our business models to comply with the new regulation, but we didn't have the margin to float all the loans while we worked to help settle everyone's debts. After weeks of trying to make ends meet, the math finally won. We'd run out of money, and our staffers—no matter how awesome our downtown office space was—wouldn't work for free.

"So my daughter's wedding is coming up," Jim continued, "and you would not believe how much stuff like flowers and the cake costs. I'm almost ready to buy them tickets to Vegas to find the nearest ordained Elvis impersonator."

He laughed at his joke before continuing. "Anyway, I was hoping to get some return on my investment so we can start making deposits on the dress, church, band, and whatever else. I was thinking that thirty thousand dollars I gave you had probably turned into, what, say fif—"

"I lost your money."

I'd been dreading this moment—this sentence—ever since Josh and Don broke the news to me. We had gone under so fast that we had to break our lease with the owner of our downtown office space. To avoid detection, we'd packed up our office in the middle of the night. Because we had to get out of there fast, we packed up four thousand square feet of brand-new cubicles, phones, and office supplies and gave them away. When the office management company realized we were gone, they told me they were going to sue me. Thankfully, the lease was in the LLC's name, not in my name, so I wasn't personally liable.

Jim didn't respond. The phone was so completely silent that I pulled it away from my face to make sure we were still connected. I didn't know what else to say other than the truth. Perhaps I could've led up to it, but no additional language would soften the blow.

"I'm so sorry," I said. "But the money's gone."

"All of it?"

"I hope to get some back," I said. "But, yeah. *All* of it."

"Do you even know what the word *investment* means?"

"I'm so sorry. That new regu—"

"You mean the regulation you told me we needed to combat, with my thirty grand?" he asked. "The one that meant you needed—absolutely *needed*—my cash?"

He didn't wait for me to respond. He was right. Josh and Don said they'd be able to pull it off with an infusion of cash. That's what I—in turn—had told Jim.

"The word *investment* means that I give you money, and then I make money on it," he continued icily. "At no point are you supposed to say to me, 'The money's gone.'"

"Maybe I could've said it better, but I didn't want to prolong this."

"I'm not talking about a point of style," he said. "I told you I didn't have the money when you came to me in the first place."

"I shouldn't have pressed you, but I've found that most people have more than they let on."

"What are you, some sort of shrink? A wannabe psychic? I wasn't playing any games with you," he said. "How much money I had in the bank is not a mystery. There are numbers in a ledger. Black and white. I didn't have it." He paused, probably in an effort to collect himself. "Sean, I actually took out a loan to give you the money you said you desperately needed to make this company a success."

"You did?" I asked, choking over this new revelation.

Then, as much to himself as to me, he asked, "How am I going to pay for my daughter's wedding?"

I had no answers.

"Are you married?" he asked.

"Not yet."

"Then you can't possibly understand how hard it'll be to tell my wife this."

When I got off the phone, I called Josh. I couldn't wait to talk to him and figure out which investors he and Don could let down easily. I wasn't sure if I had the heart to go through another call like Jim's.

It went through to voice mail, so I dialed Don.

After a few rings, I knew he wasn't going to pick up either. This had never happened in all the time I'd known these guys. If they couldn't pick up, they'd immediately either text or call me back. I stared at my phone and debated whether to call them again.

Just as I was about to dial Josh, my phone buzzed in my hand.

On the little screen, I read the name of another investor, who had undoubtedly just learned of our company's demise.

The last thing I wanted to do was answer that call.

It buzzed once. I took a deep breath. Twice. I began to feel warmth come across my cheeks. Three times.

"Hello?" I forced myself to answer, clearing my throat to hide my anxiety.

"Sean," the investor said. "Why aren't your partners answering my calls?"

Don and Josh, it seemed, were completely off the grid and appeared to be taking zero responsibility for any of the repercussions. Even while I was on the phone with this second investor, other furious investors beeped in.

I tried to ignore the constant buzzing in my ear and focus on this disappointed man. This man with whom I'd previously shared meals, good times, and dreams of wealth.

"Unless you give me my money back by the end of the week," he yelled, "I'm going to sue you personally!"

My hand began to shake as I tried to calm him down. There was no way

I could even buy him another meal. I definitely could not afford to give him forty-three thousand dollars.

"Where do you think I'll get the money?" I asked.

"I don't care where you get it," he said. "But you'll never make another dollar that isn't earmarked for me for the rest of your life if you don't come up with something."

What's going to happen to me, God? I thought as he yelled.

For the next few weeks, I was horrified of my own phone. Every time it rang I felt like I might throw up. My partners—my friends—left me to pick up the pieces. My phone absolutely blew up, but I didn't want to talk to these investors anymore.

I was alone, more alone than I'd ever felt in my life.

One night, I lay in my bed and pulled the covers up to my neck. The ceiling had a shadow on it that had moved slightly over the past three hours I'd been staring at it. I felt my heart beating wildly in my chest. I sat up, punched my pillow, rolled over to my side, and tried desperately to find a comfortable position.

"If God is for us, who can ever be against us?" I kept reciting Romans 8:31 in my head. It was a Bible verse we used in church, and it was the only thing that comforted me. I'd never experienced anxiety. I've always been a laid-back guy, so I wasn't sure what to do with this feeling—this terrible, ever-growing feeling. My face felt hot. My skin hurt. My head ached.

I'd always thought of myself as a risk taker, an entrepreneur. But when Jim asked me that question about his daughter's wedding, I realized a cold, hard truth.

I couldn't take any more chances.

Lying there in the darkness, I made a decision I said I'd never make.

I had to go into the family business.

three

WHAT A WAY
TO MAKE A LIVING

One day, Brooke showed up at my apartment with Lola on a leash and tears in her eyes. She knew the dogs needed to be together and was willing to give up Lola to make that happen. I know it was hard for Brooke to make this sacrifice, so I was deeply touched by her generosity.

The dogs were thrilled to be reunited.

Every morning I'd wake up at seven o'clock and take them out. Then I'd feed them and marvel at their canine manners. Lola ate her bowl first while Ellie patiently waited for her to finish before having her bowl of food.

"God, you know my heart," I prayed as I reluctantly left Ellie to finish her bowl so I could get dressed for my day at work with my brother-in-law at his State Farm agency. I slid on my khaki slacks—the uniform of the insurance salesman—and prayed, "You know I don't want to live a normal life. If this is your will, if you *really* want me to sell insurance, I'll do it."

Andrew, one of the top fifty most successful State Farm insurance salesmen out of ten thousand nationwide, gave me a job, my own desk, and a phone. Sadly, I had to use that phone to cold-call potential customers. I hated the feeling of holding my breath as I waited for someone to hang up on me before I even had the chance to get out my pitch.

Still, it was much better than breaking news to investors that you've lost their money.

This was my new life. I would go through the agency training program. Then, a couple of years later, I would have gained enough experience—and clients—to start my own agency. My grandfather, my dad, and Andrew had gone down that path. Now it was my turn.

"But, God, you know I hate this so much," I kept praying as I drove down Custer Road to the State Farm office located in a strip mall. "Is this the way you want my life to be?"

Ever since I decided to be an insurance agent, God and I had been having a pretty constant conversation. Not an argument, really. Not even a negotiation. I was convinced there had to be something else I could do that wasn't as office-y as being an insurance agent.

As a kid, I believed in Jesus and heard all the stories in Sunday school—Noah and his ark, Samson and Delilah, Daniel and the lions. As I grew older, I was always the nice kid everyone's parents liked. My parents brought me up to respect adults, and Mom would get all over me if I didn't say "yes, sir," or "yes, ma'am." My friends' parents knew I wouldn't get their kids into serious trouble. When I began dating, the girls' dads were always very warm and welcoming. I think they knew I was going to respect and take care of their daughters. Even though I hung with the popular kids, I didn't drink or do some of the other typical high school behavior they did. In college, I still didn't drink underage or have premarital sex, but I'm not sure I knew *why* I wasn't drinking illegally or hooking up. My Christianity wasn't fully formed. After all, it wasn't strong enough to keep me from skipping classes or cheating on exams, and I never really shared my faith with my friends or teammates.

After college, I was back in my hometown and—once again—near my parents and my church. Still, I didn't love God more than I loved myself. When I dated, I broke my promise not to have sex before I was married. I knew this was wrong, so I felt incredibly guilty afterward. Shame, however, wasn't strong enough to keep me from sinning again. Eventually, it would fade into the recesses of my mind. When I'd talk to another girl, I'd go down that path of destruction again.

I kept ignoring God, even though I felt horrible.

Something's gotta change, I thought. That's when I decided to take ownership of my faith. I wanted to—finally—be a man. I wanted to have a real faith, not a list of things I didn't do.

"All right, Jesus," I said one night. "Let's do this again."

———◆———◆———

So I got up in the morning every day, went to work at the insurance agency in the strip mall, and prayed for strength to get through the day.

The first thing I'd do, after grabbing a cup of coffee and saying good morning to Andrew, was to go into my office and open my Bible. Even though I'd drifted far away from God, I knew exactly how to get back to him. My dad always told me the Scriptures are alive—the living, breathing Word of God—and he always had his nose in his Bible. We played a game that involved me opening the Bible anywhere and reading a random verse aloud. Dad would, more times than not, be able to tell me which book, chapter, and verse. In contrast, my Bible knowledge had never gotten deeper than those Sunday school stories. When I recommitted myself to Christ after college, I recommitted myself to reading the Bible. I would read a few chapters in the Old Testament, then a few in the New Testament. The more I read, the more my faith grew—by leaps and bounds. The Bible was surprising. Unexpected. Frequently, I'd read a chapter and think, *I didn't know that was in there!*

When I asked Dad about some of the more interesting and confusing things I'd learned, he handed me a copy of a book called *When Critics Ask* by Norman L. Geisler and Thomas Howe. With that resource by my side, I read the whole Bible cover to cover over the course of several months.

Something interesting, even miraculous, happened as I read the Bible regularly. It transformed how I thought. I noticed when I got away from reading it, my mind and life got away from thinking biblically. However, when I immersed myself in the Bible, I saw the world differently.

This became my ritual. I'd pray for God to deliver me from my job at State Farm. Then, since God obviously didn't seem to be interested in delivering me from it, I'd get on the phone and beg people to buy insurance.

Every day the clock's hand swung slowly around the dial, and I'd take a break to sit in the break room, watch *Seinfeld* reruns, and eat my perfectly portioned, Sagi-approved amount of turkey and veggies.

Though I hated limiting my diet, I followed Sagi's every instruction down to the last ounce. If one of my meals was six ounces of chicken breast, a cup and a half of brown rice, and one cup of broccoli, I'd get out a scale and weigh everything. If he told me six ounces of chicken, I measured six ounces of chicken. That's how my body transformed so quickly. I never skipped a day, and I never cheated once. I saw big results in just a month.

"Wow, look at those abs," Sagi said three months after we met. "Would you consider being in my workout video?"

"Really?" I said. "Like, I'd be the guy in the back doing the routines with you?"

"You and a few other guys," he said. Sagi's new venture was a ninety-day program to help people gain muscle mass by the makers of P90X, a popular video series you can do at home to build muscle.

"Sure!" I said. "What's it called?"

"Body Beast," he said. "But I know what you're thinking."

"What?" I asked.

"Probably that when you see this handsome face, you don't think 'beast'—you think 'beauty.' Right?"

"Um, no," I said. "But I'd love to be in your video."

"You should also think about getting some professional photos done," he said. "I have a guy in Los Angeles who is an amazing photographer."

"Why?" I asked. "Do you want a picture of me to put on your desk?"

"Look at you!" Sagi said. "You've worked hard. You should see if you can get some freelance work as a fitness model."

A fitness model? Me? Could this be my path out of the insurance agency? Even though it cost me my very last dime, I packed my bags and headed to Los Angeles for a photo shoot.

* ——— ◆◆◆ ——— *

I was sitting in my office at State Farm, working up the nerve to move on to the list of people I needed to cold-call that day, when I got a text from Andrew.

Hey, send me one of your photos from that photo shoot.

I didn't think anything of texting Andrew one of the photos. Everyone in my family thought it was all a lark—the video was fun, and I'd already gotten a few magazine gigs.

Here ya go, I texted Andrew, attaching a photo.

Little did I know, this text would change the direction of my life.

A few weeks later, I was walking the dogs when my phone rang. I didn't recognize the number, but the area code indicated it was from Los Angeles.

"Is this Sean Lowe?" a bubbly person asked when I pressed my phone up to my ear. Lola and Ellie were pulling on their leashes.

"This is Tabby from the casting department on *The Bachelorette*," she began. "Thank you for submitting your application for our hit ABC show."

The Bachelorette?

Of course I knew about the show. It was the show that Shay—and even Andrew—watched. Well, I guess millions of people watch it. So do my friends Laura and Stephanie, who watch it with more regularity than some people go to church.

But I certainly didn't apply to be on it.

"I think there's been a mix-up," I told Tabby as I tried to sort through what she was saying. As she talked about "my application," it didn't take long for me to figure out what was going on. Andrew and Shay didn't want me to end up alone, and they wanted to be my matchmaker as I'd done for them.

"I'm sorry," I said, so shocked that I was having a conversation with *The Bachelorette* that I stopped on the sidewalk as Lola and Ellie waited patiently to continue on their walk. "I have no interest in being on the show."

I didn't want to subject myself to public criticism, after all. And I certainly didn't think finding real love was possible on a reality TV show.

"Just consider it," she said. "There is travel, adventure, and—of course, romance!" Tabby was one of the most enthusiastic people on the planet. "You should at least submit a video of yourself in case you change your mind and want to move forward in the future."

I agreed to think about it, ended the call, and kept walking the dogs.

A neighbor waved hello. Lola lunged for a bird that had landed on the sidewalk but lazily flitted away before coming to any harm.

The Bachelorette?

I called Shay. "What have you done?"

Shay could hardly contain her excitement. "That's great!" she said. "It sounds like they're interested!"

"Do you really want a sister-in-law who was a contestant on that show?"

"*Contestant* isn't the right word," Shay said. "You aren't going on *The Price Is Right*."

"I'm not going anywhere."

I said that sentence a little too emphatically. I was twenty-eight years old, stuck in a job I didn't love. Every day, I answered questions about floods, lightning, and automobile collisions and ate my lunch watching *Seinfeld* reruns. It wasn't a bad life, but I didn't feel I was headed to anything more. "I'm not going anywhere," may have been a truer statement than I wanted.

"It doesn't have to be trashy," Shay said. "We think you'd be great. You're nice, you're handsome, and—honestly—you aren't getting any younger."

For the rest of the walk, I couldn't think of anything else. A couple of days later, I got an envelope in the mail with details about the video and twenty pages of questions. I sat at my desk and looked at the stack of papers. Next to that stack was a stack of insurance claims I needed to get through by the time I left that evening.

Insurance.

The Bachelorette.

Insurance.

The Bachelorette.

I picked up a pencil and started to write. The form was fill-in-the-blank, like an elementary school test, except back then things were simpler.

Do you love me? Yes? No? Maybe?

"Sean Lowe," I wrote, trying to suppress a laugh as I wrote my name. *What am I doing?* I thought. I answered all their many questions, and finally got to the end of the forms.

I had to include a couple of photos. Thankfully, I had the fitness images taken in Los Angeles. But I also had to submit a video, and I knew I couldn't do it by myself. I texted my friends Laura and Stephanie: *Help!*

It was as if I'd just sent the bat signal to Batman. They agreed to come the very next day, with years of *Bachelorette* knowledge at their disposal.

"You at least should brush your hair," Laura said when I opened the door to her and Stephanie. I laughed. These girls were like my sisters, and I knew I could count on them—for support and also a little good-natured ribbing.

"Are you excited?" Stephanie asked.

"There's no harm in sending in a video," I said. "There are probably thousands of men across America who are taking it more seriously than I am."

"Yes," Laura said. "But they don't have us. Hand me the letter."

She and Stephanie looked over my letter and began reading the requirements. "Okay, so there's a list of things you have to talk about—what you do for fun, how your past relationships usually end, where you live . . . You know, the basics."

After a little strategic talk about how to shoot the video, they went to work.

"Action!" Stephanie said, holding up her cell phone.

"This is my house," I said, walking through the living room of my house.

"Cut!" she said.

"Can you make it less cheesy?" Laura asked.

"Who are you, Steven Spielberg?"

"I'm just trying to give you the best shot at this!" she protested. "Now, take two."

We were laughing so much, I'm surprised we got any usable footage.

"Okay, so this is my house," I said again. "This is the couch where I watch football on Saturdays. This is where I grill my chicken because I want to be healthy."

Stephanie and Laura, as much as we had joked, did a great job with my audition video. I took the footage we'd shot, plugged in some of my fitness photos, and I submitted the video to the producers in October.

———

During November and December, I went on with my life and only occasionally daydreamed about what it would be like to be on the show. Most of the time I trudged through my work. I was thankful to have a job—one that wasn't putting people's personal finances at risk but was actually protecting them. However, I was bored. Now, I know that lots of folks build businesses and do great things in the insurance industry. My dad put food on our table our entire lives this way, and Andrew was a third-generation insurance man. The problem, honestly, wasn't the job. The problem was me.

"Your policy covers theft, lightning, and windstorm," I was saying into the phone to one of my clients. Just then, Andrew popped into the doorway. "But I'm sorry to say it doesn't cover your watercraft."

I continued with my conversation, wondering why Andrew was grinning as though he knew a secret.

"Thanks, Mr. Elias," I said. "Call me if you have any other questions."

I hadn't even said good-bye before Andrew started talking.

"You have a call," he said. "On line three."

"Who is it?" I asked.

"Do I look like your secretary?" He smiled.

"Hey, Sean," the person on the other end of the line said. "This is Tabby from casting at *The Bachelorette*. How are you?"

My heart jumped into my throat. Andrew stood awkwardly in the doorway, waiting to get a signal from me about whether it was good news. He was texting Shay everything I said. It was pretty obvious this was more exciting for them than it was for me. Some couples grow a garden; others get an aquarium. Andrew and Shay's hobby was getting me on *The Bachelorette*.

The call was brief, friendly, and inconclusive.

"So?" Andrew looked at me expectantly.

"They were just calling to check in on me."

"Doesn't it seem like that's a good sign?" he asked.

"Well, they didn't say they wanted me," I said, shrugging. "I gotta get back to work."

"Hey," Andrew said. "I'm your boss. Shouldn't that be my line?"

———

A week later, I discovered a very strange coincidence. I was taking a road trip to Baton Rouge with my good friend Austin to catch an LSU game, which meant we had about four hundred miles of music and conversation. I was somewhat embarrassed to tell him about the possibility of being on *The Bachelorette*, but it felt weird to keep it from him.

"You're never going to believe what Stephanie and Laura got me to do," I said, bracing myself for a few jokes. When I told him we made a *Bachelorette* audition video, his eyes got big, and then he broke into laughter.

"Well, I've got some bad news for you," he said. "I'm working on the same video."

"You applied to be on the show?" I asked, stunned. Not only was it a weird coincidence, he just didn't seem like the type of guy who would want to be on that show. I guess I didn't either.

"My friends submitted an application without telling me."

"Wouldn't it be awesome if we could go together?" I asked.

"Yeah, you think that now," he said. "But you'll be heartbroken when I end up with the girl."

"Have you heard anything from casting?" I asked.

"Not yet."

Suddenly, it hit me. If Austin hadn't gotten a call—and I had—the show might actually be interested in me. I played it off in the conversation, but that night my mind reeled with the possibility.

How strange would it be if they were truly interested?

※

Christmas and New Year's came and went, and I caught myself thinking more about the show than I admitted to Shay and Andrew. But one January morning, my phone rang again.

"Hello, Sean," said Tabby. "I'm calling to invite you to be a part of a casting call in Los Angeles over the weekend."

Casting call was not in my normal vocabulary. I spent my time using terms such as *accelerated death benefits, annuitization,* and *insurance premium.* So when I rushed into Andrew's office to tell him the news, it felt nice to hear the words roll off my tongue.

Andrew picked up his phone. "I can't wait to tell everyone."

"I haven't told Mom about this," I said. Everyone in the family was aware of my new *Bachelorette* option, except Mom. There's no way my mom, a traditional, Southern woman, would like to hear that her son was heading off to be on a reality TV show.

I urged Andrew not to tell her. "There's no reason to alarm her, especially since it's unlikely to happen."

※

I flew into LAX on Friday. When I landed, there was a driver holding a sign with "Lowe" written on it. I'd never been greeted by a driver, and a shot of electricity went through me.

Is this really happening?

"Mr. Lowe?" he asked, taking my bags and ushering me to his black town car parked at the airport. We drove for a while until we got to an out-of-the-way hotel. A staff member of *The Bachelorette* met me in my room, gave me a schedule for the weekend, and told me what to expect.

"Your interview is scheduled at three o'clock. But don't come out of your room," he said. "If you need anything, give me a call."

"No problem," I said, looking around the small room that was going to be my home for a couple of days.

"But why all the secrecy?"

"From here on out," he said, "everything's a secret. There are reporters everywhere who'd love to get a photo of potential next bachelors. We have to keep you hidden."

"Okay," I said, as if hiding from roving reporters were the most normal thing in the world.

"Seriously, I'll make sure you have all the food and drink you want," he said as he was leaving. "But *don't* come out of your room."

"Wait," I remember asking him. "Am I the first guy to arrive?"

"I honestly can't say," he said before ducking out of the room.

I sat down on the bed, took off my shoes, and flipped on the television. There was a minibar that had small bottles of alcohol and candy bars, but none was on my list of Sagi-approved foods. Suddenly, all those days of eating according to my schedule seemed as though they might pay off. If the producers liked me, it would be because of my personality—but it couldn't hurt that I now had a great six-pack.

The small room's window looked out into a boring parking lot, and the television couldn't distract me from the thoughts running through my head. When it was finally time for my interview, I couldn't wait to get out of the hotel room. I was more excited than nervous about it. I was the type of guy who always hit it off with my friends' parents. How much different would it be to impress the producers of *The Bachelorette*?

"Hello, I'm Chloe Kingston," a woman said to me, extending her hand. "I'm one of the producers, and I'll be asking you questions."

The room wasn't huge. It had a small table set up with candy and soda along the wall. A cameraman had set up a camera in front of a chair. Chloe sat slightly away to the left of the camera.

"I know it's strange to be filmed, but act naturally," she said. "There are no wrong answers. We're just trying to get to know you."

"Sounds good," I said. Chloe was in her early thirties, with blonde hair pulled back into a loose ponytail. I had never met a producer for a television show, but I imagined them to be more businesslike and professional. It turns out the producers of *The Bachelorette* are very personable and not formal whatsoever. Part of their job is to befriend cast members so they'll later open up to the producers during interviews.

"What's your dream girl?" she asked.

"I want someone I can laugh with," I said, suddenly realizing I was already sounding like a cliché. "I want someone who doesn't take life too seriously. You know, someone who could be my best friend."

She nodded affirmatively as I spoke, as if what I was saying were profound.

"What are your future goals?" she asked. After I explained that I didn't want to sell insurance for the rest of my life, she followed up with, "What do you hope to get out of this experience?"

Her questions were rapid-fire and ranged from my upbringing to my football career.

After about thirty minutes, she closed the folder that had been in her lap, stood up, and said, "You did great! Now I want you to meet a couple of my friends."

She walked me into another room connected to the room where we'd just interviewed.

Much to my surprise, about twenty people were sitting in chairs in a semicircle in front of a television. Immediately, I felt my face turn red. I was overwhelmed at the thought that they'd just seen everything.

"Wow," I managed to say. "I didn't realize I had an audience."

They all looked at me with big smiles. Well, at least they seemed happy to see me.

"Please," Chloe said, motioning to a chair in front of the semicircle. "Have a seat."

If I thought the last interview was intense, this was an inquisition. They started throwing questions at me from all over the room.

"What's your biggest fear?"

"What is your biggest strength?"

"What do you hope to get out of life?"

I answered all their questions with ease. They made me feel comfortable because they laughed at my jokes. That's basically all it takes with me.

"What sort of woman do you typically date?" they asked.

"Well, I don't discriminate," I said, "if that's what you mean. I've dated a woman who is Hispanic, someone who's mixed-race, a girl from Jordan . . . I judge women based on their values, whether we get along, not their race. After all, opposites attract!"

"And what kind of values would you say you have?"

"I'm a man of faith," I said. Then I added a bit more specificity. "I'm a Christian."

When I said the word *Christian*, I wondered if that would be a strike against me. However, it seemed as though everyone liked what they were hearing. I didn't know what they were looking for. Most candidates think the show is looking for someone who has all the right answers. I later learned they were actually looking to see if I was personable and whether I would "show up" on television.

I walked back to my hotel room feeling like I'd just nailed it. I stretched out on the bed, looked at the ceiling, and laughed. *What a weird experience.* Just then, I was yanked out of my reverie when my phone rang.

Mom.

"Hey, do you want to come over for dinner?" she asked.

I was completely at a loss for words.

"Everyone's going to be here," she said. "So I might need you to pick up some things on the way."

"I'm sorry," I said. "I can't."

"Okay, well, you can come over after church on Sunday if you'd like."

"Mom," I said, realizing that the next words that came out of my mouth would hurt her. "I'm not in town. I'm in Los Angeles."

"What?" she said. "Since when? Why? Who are you with?"

I decided I'd gotten far enough in the casting process that it wasn't kind to keep her in the dark, so I was completely honest.

"I'm at a casting call for *The Bachelorette*."

She paused for a couple of seconds, then laughed.

"No, really," she said. "What are you doing?"

"Andrew and Shay submitted an application for me," I said, believing it might be a good idea to lay a little blame on them. "I didn't even know about it."

"Why would you want to go on a trashy television show like that?" she asked. Then she added, "Does Dad know?"

Slowly, Mom began to understand the situation. For months, everyone in the family knew this was a possibility, and we'd kept it only from her. I could tell she was upset by the tone in her voice and the way she clipped her sentences.

"I'm sorry, Mom," I said, realizing how hurtful this must be for her. "I honestly didn't think I'd get this far, and I didn't want you to get upset for no reason."

She ended the conversation by faking her normal "mom voice" to cover up what I knew was sadness and maybe a little anger.

"Okay, well, maybe you can make it next weekend," she said before she hung up.

I felt terrible. Mom was devastated—probably in equal amounts—that I was auditioning for the show and that we'd kept her out of the loop.

When I went back to Dallas, my life suddenly seemed duller than ever, and it didn't help that I'd alienated my mom. A couple of days after I settled back into my normal routine, my phone rang again.

"I just want you to know," Mom said in a soft voice, "that I really want you to get this. If you're selected, I'll be your biggest supporter."

I don't care that I was twenty-eight years old. I'll never get so old that my mom's approval doesn't mean something.

For the next few weeks, the casting director would call to check up on me, to see how I was doing, and to answer any questions I might have.

I was at work when "the call" came, which was appropriate since Andrew and Shay were the instigators of all this.

"Hello, Sean," said Tabby. "I'm happy to offer you an official invitation to be a part of *The Bachelorette*."

Suddenly, I was overwhelmed. But not with a desire to find true love on a reality TV show.

I wanted to win.

———— ✦ ————

"What are you going to wear?" Andrew asked as I was packing to go a few weeks later.

"Since when are you concerned about my wardrobe?" I laughed.

"Just be thankful you're not a girl," Shay said, settling in to the couch next to Andrew. "Guys can get a couple of suits, several ties, and call it a day."

"Tell that to the producers," I said, pulling out the packet of instructions they'd sent me. "I have to bring enough clothes for up to two months, including swimsuits, heavy coats, sweaters, T-shirts, tank tops, casual day clothes, gloves, and hats."

"Think about all the amazing places you'll go," she gushed. "All over the world, probably." She got off the couch, peeked at the papers, and began reading over my shoulder. "You have to 'avoid stripes, small checkered patterns, big patterns, and solid white,'" she said. "Plus, you have to 'be prepared for fourteen formal occasions for the show's rose ceremonies.'"

"Fourteen?" I asked. "That's a lot of clothes. And it's all supposed to fit in two bags."

"Don't worry," Andrew said. "You'll probably be sent home on the first night."

Shay rolled her eyes, but I didn't mind. In fact, when I was in Los Angeles for my casting call, Andrew had sent me an encouraging text:

Mark my words: you're going to win.

I made a note of the date and his exact words in my phone so I'd remember his message. Not only did I appreciate the support from my family, but it also helped that my boss was fine with me going off on this little lark to North Carolina.

The next Bachelorette, Emily Maynard, who'd gotten engaged to—and soon separated from—Bachelor Brad Womack in a previous season, was from Charlotte. Her tragic story had been repeated several times on the show: she'd been engaged to a NASCAR driver when he died in a plane crash in 2004. Just days later, she found out she was pregnant with his child, whom she named after her fiancé: Ricki. When she went on *The Bachelor*, it looked as if she had finally found love again, but her engagement to Brad was short-lived.

In my opinion, Emily was a great choice, and not just because she was gorgeous. In addition to her brown eyes and blonde hair, she had wit, grace, and Southern charm.

There was no way I'd fall in love with her.

I know, I know. It *is* a show about love. I'd watched it enough to understand that. When I was chosen to go on the show, I went back and watched the season of *The Bachelor* on which Emily was a contestant. It reminded me a little of watching film back in college as we prepared for a big football game—except with a few more cocktail dresses. At that time, only two of the official Bachelors or Bachelorettes had tied the knot. The original Bachelorette, Trista Rehn, married season 1 winner Ryan Sutter, while season 7 Bachelorette, Ashley Hebert, married J. P. Rosenbaum. No Bachelors had ever tied the knot with the girl they selected on the show.

"I want to go on a shopping spree with you," Shay said, taking the papers from my hands. "Where's the part about your clothing allowance?"

"Yeah, you won't find anything about it," I said, feeling my throat tighten. "I'm responsible for buying all of my own clothes."

"What?" Shay was incredulous. "That's going to be a lot of money."

When she stated the obvious, I took a deep breath. Anxiety crawled through me until I thought of my wonderful Granddaddy. He was raised in Alabama, poorer than dirt. His father was very abusive physically and drank a lot. Granddaddy used to tell me the story about how when he was fourteen years old, he tried to get a job to take care of his family. He applied at the movie theater, and the manager told him he'd like to give him a job. He didn't get the position, though, because they didn't have uniforms back then. The manager told him, quite frankly, that his clothes weren't nice enough. The thought of my Granddaddy as a fourteen-year-old kid having to support his family really put things into perspective.

"I'll figure it out," I told Shay.

"You can't just hope for the best." Andrew held up his hand. "You need a new suit. A good one. Let Shay and me get you one as our gift."

I was deeply touched by this kind gesture. It was an offer I couldn't refuse.

"It's only because we don't want you to make us look bad," Shay said. "We're the ones who sent in your application, after all."

"And speaking of hideous," Andrew said. "What's up with your hair?"

Shay punched her husband in the arm.

"Weren't you wondering too?"

Instinctively, I reached up to my head and ran my fingers through my hair, which was longer than usual.

"The producers wanted me to grow it out," I said. In one of my previous conversations with the producers, they told me to work on my look by growing out my hair. Maybe my All-American look was too boring for a prime-time television show.

Shay looked at my head skeptically. "I don't think your head is the right shape or . . . something."

The next day, I continued my show preparation by e-mailing the producer, breaking the news that my hair wasn't looking as good as they had hoped, and getting it cut back to its normal, short, boring length. Then I went to the mall and filled up several bags of clothing—T-shirts, shorts, socks, sandals, tennis shoes, everything. But the suits were harder to figure out. Not only were they more expensive, but it was more complicated than simply picking one up at the mall. Apparently, my brother-in-law is the kind of big shot who gets all his suits custom made, so he sent his seamstress to take my measurements. Within weeks, I had a navy blue, perfectly fitted suit. My parents also kindly bought me a couple of suits, which completed my wardrobe for the show.

Emily's season was not going to begin in Hollywood. Because she didn't want to disrupt her daughter's life too dramatically, ABC agreed to bring the show's production to her hometown. On the morning of my flight to Charlotte, North Carolina, I placed my new purchases on the table and began stuffing them into my bags.

"Wait, wait," Andrew said. He and Shay had come over because they agreed to take me to the airport. "Fold your shirts like this, and hang them up as soon as you get there," he said as he situated my clothing in the bag.

"There's just not enough room."

"Well, you can't show up looking like you slept on the street," he said. By the time I had to leave, I threw five bags into the back of Andrew and Shay's Tahoe. Yes, that was more than I was supposed to be allocated, but there was no way to fit all those clothes for all those climates in two bags. As we drove to the Dallas/Fort Worth International Airport, I called Dad.

"You busy?" I asked.

I could tell from his voice he was in a public place.

"I'm in the locker room at the gym, getting ready to work out," he said. "What's going on?"

"I'm on my way to the airport and just wanted to tell you good-bye. I won't be able to talk to you for several weeks."

"Your mom and I have and will continue to pray for you, son," he said. "I love you, and I know God will use you somehow in all of this."

When I hung up the phone, my mind raced. What was I getting myself into? What would it be like to have cameras following me around all the time? What would the other guys be like?

But the one thing that kept coming back to me was the text Andrew sent me when I was auditioning in Los Angeles.

Mark my words: you're going to win.

four

A NOT-SO-MEMORABLE
FIRST IMPRESSION

The producer smiled, with her hand outstretched. "Hand it over."

I arrived in Charlotte about three days before filming was to start, and the first thing I had to do was give up my phone. The producers wanted to control every aspect of our lives, for obvious reasons. They didn't want to invest time and money into our potential relationships with Emily, only to have their investment ruined by former flames wooing us away via e-mail, phone, or text. Also, they didn't want any confidential information leaking out to a hungry press.

For many people, this was the hardest moment of all—handing over the one thing that connects you to friends, family, and—really—the world. But I couldn't wait to get rid of my phone, which had haunted me for months. Every time it rang after the collapse of our company, it meant bad news or a terribly uncomfortable conversation. After things settled down with that situation, it became my connection to work e-mails. I was thrilled that I no longer had to respond to the constant noise of work communication. *Good riddance*, I thought as I turned off my phone and handed it to the producer.

Though I was glad to be free from my phone, it meant there was no easy way to kill time while I was on *The Bachelorette*. My hotel room had nothing for entertainment but a minibar and a hotel television. I'd been on Sagi's diet so long I wouldn't touch the minibar, and watching television got old after about an hour. I sat on the bed, looked out the window, and wondered if any of the guys I saw walking in from the parking lot were my competition. Looking back, I realize those days in the hotel room alone were a big part of the show prep. When I'm bored in normal life, I would've checked scores on ESPN, read the news, or texted my friends. But there, alone in my room, my only real option was to think about Emily. Would I like her? Or, more importantly, would she like me? Would I meet her daughter? What would it be like to date a mom? What should I say to her when I got out of the limo?

My thoughts were interrupted only when staffers would come and grab me to do various tasks—extremely awkward tasks. The first thing I did was take a written psychiatric evaluation.

When you get mad, do you ever think of hurting animals?

How do you feel when you lose twenty dollars?

After I answered five hundred questions, I had to meet with a psychiatrist who traveled with the cast. She read my questionnaire and asked me a few more questions.

"So what's the verdict?" I asked at the conclusion. "Am I normal?"

She didn't declare me "normal," but she did give me the go-ahead on the show. Then I underwent an extensive background search.

Have you ever been involved in pornography?

Have you ever sent anyone nude photos?

Have you ever been convicted of domestic violence?

To ratchet up the awkward a few more notches, the producers had to make sure we had no sexually transmitted diseases. As the nurse drew my blood, I thought, *What have I gotten myself into?*

Of course, we also had photos taken—headshots that would soon be put on *The Bachelorette* website for people to evaluate and judge.

Other than these things—which didn't take up a ton of time—I sat in my hotel room and went stir-crazy. The night before filming was to begin, I was told the producers were scheduled to drop in and introduce themselves. I prepared myself for two or three visits—four, tops. I was surprised when one producer after another after another showed up. By the time I went to bed that night, about twenty people had stopped by, introduced themselves, and gauged whether I was ready for this adventure. One of the producers pulled me aside and lowered his voice.

"Traditionally, we try to pick the two guys we think have the best shot ending up with our girl to be the first and last out of the limo," he said. "We want *you* to be first."

I was so honored by this news that I could barely sleep that night.

———————

The next morning, since I had nothing else to do, I started getting ready early. I paired the custom-fitted navy suit with a white shirt that had a blue checked pattern. I took a deep breath, looked in the mirror, and marveled at how much the cut on a suit can improve your look. *Thank you, Andrew and Shay.* When the knock came on my door, a producer telling me it was time to go, I couldn't get out of that hotel room fast enough.

My limo had three other contestants, to whom I quickly introduced myself. On the show, the guys all seemed to go by their first names (or, even worse, descriptions: "the guy with the bad suit" or "the guy with the crazy eyes.") But in the limo, in the last few moments before we entered the world of *The Bachelorette*, we still had last names, and I met Arie Luyendyk, John Wolfner, and Joe Gendreau.

"Luyendyk?" Joe asked when he met Arie. "Are you kin to Arie Luyendyk, the racecar driver?"

"Yeah," Arie said. "That's my dad."

John (whom we frequently called Wolf) was a data destruction specialist, and Joe was a field energy adviser.

I have some stiff competition, I thought. I don't know what I was expecting, but they all seemed like nice guys—and they in particular became great friends. Of course, I shouldn't describe them as "contestants." The producers of the show didn't want us to view this as a game but as a chance to pursue a real-life love connection between Emily and, well, one of the twenty-five guys sitting in the limos lining the drive.

The show had tried to keep the shooting location under wraps, but word got out fast. I looked up and saw a local news helicopter getting footage for their evening broadcast. The mansion was in a beautiful, gated community, but that didn't stop some fifty to sixty fans from trying to sneak on the property to catch a glimpse of the action. The show had hired off-duty police officers to keep the crowd at bay.

On the way, through a handheld radio a producer in our limo was holding, I heard that one of the limos had a collision with a manure truck.

"That doesn't happen when we film in Hollywood," Scott said. Scott was one of the two house producers who spent all his time with the guys.

I readjusted my tie and took a deep breath. Through the tinted windows, I could see the mansion at the end of the fifty-foot drive, and I knew Emily was in there somewhere, waiting to meet us.

"This must be the biggest thing to happen in North Carolina in a long time," said Scott. I followed his gaze, looked through the tinted glass, and saw what looked like some sort of monster—a gigantic glob of tree branches and leaves—amid the trees.

"Is that Chewbacca?" one guy asked. A security guard had camouflaged himself with special clothing designed to resemble heavy foliage. It was the sort of gear hunters use, which was appropriate since this guy was hunting for photographers and reporters trying to get some sort of scoop. I watched as he crawled toward us making sure no one got a glimpse of the behind-the-scenes action. Preseason spoilers are a big business and earn prestige, page views, and money for the person who gets the goods.

The biggest spoiler happened during season 13 of *The Bachelor*. In the show's 2009 romantic finale, single dad Jason Mesnick proposed to former Dallas Cowboys cheerleader Melissa Rycroft. Viewers at home swooned as Jason and Melissa began "happily ever after." But just seconds after the show aired, the after-the-rose ceremony came on, showing Jason and Melissa sitting as far away from each other as humanly possible while still being on the same couch. Jason then proceeded to dump Melissa on live television, saying he actually had feelings for the first runner-up. Viewers reeled from the turn of events, but attentive readers of the spoiler blogs had seen it coming for weeks. Somehow, someone had correctly predicted the biggest shock of the franchise's history—weeks before it happened.

Understandably, the producers were nuts about secrecy. Even though we signed confidentiality agreements, gave up our phones, and were forbidden to speak to the press, information still leaked out. I think this happened for two reasons. First, it's basic human nature: if someone knows something juicy, he or she can't wait to tell it. People send bloggers tips such as, "Hey, I'm a friend of so-and-so's and I heard that . . ." Plus, I wonder if some of these spoilers have a few people inside the show, too, who give them the valuable inside scoop.

The quest for that inside information was why there was a security guard in a ghillie suit inching toward us, reporters crawling over this small town, and helicopters flying overhead.

<hr />

What is going on? I thought. Only days ago, I was sitting in my cramped office asking people to buy more life insurance.

"First limo," I heard come out of the radio in the hand of one of the producers, Mary Kate. "Let's go."

The driver pulled around slowly under the carport of the mansion. The doors to the multimillion-dollar house were propped open, revealing an ornate hallway with a gorgeous staircase. The show's lighting technicians knew just how to shine a light here, dim a light there, and burn a few candles to transform a regular room into something out of a fairy tale.

When I drove up, Emily was standing in the foyer, wearing a gold dress and a nervous smile. Candles were everywhere—on tables, on the steps, on pillars, on the floor—and light sparkled off her dress. It sounds cheesy, but she really looked like an angel.

I opened the door of the limo and had two thoughts: *Don't trip over your words*, and *Don't make a fool of yourself.*

My memory blacked out at that point, because I don't even remember meeting her.

According to the broadcast I watched later, here's how it played out: I climbed out of the limo, straightened my jacket, and climbed up ten stairs.

"Welcome to Charlotte," Emily said.

"You look amazing," I said.

We hugged. I told her I looked forward to getting to know her more. We hugged again.

After my intro, I walked into the mansion, settled in for a long night, and felt glad I didn't trip over my words or feet. Certainly I'd held my own compared to the parade of guys who made their introductions *after* me. As the guys came in one by one, I heard about the gimmicks they came up with—or the producers came up with—to make a memorable first impression. One guy dressed up like a grandma, another brought in an ostrich egg (for reasons I can't quite remember), one brought her a real glass slipper, and another broke into dance moves. Oh, and one guy—named Jef Holm—came in on a skateboard while clinging to the limo's bumper. The host, Chris Harrison, admitted that the limo came in much faster than they'd hoped, but Jef rolled in fast, tossed the skateboard into the bushes, and wowed Emily. I was interested to see who the last guy to arrive would be, especially considering that the producers took special care to relegate the guys who seemed most likely to end up with Emily to the first and last slots. As we waited for the last guy to get out of the limo, we realized he wasn't even in the limo at all. Overhead, we heard a chopper.

"Is that a news helicopter?" someone asked, peering out the window.

"Nope," another said. "It looks like a guy is getting out of that."

Sure enough, it happened. A guy jumped out of the helicopter in a move that definitely upstaged Jef's skateboard.

When I heard about all this, I wondered if my two hugs and polite "nice to meet you" would be enough to stand out.

A few minutes later, Emily came in on the arm of "helicopter guy," followed by a camera crew. It was amazing to see this in action. At the casting call, I'd been filmed with a single, stationary camera. Having an entire crew of people standing around in various places catching everything you do on

film was quite a new experience. Between the lighting, the fairy-tale setting, and the camera and sound guys, nothing felt real.

Emily made her way around the group, chatting and pulling some guys
aside for private conversations in areas that the producers had set up with
cameras and romantic lighting. Getting time with her was crucial, because
there was the all-important "first impression rose" at stake. It seemed a
little odd that all these guys were competing for a rose, but the flower was
just a symbol. It represented an invitation to stay longer. Emily's job was to
give this rose to one of the guys who really stood out, thereby protecting
him from being sent home during the first rose ceremony.

No one was looking forward to the rose ceremony. At the end of each
cocktail party, Emily would hand out a single red rose to each guy she'd like
to get to know better. On the first night, we were told, she was sending *six*
guys home. As the evening progressed—and beer glasses got drained—a
palpable sense of desperation came over the group. Thankfully, everyone
was aware of the general flow of the evening. Tonight was about starting
casual conversation, making an impression, and not taking up too much of
her time. It was only considerate to make room for the other guys.

Not everyone felt this way.

"Helicopter guy" was having his private moment with her in the courtyard as the rest of us milled around inside. I kept asking producers when I
could talk to her. Finally, Scott pointed at me and said, "You're up."

"Mind if I steal her for a minute or two?" I asked politely after making
my way out to them. I normally wouldn't interrupt people having a conversation like this, but I was now on "Planet Bachelorette," where normal
behavioral rules didn't apply.

"I certainly mind," the other bachelor said pointedly. "But I don't know
if I can object."

Awkward silence.

"Well," I said. "I'd appreciate it."

He didn't budge.

"Well, thank you," Emily said to him, indicating it was time for him to
go. He muttered something about how I needed to treat her like a princess as

he walked back into the mansion. Inside, some of the guys who'd witnessed his weird response confronted him about it, and a *Bachelorette* villain was born. I'm no expert on the show, but it seems as though every season there's "that guy." (Or on *The Bachelor*, "that girl.") That's the person who isn't there to make friends and proceeds to make sure he is the most unfriendly person there—except to the Bachelorette's face, naturally.

It didn't matter to me, because I got a chance to talk to Emily. While these cocktail parties were supposedly casual meet-and-greets, I had a strategy. Every time I talked to her, I had one idea that I wanted to get across. On the first night, for example, I wanted to tell her about my family back home. I was just able to get the words out when someone interrupted. However, our conversation went well, and I couldn't wait to get to know her better.

The night stretched out longer than it probably appeared on television, because it took time to set up cameras to capture Emily talking with each and every guy. Before she was swept away by the host, Chris Harrison, she gave the first impression rose to a single dad whose kid had handwritten Emily a letter.

Well-played, Single Dad.

While Emily was deliberating over whom to send home, the producers lined us up to hear the verdict. We waited while Emily made her final decisions and the producers arranged the guys' names into the order they wanted her to call them out. Since it was the first night, no one knew all the guys' names yet. A producer stood off to the side, to give her helpful name prompts.

When the cameras started rolling, Chris Harrison walked in and clinked a champagne flute. Once he had everyone's attention—which he certainly already had—he began explaining how everything would work. I suddenly felt anxious. I don't remember what Harrison said, but I knew the score. If she gave me a rose, I'd stick around. If I didn't get a rose, I'd be on the next plane departing from Charlotte Douglas International Airport.

Emily picked up a flower from the tray and paused.

"Coming into this, I was really scared—scared that maybe you guys weren't going to be into me or I wouldn't have the feelings I hoped I would have, especially on the first night," she said. "You all have exceeded my expectations a million times over. It made me really hopeful, and I'm really confident that it can really work out this time!"

And with that, she began handing out the roses.

Charlie.

Kalon.

Arie.

Jef.

I honestly didn't think I'd be one of the first to leave and had a quiet confidence as I stood there. However, I have to admit, my heart pounded as she went down her list. Shay and Andrew had joked around about how I didn't want to be the guy sent home on the first night.

Aaron.

Joe.

Chris.

Alejandro.

Finally, when I heard her say, "Sean," I sighed in relief. I didn't realize I had been holding my breath. Emily sent home six guys that night and—thankfully—I wasn't one of them. By the time I got my rose, it was two o'clock in the morning—and we weren't finished yet.

Much behind-the-scenes action happened that made the initial cocktail party—and, really, everything on the show—take up so much time: Every guy had "In the Moment" chats (known as ITMs) with the producer and a more formal sit-down with Emily. Cameras were set up for the ceremony—and then taken down. Emily had to take occasional breaks during the night to rest or eat because it's such an exhausting evening.

In fact, we didn't wrap filming until six o'clock in the morning. As soon as the cameras stopped rolling, Harrison went into the kitchen and made everyone breakfast burritos.

The first evening on *The Bachelorette* was certainly memorable. I headed back to my room, clutching that rose.

I knew it wouldn't be my last.

five

THE BIG BABY

"Gentlemen, good morning. Let me tell you how this works," host Chris Harrison said to the bachelors after he called us out of the mansion. There were a total of sixteen guys left vying for Emily's attention, and we all waited anxiously as Harrison laid out exactly what was going to happen next.

"Each week, you'll be going on dates with Emily: one-on-one dates and group dates. There will be roses up for grabs on each date. If you get a rose, you're safe during the next rose ceremony."

It was hot that March day in Charlotte, and the guys shuffled in their seats. "Now let me tell you about the individual dates. They're a little more complicated. You need to have your bags packed, because if Emily decides not to give you a rose on those dates, you'll be going home immediately.

"A word of advice," Harrison said. "Not all of you will be going on dates this week. If and when you get time with Emily, take advantage of it. It might be the only time you have with her. Who gets to go on what dates? Or who doesn't get a date? Well, you'll be told on date cards. I have the first one right here." He placed the card on a table and walked away.

Someone grabbed the card and read it aloud. I'm not sure who went on the first one-on-one date, but it wasn't me. This sent me into a waiting pattern—very common in the world of *The Bachelorette*. A date card would come, guys would get pumped for their dates, and the rest of us would hang out at the mansion. Not a bad life, of course. Since there was no way to kill time by surfing the net, checking e-mail, or texting friends, we hung out at the pool, ate some of the great food they left for us, and relaxed with the other guys. In the mornings, I'd go out onto the second-floor porch that overlooked the courtyard and read from the book I'd brought.

Jesus Calling had a devotion for every day of the year. The author— Sarah Young—wrote from Jesus' point of view, so the book is like Jesus talking to you. Because the readings are based on Scripture, I couldn't wait to read them when I woke up. Ever since my spiritual renewal after college, I felt like I needed the Bible to get through the day with the right mind-set. And since I was in such an extraordinarily unusual environment, I needed God even more.

"I will not show you what is on the road ahead, but I will equip you for the journey,"[4] I read one muggy morning in the courtyard of the mansion. As I read the words, I really felt like Jesus was speaking to me.

"Hey, what are you reading?" asked a voice from behind me. It was Alejandro, a bright, urban mushroom farmer from San Francisco who'd been on *Forbes*' "30 under 30" list. Being a mushroom farmer seemed so much cooler than being an insurance salesman. It was hard not to compare myself to these accomplished guys.

"This is my daily devotional from a book," I said. "Every day, it's like a message from God." As soon as I said the words, I knew I was labeling myself as "the evangelical Christian guy," but I wasn't going to hide who I was.

"Cool," Alejandro said before walking back into the house.

And so we whiled away the hours, waiting until the next date card would arrive. I didn't have a date during the first week. But on the second group date, finally, my name was on the card, along with a bunch of the other guys' names. The invitation simply read, "Let's play."

The coy wording left me wondering what on earth we'd end up doing. The producers never told us what we would be doing, only what we should wear. The word came down that we were supposed to dress for outdoor sports. *This*, I thought, *could benefit me because of my football background.*

When we arrived at a park on a sunny day, Emily was waiting for us, holding—you guessed it—a football. *I've got this.*

We tossed the football in the park while all the guys tried to impress her. It was hard to figure out the dynamics of a group date, something that would never happen in real life. Because I'm not the type of guy to aggressively pursue women, I hung back as some of the others flirted and joked with her. Then, suddenly, she left.

"What do you guys think we're going to be doing today?" someone asked.

Well, you have to hand it to the producers. They knew how to put us in uncomfortable—and revealing—situations. Instead of tossing the pigskin, Emily introduced us to a group of her friends. Their job was to interview us individually, to see who would be a great dad for Emily's six-year-old daughter. Nothing was off limits, so they asked us: *Have you ever cheated? What things do you have in common with Emily? Have you ever dated someone with a child? What is the worst quality about yourself?* And my personal favorite, *What's up with the guy with the egg?*

Watching the guys go before me was nerve-racking—I saw one of the guys dance and another do push-ups on a picnic table. When it was my turn, they didn't hesitate to start grilling me. After a few warm-up questions—what I did for a living and where I was from—they got down to business.

"So why do you think you have a connection with Emily?" one of her friends asked.

"I think we've connected on a few points," I said.

"Like what?"

"Well," I began, "I come from a family that's centered on faith. That's who we are and what's most important to us."

The ladies seemed to like that answer but pressed harder.

"Are you ready to be a dad?"

"Well, I don't have kids, so that would be new to me," I said. "But my dad has taught me how to be a man for the past twenty-eight years, so I think I'm prepared."

The women relaxed a bit after that, telling me I was cute and asking me if I worked out.

"Only occasionally," I said, probably causing Sagi back home to yell at the screen.

"Don't lie," Emily's friend Wendy said. "What would your superhero power be if you could choose one?"

I knew they liked me because the questions seemed to be getting sillier. "I guess I'd like to fly."

"Yeah, you'd look good in a cape," Wendy said. "Or Spandex. Hey, will you take your shirt off?"

I was taken aback by the question and laughed. When I saw she was not laughing, I asked, "Seriously?"

"Yeah, we need to know what we're dealing with."

Of course, there was no way I was going to be "that guy." I wasn't going to be parading around without a shirt on national television. Yet the ladies insisted—and the producers encouraged me from behind the cameras. "Come on, Sean," they said. "It'll be fun."

I certainly didn't want to be a spoilsport, so I dutifully took off my shirt and did push-ups, as requested. Wendy sat on my back as I did them and said, "This is like a dream come true."

That's when I knew I'd officially won over Emily's friends.

And I'd officially become "the guy with the abs."

After playing with a couple dozen kids in the park while the ladies compared notes with Emily on us, it was time for the evening portion of the date. We went to a restaurant and club in Charlotte that had two stories. The guys were on the second floor, while Emily was down below. There were about twelve guys on the group date, and they went down one at a time to spend a few minutes with her alone.

I knew I'd killed the date portion with her friends and had a feeling Emily was digging me. I didn't know what had happened with her and anyone else. I'd been back at the mansion reading my book and taking dips in the pool. But I felt good about my position in the pack.

It was time to make a move.

I made a paper fortune-teller, which is a piece of paper folded into a certain shape that allows you to write questions and answers underneath flaps. The way it works is simple: Someone picks a number and the person with the paper fortune-teller moves the flaps back and forth depending on the answers. Normally, the questions are pretty silly—who's your favorite singer, what's your favorite color, and so forth. Every junior high kid knows how to make them to pass time during math class.

Of course, I didn't care who her favorite singer was. Instead of playing the game by the conventional rules, I wrote, "Can I have a kiss?"—or some variation—under every flap. I was the last bachelor to have alone time with Emily. We chatted for a few minutes, and I could tell it was going really well.

"You're perfect," she said, reaching for my hand.

"Wait a minute," I said. "I'm far from perfect."

"Well, you seem like you're just the whole package—you've got it all."

That's when I decided to give the paper fortune-teller a chance.

"Want to play a game?" When she picked a corner, I lifted the paper flap to reveal my question.

"Can you have a kiss?" she read and smiled.

That's when I leaned in and we had our first—amazing—kiss.

Later, when watching the episode on television, I realized they didn't show this moment. I think the producers decided to build up our second kiss (at the rose ceremony) and portray it to viewers as our first. Nevertheless, I carried that moment in my heart from that point on, and it gave me such confidence. I really wanted the rose to show the other guys where I stood, and that's exactly what happened.

"I'd like to give the rose tonight to . . . Sean," she said. "You backed up everything you've been saying since day one. And I'm very thankful for that."

◆———◆

I sat outside by myself the next morning with my coffee, my *Jesus Calling* book, and a million thoughts running through my head. As I settled down to read my devotional, Alejandro and Charlie came up and sat on the furniture around me.

"What's Jesus saying today?" Alejandro asked. Charlie laughed.

I realized my Bible study probably was strange to most of the guys there. Few, if any, of them were Christians, so I didn't advertise that I was having a morning devotional. I never said, "Hey, guys, listen to this." But I'd definitely oblige if asked.

"'Come to Me with a teachable spirit, eager to be changed,'" I read. "'A close walk with Me is a life of continual newness. . . . Seek My face with an open mind, knowing that your journey with Me involves being transformed.'"[5]

Soon, word spread that I had daily devotionals, and guys started showing up. I really liked the guys, and being in such a strange situation bonded us together. Even though most of our time was spent lounging around waiting for dates—or recovering from them—the mornings were dedicated to our little devotionals. Without even meaning to, I found myself leading this Bible study on the set of *The Bachelorette*.

During the next rose ceremony—with the rose firmly attached to my lapel—I had nothing to fear. I watched as the other guys ushered Emily to various locations on the property, competing for time and conversation. As with most of these cocktail parties, there was no shortage of drama. The egg guy finally decided to break his egg, which he had named Shelly. Then, when Emily was talking to one of the guys, he called her situation—the fact that she already had a child—a "compromise." Of course, this was the same guy who admitted to Emily's friends that he'd cheated on an ex-girlfriend (his third cousin) and had a one-night stand. When Emily stormed through the house—wearing boots instead of her heels, because she didn't even care to keep up appearances for the camera—I knew things wouldn't end well for the guy. She promptly escorted him to the door without waiting for the ceremony.

She was still a little shaken by the time I caught up with her later in the evening.

"It's only been forty-eight hours," I said, sitting down beside her near the roaring fire. "But I kind of missed you."

"You did? Why? Flatter me for a minute." She smiled, taking my hand. "I need it."

Emily's Southern charm was evident, even when she was distressed.

"Normally, if I had such a connection with someone, I wouldn't have waited two days to talk to you," I said. "I would've texted you to tell you how much fun I had being with you."

"You wouldn't play the 'two-day rule'?"

"I wouldn't have played a game at all."

I'd never felt closer to her. Since our kiss, I felt confident in our relationship. I knew in my heart that none of the other guys would have the connection we had. Not only did we already share a special moment after the group date, but faith was also important to her. The other guys were great—I was becoming good friends with Charlie, Alejandro, Jef, Arie, and John Wolfner. But I didn't get the feeling they shared her Christian faith. In my heart, without losing sight of the fact that we were on a reality TV dating game, I knew we had an undeniable connection.

"I want to talk to you about something your friends brought up," I said.

"Oh no." Emily laughed.

"They asked if I could be a good dad to Ricki. For the past twenty-eight years, my dad has taught me how to be the greatest father," I said. "I don't want to get ahead of myself, but if we were to get married, Ricki would be my daughter. She can call me Sean; she can call me whatever she wants. But she'd be mine."

"That was exactly what I needed to hear. I know you are good-looking," she said, "but I wanted to thank you for also being so sweet."

I could tell I'd touched Emily deeply. When I leaned in and kissed her, the producers made it look like our first kiss for the viewers at home. But to me, this was another moment in a fabulous week solidifying our relationship.

Our time together was quickly interrupted. I never had quite enough time to hang out with her and longed for a one-on-one date to spend real time with her. When I relinquished her to whichever guy came in next, I went back out to the mansion's main room with a full heart. Though it seemed improbable, I felt like I could really be interested in Emily.

When I got back to where the guys were sitting, I could tell they were agitated.

"I saw Emily kissing Arie," one of the guys said. "Right there, in the hall."

I couldn't believe my ears.

"When?" Of course, I'd just kissed her two days ago—not to mention two minutes ago. How could she also be kissing Arie? Looking back, I realized this was a "How naive could you have been?" moment. But it felt like a punch in the gut. Planet Bachelorette was a new world for me—everything that I'd been taught about loyalty and dating was on temporary hiatus.

When the show broadcast, all the viewers saw between Emily and me was a sweet kiss and a declaration that I'd consider Emily's daughter my own. But behind the scenes, I was furious.

"It's offensive she'd kiss Arie in plain sight of the other guys," one of the bachelors said. This is the convoluted world of the show. In normal life, a guy would be angry if a girl he was interested in kissed another guy, period. But normal rules didn't apply, so we tried to find new boundaries. Since it wasn't reasonable to ask Emily not to kiss the other guys—whom she was technically dating!—we drew a new moral line: it was wrong to flaunt it in front of our faces.

During the rose ceremony, I didn't make eye contact with her and stood as rigid as a soldier. Because I had the rose, I didn't care what names she was saying. I was safe, but did I really want to be there? After another guy was sent home in the "limo of shame," the producers passed out the champagne to the guys as they did every week. Then they had us gather in the middle of the room, raise our glasses, and toast with a "Here's to another great week" type of thing. By the time they got around to pouring the champagne, I was so steamed I couldn't even raise my glass.

"Sean, aren't you going to toast?" Emily called me out, playfully.

I gave a halfhearted shrug.

In case you're wondering, that's what it looks like when I'm being a baby.

Typically, when the camera crew is done with that final shot, guys linger to see if they can talk to Emily before the producer pulls her away. Face time with her when the cameras aren't rolling is at a premium. That night when they yelled, "Cut!" I darted into the courtyard, took off my tie, and threw off my jacket.

I was done.

As I sat on the outdoor furniture, fuming, I heard someone come up behind me.

Emily put a hand on my shoulder. She was followed by her producer.

"Listen, guys," Mary Kate said. "I'm not supposed to let her talk to you off camera, but she begged me."

Without a word, I motioned for her to sit down.

"Sean, I'm so sorry if you heard anything or saw anything," she said, her voice soft with emotion. "I really care about you."

Her words couldn't cut through my anger.

"Yeah, okay," I said. "Whatever."

When she and Mary Kate left, I knew I hadn't handled the situation very well. My friend Charlie came out with a producer named Jonah to commiserate. Jonah is the kind of guy you can't imagine living outside of Hollywood, with his wild hair he wears like an Afro. He looks like Sideshow Bob from *The Simpsons*, but with an unkempt beard. (His hair even has its own Twitter handle.) Normally, Jonah and I kicked back and had a great time on set.

Not that night.

"I want to go home," I told him. "I don't need this, and I don't need her."

He let me rant for a while before he finally decided to push back a bit.

"Listen, Sean. This is a show about making relationships with multiple people. Maybe she shouldn't have done it in the house where someone else could have seen her, but of course that stuff is gonna happen."

We spent the night in front of the fireplace in the courtyard talking about the situation. By around four o'clock in the morning, I'd finally managed to cool off.

Reluctantly, I realized Jonah was right.

I'd signed up for a show with a premise that flew in the face of the way things were normally supposed to work. Being mad at Emily for following the rules of the show wasn't fair. Plus, she was concerned enough about it to follow me into the courtyard. It made me think, *Okay, she really doesn't want me to leave. She wants me to be in this.*

I shuffled back to my room, exhausted but satisfied that Emily did care about me.

In my heart, however, something didn't feel quite right.

six

GETTING ON
MY SOAPBOX

"Love takes no prisoners," the date card read.

Though I had no idea what that cryptic message meant, I was excited my name was on it so I could—finally—spend real time with Emily.

It had been a long time coming.

The morning after the cocktail party, Chris Harrison told us we were leaving Charlotte for good. Within two hours, we were packed and on our way to Bermuda. While there, I'd done nothing but sit around in the sun while she went out on group dates and two-on-one dates with the guys. Without a cell phone, laptop, or any ability to connect with friends back home, I was left to hang out with the guys and my thoughts. The guys were great, but almost all my thoughts were of Emily. Sadly, I wasn't able to spend too much time with her until my first one-on-one date during our next stop: London, where—apparently—love would take no prisoners.

The show makes a big deal out of location changes, and they really played up London. Chris Harrison met us in historic Trafalgar Square around seven o'clock in the morning. There weren't many people out and about, and the morning sun was reflecting off Big Ben down the street. It was a great moment, even before Harrison put things in perspective for us. "Only one of you will become Emily's husband. Yeah, I said it—*husband*."

Just hearing that word sobered us. Well, some of us. It was evident by this time that some of the guys were into Emily and some weren't. Though I had always maintained that it would be ridiculous to find love on a reality TV show, I was gradually being convinced. Maybe I was wrong.

When I met Emily the next day for our one-on-one date, she didn't look as radiant as normal. Somewhere between Bermuda and London, she'd gotten pretty sick.

"We're going to take a tour of London, in the most perfect and iconic way," Emily said after greeting me. As she was talking, one of those red double-decker buses came around the bend and stopped just for us.

"Are you sure you're up for this?" I asked as we sat in the open-air bus with the wind cutting through our jackets.

"I wouldn't have done this," she said, holding back a sniffle, "had it not been you today."

We drove around the city, seeing Big Ben, Westminster Abbey, and Buckingham Palace. It felt so natural to be with Emily, and I looked for any sort of reassurance that I might be winning her heart. Because of the context of the show, Emily couldn't openly express preference for one guy over another. Even if she developed feelings of love, she wouldn't be at liberty to express it to anyone until the proposal.

This is not a show policy. Rather, it's just how things work out. It would be inconsiderate to tell one guy she loved him when she might not necessarily have had the time to develop feelings for the others. That meant, on our date, I began looking for clues to how she really felt. In the meantime, I enjoyed putting my arm around her and pulling her into me to keep her warm. Plus, I thought it was cool that she didn't complain about being under the weather.

"I'm really glad today's date is with you," she said. "Normally, when I meet guys who look like you, they're really boring. But you're the opposite of boring." Throughout the day, she grabbed my hand several times and said, "You're just perfect."

There was that word again. Every time she called me that, I felt flattered but corrected her. I knew—and she'd soon find out if we got to spend real time together—I was far from perfect. Nevertheless, I appreciated the fact that she seemed to be falling for me. Emily was beginning to seem like the ideal woman for me—not because of her outward beauty, but because of her faith.

One-on-ones were daylong affairs, followed by an evening dinner date. Though, it must be said, the dinner portion was never as romantic as it seemed. Before we went on the date, the producers sent food to our hotel rooms. We ate in our rooms and then went out for dinner, where we were given beautiful food arranged nicely on the plate. This was just for show. No one looks good eating, and microphones pick up all kinds of chomping. (Just listen during the next season when someone slurps wine during the date.)

We were told to keep things light during the day portion of the date. If we had something serious to bring up, we waited until the evening. Throughout the date, the producers pulled us aside individually for ITM chats. The at-home viewers saw us doing our various activities, but periodically the camera would cut to Emily or me talking about the date. The producers did this so the viewers at home could sense our feelings about how the date was progressing in real time.

"How do you think the date is going so far?" they might ask. "What did you think when Emily said this?" and "Are you excited about tonight's dinner date?"

During one ITM chat in Hyde Park, the producer named Scott—who became a great friend—said, "We have an idea. We're going to go on a walk, and we're going to come to Speakers' Corner."

Speakers' Corner, I soon learned, used to be a site for public hangings, but now it's a spot where people bring their soapboxes—little stepladders—to say whatever they'd like: religious sermons, political diatribes, or jokes. It's located on a famous strip of land between the green lawns of Hyde Park and the city's bustling traffic. Only two things are off-limits: profanity and insulting the queen.

"We think it would be really cool if you got up there and spoke on love," Scott said.

"Love?" I asked, incredulous. I've always been deathly afraid of public speaking. I'm even more afraid of public speaking on topics that might sound cheesy. "What specifically?"

"Just whatever comes to mind," he said. It didn't take me long to relent. "Once you walk up to the crowd," he said, "look for a guy on a soapbox giving a speech. Emily doesn't know anything about this, so just act like you're listening to him. We've arranged for him to ask you if you want to come up and say anything. Then it's up to you."

When we approached Speakers' Corner, the energy was palpable. People were pontificating, hecklers were punctuating speeches with insults, and the crowd was very attentive to some guy's rant. Suddenly, one of the guys he was jarring with looked at me and asked, "What do you think?"

"About what?"

"Freedom of speech," he said.

"I agree with that one hundred percent."

"Why don't you come up here so everyone can hear you?"

Even though I knew it was coming, I had no idea what I was going to say—absolutely no idea. I got up on the soapbox and started saying what came to mind.

"Let me tell you what I think about love," I began.

"Okay," a man said from the crowd. "All right." The atmosphere was part political rally–part church revival.

"Love is about giving yourself completely to someone . . . with an eternal type of love. Love is a bond much deeper than most people can comprehend."

The crowd was getting into it, and their enthusiasm was energizing. "Now, I've never experienced that type of love, but I've been in the presence of it. My parents have it, my grandparents have it, and I'm searching for it."

"You haven't found it yet?" someone yelled.

"I'm with this beautiful woman today. I'm not saying love is there yet, but I'm hopeful it will develop."

At least, that's what the viewers at home saw. In real life, my speech was interrupted by a guy on the front row who kept yelling out political questions.

"What do you think about double taxation?" he yelled.

"Hey, I'm talking about love here, buddy," I said. I tried to ignore him, but he kept asking me weird financial questions.

This speech was a turning point for me. Making a speech at the famous Speakers' Corner about love was about as far out of my comfort zone as I could get. I didn't want to say those things in front of the crowd in London, and I definitely didn't want to deliver a speech in front of the millions of people watching from home. By the time I stepped down off the soapbox, I was glad it was over but felt proud of myself.

We toured the city all day. We took a break to change and get ready for dinner, which gave Emily and me about an hour to rest. During that hour, we nestled into a couch, and I had my arm around her. Every once in a while the cameras had to reposition, so the crew would leave us alone. Those moments with just the two of us always felt special. During those times, I held her.

"I'm having such a great day," I said.

"Me too," she said, giving me a light kiss.

I was very aware that her lips should've been the last thing I was putting on mine, but there's no way I was going to miss out on this intimate time with her just because of her cold. (When I got back to my room, I dropped Emergen-C vitamin tablets into water and probably drank ten glasses of it.) By the time we made it to our evening date, Emily's voice was as raspy as a five-pack-a-day smoker.

The date card's mysterious "Love takes no prisoners" referred to our evening dinner in the Tower of London's dungeon, a former prison where Anne Boleyn was famously beheaded in 1536 for treason against Henry VIII. *Bon appétit!*

We managed to have a nice evening, even though Emily didn't feel well. I could tell she was trying to figure out if I was as perfect as she'd thought.

"So is this the night when you're going to drop the bomb and tell me that you're divorced three times and have seven children?"

"What you see is what you get," I said.

"You have everything that could make you perfect, but you are humble in a way that you don't try to sell yourself," she said. "I like that."

By this time, I had zero doubt I was the guy. This was partially due to the fact that I'd gotten to know all the other bachelors really well. My friendships with the guys—Jef, Arie, Wolf, Charlie—were a great bonus. While they were all nice guys, I knew from a faith standpoint I was really the only one who matched up with Emily's beliefs. I noticed she was different around me than she was when she was with the others. It gave me hope—almost a certainty—that I was the one for whom Emily was falling. Plus, she kept sending me messages: she told me she wanted to have a big family; she told me I set the whole tone of the show ever since I got out of the limo first. At the end of the date, she told me something that I took as reassurance.

"Days like this make me excited for what's next," she said.

What's next, of course, implies a future.

"I know what this show is all about," I said. "But I'm confident in what we have."

"Me too," she said.

———————

My sister was right. Being a part of the cast of *The Bachelorette* took me all over the world. We went from North Carolina to Bermuda to London to Croatia. In Croatia, I didn't get to spend much personal time with Emily since I was relegated to the group date. We were able to steal a bit of private conversation, however.

"You know where you stand. Don't worry if you're not spending as much time with me as you want," she whispered. "More time will come, I promise."

Every week, Emily sent another disappointed guy home, but I never got nervous during the rose ceremonies. I was confident we aligned better than anyone else.

By the time the group had been narrowed down to six, we went to Prague. Chris Harrison set the stage, once again, by filming that episode's opening scene at Prague Castle—the largest ancient castle in the world and home of the president of the Czech Republic.

It was a chilly morning, and the streets were virtually empty. "This is by far the biggest week. Your relationship is about to take a huge step forward," he said. "The four of you who receive roses this week will be able to take Emily back home to meet your family—a huge step in any relationship."

Right in the middle of shooting, we were treated to a private performance of the changing of the guards, which happens every hour, on the hour. It was a memorable moment as we stood atop that chilly hill, with an amazing view of this historic city. Afterward, Chris continued with his speech.

"This week, there will be four dates—three romantic one-on-one dates and a group date," he said. "The man who gets that rose is guaranteed to get that hometown date and introduce Emily to your family."

I was staying with the guys close to Prague Castle and the Charles Bridge, at a hotel called Aria. Emotions were high among Arie, Chris, John, Doug, Jef, and me, because everything was accelerating. When the prospect of bringing Emily home to meet family came up, things got serious fast. The three one-on-one dates were more critical than ever.

I didn't get one.

There I was in the hotel in this gorgeous city, alone. Well, I was never truly alone. I almost always was surrounded by the guys, producers, sound technicians, and cameramen. One night, however, I managed to sneak out of my room and go to the first floor of our hotel, where there was a community computer.

Of course, this was forbidden. We were supposed to disappear completely during our ten weeks on the show. But I'd never experienced any type of fame at all. I knew that if I could just log on to that computer, I could Google my name and find articles about me and the show. It was a strange feeling to know there was Internet chatter about me—when I was previously an unknown insurance salesman. The show had not yet begun to air, but I knew the spoilers had already been on the case and revealed our identities.

I got into the lobby and looked around. No producers. No cameramen. No problem.

My heart raced as I slipped into the chair in front of the computer and logged on for the first time in almost two months.

"Sean Lowe Bachelorette," I typed into the search engine. Within a matter of seconds, a few articles came up about the upcoming cast of *The Bachelorette*. It was all generic stuff, a description of where I lived, what I did for a living. But it was the first time I had my own Google footprint—small as it was—and it felt pretty weird.

When I got back into the room, no one had noticed I'd been missing. A couple of the guys who didn't get one-on-one dates were devastated. I was disappointed, too, but I felt good about where I stood with Emily. Now that we were deeper into the season, the producers—with whom we spent so much time—started asking more personal and probing questions. Scott, the producer assigned to me, pulled me aside in Prague and said, "It's obvious you and Emily have a special connection."

This scratched exactly where I itched. Unlike people who would later be watching at home, I had no idea what sorts of connections Emily was making with the other guys. My only way of gauging our relationship was through our personal interactions—and those were few and far between. The producers, on the other hand, saw everything that was going on. Since one of the producers, Scott, said we had a connection, it confirmed what I already felt.

"Do you think you could see yourself marrying Emily?" he asked.

These chats with the producers really stirred emotions inside me and made me think about it. *Do I? Yeah, I guess I kind of do.*

"I just hate that I can't spend time with Emily," I confided in Scott the evening that my good friend John Wolfner was on his one-on-one date with her.

"Let's figure out a way to get you alone with her," Scott said. "She's going to come home, drop Wolf off. Let's make a move."

"What do you mean?" He had my attention.

"Let Wolf tell you about his date," he said. "Then you can slip out and try to find her."

I was thrilled at the idea of having a private one-on-one. (Well, as private as you could get on a televised dating show.) After Wolf came home and told us the evening went really well, I excused myself and slipped out the door.

Scott, my coconspirator, was waiting for me outside. "We're going to have to hurry to find her."

I knew Emily was staying at another hotel just around the corner from us, but I had no idea where she was.

"She has to be close because she just dropped Wolf off, right?"

I remember thinking, *I hope I can find her.*

I was so naive.

Of course I was going to find her. I was running through the streets of Prague with producers and cameramen running alongside me. They even gave me directions.

"Turn here," Scott said. "Turn there."

After about twenty minutes of jogging, I found her in a tunnel, and she was legitimately surprised. "I was thinking of you all day!" she said, giving me a big kiss. "I missed you."

We ducked into a pub right by her hotel and got to spend time just the two of us.

"This is perfect," she said. "Just like you."

At the end of the evening, the producers had planned that we say good night in that tunnel up the street. I kissed her there—in perhaps the most romantic setting imaginable—and slipped back into the hotel. The guys had no clue I was gone.

Our group date the next day, with Doug and Chris, was once again in an old dungeon. I was beginning to think the producers believed nothing said romance like historic torture chambers. When I saw her, Emily and I exchanged mischievous glances over our secret rendezvous before she took Doug off for their personal chat.

During their conversation, she decided to send Doug home without waiting for the rose ceremony. Chris and I were left hanging out in this freezing, damp, and dark medieval dungeon.

"What do you think is taking so long?" I asked.

What viewers don't realize when they're watching some of those dramatic dismissals is that it takes at least two hours to send someone packing. Emily had to talk to Doug, and then they had to film him leaving. Then they had to film his reaction to leaving. When Emily finally returned to Chris and me at the end of the night, we were so glad to see her.

"One of these keys opens this door," she said, holding two gigantic keys. "I'm going to spend time with whoever has that key."

She took the two keys and handed them to us, and I was thrilled when my key unlocked the door. Once we got inside the room, she whispered, "That wasn't luck. Of course I gave that key to you because I want to spend time with you."

When she gave me the rose that evening, guaranteeing she'd be coming to my hometown to meet my parents, I knew her feelings for me were real. On that flight home, it began to dawn on me: I was starting to fall for Emily, and there was a real chance I could spend the rest of my life with her. I had alternating feelings of joy and a profound sobriety over it.

I might be a dad pretty soon!

I got as comfortable as I could in that airplane seat as I tried to sort out my feelings. The producers always made Emily and the bachelors take different flights, probably because they knew there'd be no way to keep us all separated on the same flight. We had to stay separated because the producers wanted to make sure all interaction was on film. Since the cameras weren't rolling, we couldn't get near each other.

I wondered where Emily was and whether she was thinking of me. When we reached cruising altitude, I put down my tray table and started writing a letter to the little person who might one day be my daughter.

Dear Ricki,

I'm writing you this letter before ever meeting you. I think it's important that I tell you a few things that I hope you'll never forget. You may not fully understand the true meaning of this letter until you're older, but I feel compelled to share these things with you now.

I want you to know that I will always love you with all of my heart. God has blessed me in so many wonderful ways, but bringing you into my life has to be at the top.

It's important to remember that I'll never try to replace your father. But please don't ever forget that you will forever be my daughter. I hope to shower you with the kind of unconditional love my dad has always shown me and I promise to thank God for the chance to do so. It's just as important that you understand something else as well. I'm so in love with your mom.

I hope to honor you by loving your mom with every ounce of my being. Your mom makes me so very happy, and I plan on spending the rest of my life doing the same for her. The thought of spending the rest of my life with you and your mom overwhelms my heart with joy.

The last thing I want you to remember is that I'm always here to protect you and your mom and I'm always going to be here for you.

Love always,

Sean

Before this show, I hadn't given any thought to suddenly being a dad. As the international flight droned on and on, I drifted off to sleep—my mind filled with images of having my own instant family.

seven

THE *L* WORD

"I'm going to take Emily to my family's ranch in Utah," Jef told me. I knew his parents were loaded, and their wealth was more than evident during his hometown visit. He escorted Emily around in a dune buggy on his parents' property, which included its own shooting range, their private lake, and hundreds of acres of natural beauty.

Oh no, I thought. *I've got my work cut out for me.*

"I'm gonna take her to the racetrack and take her in my two-seater Formula 1 racecar," Arie told me.

What am I gonna do? I thought as I tried to figure out my hometown date. *How can I compete with that?*

I decided to play it straight. Honestly, my life wasn't that elaborate, so I decided to show her what I did on a typical Saturday. When the producers' vehicle pulled up in Dallas, I was already at the park with Lola and Ellie. I never have my dogs on a leash, so they ran up to greet her.

"It's just us hanging out at the park at the lake today," I said, hoping she enjoyed being outdoors and with nature as much as I did. I couldn't imagine a wife who didn't enjoy the fresh air of nature. "I hope that's all right."

"This is just what I wanted," she said.

She leaned down and greeted Lola and Ellie, who didn't jump on her and walked without a leash by our sides to the picnic blanket the producers had set up overlooking the lake.

"Even your dogs are perfect."

Emily threw that word around so much that people started associating "perfect" with my name. I was surprised I came off that way. When I signed on to do the show, I had no idea how people were going to perceive me. I knew full well *The Bachelorette* producers could make me look bad, great, or crazy. I feared they would edit me to make me look a certain way to fit in to the narrative of the show.

I was glad that they had portrayed me so well—more than once, someone referred to me as a "genetic gift." The truth is, however, I'm far from perfect, and I had a sinking feeling Emily was about to realize that during my hometown date. Like everyone else, I have insecurities. One of my greatest is that my family still treats me like a child. Another insecurity is that I've never fully reached the point of financial success I wanted so desperately. Plus, the sound of my mother's pained voice when I admitted I was in Los Angeles at that first casting call still rang in my ears. How would she respond to having Emily in her home?

We settled down on the blanket for a conversation to set up the moment when Emily would meet my family. Here's a confession: one of my biggest fears is sweating in situations in which it's inappropriate to be sweating. On that day, the sun was hitting me just right, and I felt my face get red with heat.

"Are you hot?" I asked her.

"No, I'm fine," she said. Of course, there's that old saying that Southern ladies don't sweat; they glisten. I felt as though Emily—ever the proper lady—was probably a "glistener."

I, on the other hand, was sweating my tail off. I tried to ignore the sweat running down my back.

Usually, the producers tried to stay out of our dates, to let the conversations happen naturally. Thankfully, they didn't often need to interject to spice things up. However, if the conversation started to lag, they might shoot out a suggestion for a topic of conversation. "Sean, why don't you tell her about . . ." Or they might say, "Sean, didn't you say something about a certain childhood drama?"

The producers didn't interrupt us on that day because our conversation was going so well—other than the fact that by the end of it I'd sweated through my clothes. They broke us up to do our ITM chats, and then we headed to my parents' house in separate cars.

I was so excited for Emily to meet my family because they were part of my strategy. It isn't easy to express what kind of person you are on a televised dating show. So every chance I got, I told her about my upbringing, my values, and my parents. I also emphasized how I wanted to create a family with her that's just as great as the one my parents created for me.

Mom, Dad, Shay, and Andrew were in my parents' backyard with my nephew, Smith, and my niece, Kensington. This was the first time they had gotten involved in this production, and it was very strange to have cameramen cowering around our yard. Plus, they'd all seen Emily during her season on *The Bachelor*. When I walked in with Emily on my arm, I could tell by their faces it felt like seeing a celebrity. It didn't hurt to have film crews following our every move.

"Your son is so great," she said. I could tell my parents noticed when she reached for my hand. Shay has always been very open with my family. In fact, she never stops talking. Every problem she's ever had in her life, she's immediately shared with my parents. I, on the other hand, hide everything. I'm perfectly content being alone to work things out in my own head. I don't want to sit around and discuss my situation with other people, especially my family. Out of all the girls I've ever dated, guess how many I've talked about in a deep conversation with my parents?

None.

Sometimes on the show, the parents really grill the person being brought home, but my parents are nice and unfailingly polite. Because humor is so big in my family, the producers thought it would be hilarious for me to tell Emily that I still lived at home. It was a little cheesy, but we decided to go ahead with it. After we chatted out in the yard for a bit, the producers gave me a signal.

"Emily," I said. "I need to come clean on one point." My family pasted stern looks on their faces. "I still live at home with my parents. I don't *have* to live with them, but I *choose* to live with them."

"I don't blame you," she said graciously, motioning to my parents' well-kept yard with flowering bushes, green grass, and a beautiful cottage for their granddaughter. "I want to move in too."

"Let me show you around," I said. When I took her to "my room," there was an unmade bed, half-eaten cookie remnants, and a lot of filth. "This is Whiskers, Buddy, Mumu, and Froggy," I said, pointing out the various stuffed animals they had placed around the filthy room. "I kind of wish my mom would've cleaned up a bit."

I'm not sure she bought it. It was so over the top. "That's okay," she said kindly. "I know how to clean."

The girl was unflappable, even when my mom and dad tried—as another joke—to serve her baked armadillo. When we revealed that these were hoaxes, she took it all in good fun.

The day was a whirlwind, and almost no second passed when a camera wasn't pointing at us. Producers wanted everything to be documented, of course, so they tried to make sure there were no private moments. However, one exchange did happen off camera that was pretty significant. Emily and my dad had gone inside the house to talk and were about to go back outside to meet with everyone else. It was all staged, of course, which takes a little time. As the producers were discussing camera angles, Emily stole a short, private conversation with my dad.

"Sean's so much different than the rest of the guys," she said.

"How so?"

"His faith is so evident in the way he acts around me."

"Well, can I tell you a little story?" he asked. "The day Sean was on his way out to the airport to fly to Charlotte to start filming the show, he called me. I was in the locker room at my gym, but I made sure to pick up."

"All right," the producers interrupted. "Let's go back and regroup with the family."

"Hold on," Emily said. "I want to hear this."

The producers, always on a tight schedule and reticent to let any meaningful conversations happen off camera, stood around as my dad continued.

"So I was telling Emily that Sean called me on the way to the airport when I was at the gym. I told him that Sherry and I would pray for him, that I loved him, and that I knew God would use him somehow in all this.

"Fifteen minutes later, I was out in the gym exercising when a guy tapped me on the shoulder. He said, 'You didn't know it, but I was standing behind you when you were on the phone.'"

Dad could tell he had the attention of Emily and even the producers.

"He said, 'I heard what you said to your son, and it made me think that I need to get my life right with God. Just hearing you say you loved your son and that you would be praying for him made me realize how far away I have gotten from God. Anyway, I wanted you to know that God is already using your son because your conversation got my attention.'"

"Really?" Emily asked.

"Yes," my dad said. "That's when I knew God does have something in store for Sean in all of this."

It was a special moment, because Emily's interest showed my dad she had a very soft heart. I was glad my hometown date allowed Emily to get a sense of my family's faith, kindness, and fun-loving ways—even if we weren't racing around a track or traversing a huge farm in a dune buggy. As simple as it was, the hometown date helped me become more comfortable with our escalating romance. By the time Emily was whisked away, Mom—who'd been skeptical—said she'd be thrilled if Emily and I got engaged. I'd like to say I'm the kind of guy who would pursue romance no matter what my family said, but their stamp of approval went a long way in confirming the feelings I could no longer deny were developing for Emily.

Jef, Arie, Chris, and I—the final four—reconvened in Los Angeles for the rose ceremony after the hometown visits. Just like every other rose ceremony, I wasn't nervous at all. I was the second person Emily called that night. Whether I was the first or the last person she called, it didn't matter. I knew she was going to call my name.

I knew I had something really special that no one else shared with Emily—mainly our faith. I didn't question it.

When Chris went home that night, I went to our final destination knowing one thing for certain.

Andrew's text had told me so many months ago: I was going to win. But by this time, I'd realized I didn't want to win.

I wanted to spend forever with Emily as my wife.

———

"Wear shorts today, but make sure you bring a swimsuit," Scott told me when I woke up on the tropical island of Curaçao in the southern Caribbean Sea. We had finally reached the end destination of the season's *Bachelorette* journey. In a few days, Emily and I would be engaged in a jaw-dropping romantic setting. At least, that's what I knew in my heart. We still had to go through the formality of one more rose ceremony. At that point, two remaining guys would both propose to Emily in the show's finale. She'd say yes to one, and then cue happily ever after.

I grabbed my swimsuit and headed out to the van. They drove me down a dirt road and then stopped randomly in the middle of nowhere.

"This is your spot," the driver said, putting the van into park and rolling down the windows. I looked out and saw the cameramen getting into position, probably for about fifteen minutes. Everything about this show was hurry-up-and-wait, but today it seemed particularly cruel. My thoughts were racing. This was going to be a big day for me, because I was finally going to tell Emily I loved her.

"Is there anything you want to talk to Emily about specifically today?" Scott asked before jumping out of the van to help the camera crew. He asked this question before every date and then figured out the best time to bring up that particular topic.

"Yep," I said. "Today's the day."

"The *L* word?" He smiled.

I knew it was time. Saying "I love you" is a big moment in every relationship. It's even more challenging to say it on a television show to a person who can't return the sentiment. I didn't realize it at the time, but I was the only guy who hadn't come out and told Emily I loved her.

"Okay, well, please wait to tell Emily during the evening portion of the date when things are supposed to be more serious," said Scott. "Oh, and good luck!"

Officially putting it on the agenda made me feel uneasy. I didn't want to overthink the moment. *Surely it will come up naturally in conversation*, I thought as I sat in the van alone. However, my mind kept going back to it as a tongue finds a bad tooth. Even though I was so happy to give up my phone two months ago, I regretted that there was never any distraction. No texts. No Nigerian e-mail scams. No weather alerts. No Angry Birds. Unable to properly waste time, I sat there in the heat as the anticipation built.

This was the week the producers would offer Emily the option of overnight dates with each guy. At the end of each of her three evening dates, Emily opened a card from Chris Harrison inviting her and her date to use the "fantasy suite." This card, for some reason, is usually accompanied by a ridiculously old-fashioned key, presumably because a magnetic key card doesn't conjure romance in the same way. While I normally would've been nervous about such a prospect, I knew premarital sex was off the table for this Southern Christian bachelorette. When Emily was a *Bachelor* contestant, she turned down an offer for an overnight date from Brad Womack, saying she didn't want to set a bad example for her daughter. I didn't even wonder how she was handling this potentially awkward situation, because I knew she'd do it with grace and charm.

I jumped when Scott knocked on the window and motioned toward the road. "Okay, it's time to start walking."

I climbed out of the van and placed my feet on the dirt. I hadn't seen Emily for several days and had no idea what to expect. When I came around the bend, there she was. Radiant. At this point I had a choice to make. Some people try to continue walking casually, which is super awkward. (I noticed that when a camera was on me—and me alone—I suddenly forgot how to walk. *Do I swing my arms, or do I look like Sasquatch? Am I going too slow?*)

But it's also odd to break out into a sprint. Presented with two equally uncomfortable options, I chose the one that more accurately reflected how I felt. I jogged up to her and gave her a big hug.

It was wonderful to have her in my arms again. At this point, the dirt road had yielded to a view of the ocean, and we took a moment to absorb the amazing scenery. *The Bachelorette* had taken us all over the world, and it was poignant that this was our last stop. As we stood there, arms intertwined, a helicopter appeared in the sky.

"Our date is going to be on our own private island," Emily gushed.

I'd never flown in a helicopter before, so I made sure to buckle up. There was a moment after we climbed into the helicopter and before we took off during which the cameras were getting in position. I remember like it was yesterday. She leaned over and said, "Make sure you don't tell anybody this, but I have a plan."

"For me?"

"Yes." She smiled. "For you *only*."

"When I open the fantasy-suite invitation tonight, I'm going to say no on camera," she said. "But after we finish filming tonight, come back to the suite and we can hang out."

"Really?" I asked, my heart in my throat.

"Don't get any ideas." She smiled. "I want so badly to be able to talk to you without the whole nation watching. No cameras. Just us."

I'd never felt more certain of our relationship as I looked out the window and watched the ground grow distant beneath us. The private island, of course, was amazing. Before we got to get out into the ocean, we were to partake in another picnic by the water. As I sat there, looking at her over our prop food, it was all I could do not to break out into laughter. It was so fun to share secrets with her.

Emily, apparently, had other things on her mind—mainly my past relationship with Brooke.

"You sister told me you treated your past girlfriend like a buddy," Emily said. "How so?"

The last thing I wanted to do was talk about Brooke, especially while being filmed. But I was developing a real relationship with Emily, even though it was playing out on a television show. That meant we had to have real conversations.

"I loved her, I really did," I said. "There came a point when I realized I wasn't supposed to spend the rest of my life with her. Because I wasn't in love with her, I didn't do the sweet things a boyfriend was supposed to do," I said. "Like, when I'm around you, I can't stop holding your hand or kissing you. I didn't necessarily have those feelings around her."

"Did you ever talk about marriage?" Emily asked.

"Yes, she brought up marriage all the time, but I'd always try to deviate from the conversation," I said. "That would cause arguments. She knew something was up."

Of course, this was an oversimplification of our relationship. Brooke's one of the best girls I've ever met. However, it's not easy to put a three-year relationship into a nutshell. Because the cameras were on me, I left out the fact that I went back to Brooke and told her I regretted ending everything. I left out the fact that she was the one who told me that she didn't want to be with someone who was willing to leave her for so long.

After our chat, Emily and I snorkeled and wrapped up the day portion of our date. The producers called, "Cut!" and gave us enough time to shower and get ready for the night portion.

It didn't disappoint.

※ ———— ※

The technicians had set up a beautiful picnic area right on the beach on our resort in Curaçao. Again, the lighting department was amazing, because they could transform any place into the most stunning spot in the world. A blanket was covered in lush pillows, a fire crackled in the background, light hit the rocks just right, and the stars and the moon sparkled. (Though I'm not sure the lighting technicians were responsible for the appearance of the stars and moon.)

During the evening portion of the dates, the producers liked for us to begin by rehashing the day. *Yeah, today was so great—I enjoy spending time with you—Snorkeling was fun*—before getting into more serious conversation.

"I so enjoy spending time with you, Sean," Emily said before going back to her favorite topic. "You're the perfect man."

"I'm far from perfect."

"What's not perfect? I feel like things have been going so perfect . . . at least that's how I've been feeling."

My heart was beating in my chest as I prepared to express my feelings to her for the first time. "I don't want you to worry about how you will fit into my life."

"It's not just me—it's Ricki and me," she quickly corrected.

"I want that," I said. "I want to be a soccer dad. Actually, I wrote Ricki a letter on the way home from Prague."

I pulled out the paper and cleared my throat.

When viewers were watching the show on Monday nights, they saw these wonderful, intimate dates. What they didn't see was all the activity going on about ten feet away. Right outside the camera's gaze were about twenty people standing around watching us. There were camera operators, sound technicians, producers, directors, storywriters, lighting techs, and more. Not to mention the millions of people who were watching this unfold at home.

Even though the setting was less than private, the moment I was having with Emily was as real as any I've ever had. Maybe more real, because I'd never even considered adding a little girl into my life. I'd never talked to anyone about being the father of her children.

"Dear Ricki," I began, and my voice broke a bit. "I'm writing you this letter before ever meeting you . . ." By the time I reached the end, I'd regained control of my voice and emotions. "The thought of spending the rest of my life with you and your mom overwhelms my heart with joy," I read. "The last thing I want you to remember is that I'm always here to protect you and your mom and I'm always going to be here for you."

I'd been confident that Emily believed I was the one. But in that moment, when I saw that look in her eyes after I read the letter, I knew. My loving letter to Ricki had sealed the deal. I folded up my letter, handed it to Emily, and thought, *That's it. I'm about to be a husband and a dad.* With my newfound confidence, I took a deep breath and decided to go for broke.

"I can't stop thinking about you, and I can't picture my life without you," I said. "Never in a million years did I think I would have these feelings or find the woman I wanted to be with forever. But I've fallen in love with you, and I know this beyond a shadow of a doubt."

Normally, in an untelevised relationship not involving two other guys, a woman might respond with, "I love you too." In this context, however, it's forbidden. So Emily simply beamed with joy instead.

"That makes me so happy to hear." That's when she reached behind her back, pulled out an envelope, and asked me to read it. "Tell me what you think."

"Emily and Sean," I read aloud. "If you choose to forego your individual rooms, please use this key to stay as a couple in the fantasy suite."

I put the card down and said, "Well, I'd love to stay up, talk to you, and be with you."

"I'd love nothing more but to spend every minute with you that I can get," Emily said.

Viewers at home hoping to see fireworks were, of course, disappointed. We walked into the suite, admired the décor, took a dip in the pool, and she promptly showed me to the door.

On the episode, Emily said, "I'd like nothing more than to spend this time with Sean. But I'm a mom, and it doesn't line up with what I believe in or the example I want to show my daughter."

Of course, I was only pretending to walk back to my room. When they stopped filming, I walked right back into the suite for my first opportunity to talk to Emily freely since we arrived. I had a pretty good sense of who Emily was simply through our casual conversations over the course of the first few weeks. This would give me a chance to talk to her more specifically about things that were important to me—whether she grew up going to church, how many children she wants, that sort of thing. The fantasy-suite farce Emily concocted allowed us to talk honestly and candidly for the first time ever.

When I walked back to the suite, she was off doing her ITM interview, so I let myself back in. As I waited in the condo, I heard the door open and her sweet, Southern voice. "Where's my boyfriend?"

That was the first time she'd ever used that term for me.

It definitely had a nice ring to it.

At least it would do until next week, when she would call me, simply, her fiancé.

eight

THE ONE WHERE I
GOT MY HEART BROKEN

For the past two months, I'd been living with an ever-dwindling group—in North Carolina, Bermuda, Croatia, London, and Prague. When we began the hometown dates, the producers officially separated the final four. Now that we'd gotten down to three, perhaps the producers didn't want us to compare notes during the overnight dates. Since the element of surprise is key to a good show, they took every effort to make sure the drama unfolded on camera in real time—not during a late-night conversation after the crew had gone. Even though we were competing for the same girl, Jef, Arie, and I had become close friends. I hated suddenly being separated from them when we made it to Curaçao.

The producers assigned us each a handler at this point. Mine was a guy about my age named Mark Brenner, whom I always referred to by his last name. To my surprise, his sole job was to make sure I showed up on time, was well fed, and had anything I needed. I mean anything. If I said, "Brenner, I need a massage," he would call the masseuse and have him show up that day. Or if I said, "I need this specific type of protein from GNC," he would be out the door and back in half an hour. If I said, "This is what I want my diet to look like," he'd go to the grocery store and come back with the exact fresh produce I'd requested. Brenner, a man with a true servant's heart, was unfailingly kind and always willing to serve.

He also became a good friend. Since I'd had the first date of the week, I sat around and waited for Jef and Arie to go on their dates. The overnight dates were scheduled with a day between each of them. Of course, there would be no actual overnight dates with Emily. I hadn't stayed "overnight" technically, because I went home at around three o'clock in the morning. Even so, those moments felt like "stolen time," and I was so honored that she chose to have that time with me and me alone.

While I was down at the beach, waiting for the rose ceremony, I went over our secret rendezvous in my head. It was so intoxicating to be able to talk without the cameras on us. I could tell by our conversation that Emily was serious about the details of our lives together with Ricki. She asked me about my job back home. I told her about the family insurance business, which I admitted I didn't want to do indefinitely. Even though I wasn't sure of my future occupation, I told her that I could take care of her and Ricki—I would work hard and do the right things to make sure I was a good provider for them. She even asked me about insurance, to make sure that we could all be on the same health care plan. We talked until three in the morning—about faith, kids, where we wanted to live, and so on. The details swirled in my head as I waited and waited to see her again. Though I was in a Curaçao resort—how torturous could it be?—I missed Emily so badly the week felt like a month.

I spent all my time with Brenner and Scott, the producer assigned to me. Without contact with family or friends, everyone I knew was *Bachelorette*-related. That meant we mostly talked about Emily, leading up to the multiple interviews I'd have every day. Being so singularly focused on a person creates perhaps an unbalanced need to spend time with him or her, but that's where I was—on a beach waiting to be reunited with my future wife.

Not once—during the entire time I was hanging out getting sun—did it ever occur to me to think, *What if I don't get a rose?* I was as sure of my relationship with Emily as I was sure that the resort was luxurious, the ocean water was salty, and the ground was firmly beneath my feet.

Of course, I was actually standing on sand.

When the night of the final rose ceremony finally arrived, I buttoned up my white linen shirt and took a deep breath. When you get to this point, the show is absolutely paranoid about spoilers. Security was everywhere and had set up so many checkpoints that it was like we had our own resort inside of the resort. No one was going to get within the parameters without being tied directly to the show. The producers feared that a photographer would snap a photo of us and the entire buildup of the season—*who will be Emily's final three?*—would be ruined before the first episode even aired. With the millions of dollars they had invested in this show, I didn't blame them. However, it was odd to be surrounded by so many sober-looking security guards trying to keep my identity secret from prying eyes. No one had ever cared who I was. Even when our college football games were televised, I was just a small cog in a big machine. I'd never experienced anything like this.

When our car pulled up to the location of the ceremony, I smiled at Brenner and said, "One more to go."

"Okay, walk down the path," he said. "You'll meet Chris Harrison there. He'll lead you to where you should stand."

I was so happy to see Harrison, Jef, and Arie that I gave them each a bear hug.

"Arie," I said, "didn't you get the memo? You were supposed to dress up."

"Did you spend all week getting your hair to do that?" he asked. "Or is that not intentional?"

"Check out this guy's," I said, pointing to Jef. "Without his hair, he'd be half his height."

After spending the past two months living with one another and traveling to the most exotic locales, I considered these guys dear friends. We were so happy to see one another that we were joking around, laughing, and carrying on before Emily arrived—even though we all loved the same girl.

"Guys!" one of the producers yelled from the darkness outside the lights of the makeshift set. "This is serious. Stop clowning around!"

Like obedient schoolboys, we stood on our marks quietly. I knew that

Emily was back in the deliberation room, deciding what order she should call out the names. While Emily and Chris were back there discussing who was going home, the producers interspersed footage of the three of us standing silently on our marks, waiting for her to arrive and pronounce our fate. The producers were right. This was a serious moment, and we needed to act like it. I hated to think about Arie or Jef being sent home. This fun adventure would all come to an end for one of them in a few moments. Mostly, though, I was excited to see Emily.

Finally, a serious-looking Chris Harrison approached and set the stage for what was about to happen.

"It's been another great week and another great destination. But I know being on this beautiful island is the furthest thing on your mind," he said. "This is the last rose ceremony. The next step is a proposal to Emily."

When he said the word *proposal*, I felt a surge of joy. I'd already rehearsed what I'd say to her when I got down on one knee.

"After all of this, however, there are only two roses tonight," he continued. "One of you is going home."

I heard a swishing noise coming from my right. The dress Emily wore that night was stunning—it looked like a tank top above the waist, but the bottom looked as though it were made of metal. It was shimmery and made a rhythmic sound when she walked. I remember hearing her before actually seeing her.

My future wife.

She stood before us and gave her obligatory "this is a hard choice" speech. "I can't believe we're at this point, and I have my three guys here," she began. "I had to make a decision, and I want each of you to know that I care so much about each of you." She paused. Was she about to cry? Emily had done such an amazing job navigating this complicated dating scenario. I admired the way she was letting Arie or Jef down so easily. "And I want you to know that . . . I'm sorry."

She picked up the first of two roses and held it. Frequently, the most obvious person is called first. If there's a favorite, the producers get him out of the way so they don't ruin the suspense. I'd gotten the rose first during many of the rose ceremonies—and in others, my name was never called because I'd gotten a date rose. I figured I'd probably get called first that night.

"Jef," she said. I exchanged a sympathetic glance with Arie as I watched Jef walk up to her and the rose.

Oh, man, I thought. *Arie's going home.*

After a seemingly long pause, Emily picked up the final rose and said two syllables that absolutely shattered the dreams of my future life and family.

"Arie."

I froze.

Did I hear her correctly? What just happened?

I wasn't sad. I wasn't mad. I was shocked. I didn't know what was going on as I watched Arie go up and receive his rose.

I gave Jef and Arie a hug. "I love you, man," Jef said to me as I pulled away to talk to Emily.

"May I walk you out?" she asked.

We sat on a bench away from everyone. A dog barked in the distance.

"What are you feeling?"

"I feel stupid," I said. There were a lot of words that I could've used, but *stupid* was the one that came out. How could I have been so utterly and completely wrong? Had I misread her cues? Her many cues?

"Why?"

"Because I knew with certainty that I was ready to spend forever with you. I didn't see this coming, obviously. I think you should know it's going to hurt me."

I got up to leave, but there was no vehicle for me to get into.

"Come on, man," said Scott. "We just need to get you guys talking a bit more."

Reluctantly, I sat back down on the bench.

"I don't feel like I deserve you," she said. Suddenly, all the moments she said the erroneous word *perfect* to describe me came flooding back. Did she really believe I had my act so together that I was unobtainable?

"Going into this final week," she said, "I thought you were the one."

My mind was reeling. If she thought I was the one going into this week, what had happened to change her mind? Our date had gone so well—even with our secret overnight date that she'd told me was a privilege only I had shared. It just didn't add up. Was she upset that I didn't have a job I loved back home and might not be as wealthy as the other guys? That was the last thing we talked about before the rose ceremony. Did that factor in to it at all?

Of course, I had no answers.

"Well, so did I," I said, barely able to get the words out. "I thought I was the one. I thought you were the one."

"I wanted it to be you so bad," she said, no longer holding back her tears. "I've loved every minute."

"I care about you ultimately," I said, wanting desperately to get out of this situation. "If this is the best for you, you have to do what's best for you." Though I didn't plan on being in this situation, I didn't want to be the guy who gets angry and leaves on bad terms. I climbed into the Suburban, which was full of sound technicians, producers, and a host of other people who'd come along with me in this journey. I wasn't really supposed to talk to the behind-the-scenes guys, but I couldn't help but notice it was as quiet as a morgue.

I stared out the window into nowhere, unable to speak. I only turned around when I heard loud sniffling. The camera ops and sound techs were not supposed to be involved in the show in any way except behind the scenes, of course. One really sweet sound tech named Kittye was in the backseat with me. Even though we weren't supposed to interact, I'd gotten to know everyone by name. We'd spent so much time together over the past few weeks. About a foot of space separated Kittye and me as the cameras rolled. Obviously, she couldn't be in the shot, so she had pushed herself as far away from me as possible in the back of a full Suburban. When I looked over at her, I noticed her back was turned away from me. She was staring out the window too—crying.

"Are you okay?" I instinctively asked, breaking the rules.

"I'm just"—she sniffed—"sad that you've gotten your heart broken."

In that moment, seeing her kindness, I couldn't help but smile. I whispered, "Thank you, Kittye."

I looked up and saw that the producer, Jonah, and my handler, Brenner, were both bawling. Jonah, who is prone to being a tad dramatic, had his head in his hands sobbing. You would've thought our Suburban was following a hearse. Honestly it did, just a little, feel like a death. In my mind, I'd mapped out my entire future with Emily and her daughter. *Our* daughter. Suddenly, having that ripped away was the worst thing I'd ever felt.

Amid such despair, the fact that almost everyone in the vehicle was grieving with me was very touching. Even though I hadn't found true love, I'd made friendships that would last a lifetime.

When it became apparent that the producers were going to keep us driving around in circles until I said something, I mustered up the strength to speak. Even though the feelings I had were real, they still had a television show to make.

"Can you tell me what you're thinking?" the producer asked me one more time.

"I had a beautiful picture of what my life was going to look like. And now it's gone," I said. "It feels like it was stolen from me."

nine

NEWFOUND NOTORIETY

"Hey, buddy," Brenner said when I finally got to the hotel after my Suburban ride of shame. I had already gotten out my suitcases and started shoving my clothes into them. "We really need you to do us a favor."

"What?" I asked, barely able to get out the word. I'd stuffed all my socks into the side of my suitcase, and the zipper wouldn't close.

"We need you to stay a little bit longer," he said.

"All I want to do is go home," I said with as much control over my voice as possible, but it may have sounded more like a plea.

I looked up and Brenner was still standing there. "Just a little longer," he said gently.

"What does 'just a little' mean, specifically?" I asked. *An extra day wouldn't kill me*, I thought as I took a deep breath.

"Just stay another five or six days?" he said.

"Five or six?" I said, unable to believe my ears. "That's almost a week."

"Listen, it's simple. If you're seen in Dallas before Jef and Arie are home," he said, "it would jeopardize the whole show."

I paused, gripping my socks so hard my knuckles were white. I loved Brenner—and the other producers—and wanted to treat them well even in this horrible circumstance. The show had invested millions of dollars into this story, and I didn't want to accidentally give away the ending.

A story.

I felt a little queasy that all the heartache I felt was just a part of a story—and I wasn't even a main character. If this had been a real fairy tale, I would've fought a few dragons and ended up with the girl in the end. But Prince Charming never got sent home in a Chevy Suburban.

"Sorry, man. I need to get back to normal life," I said.

"Of course," he said. "I understand." I took one look at the guy and realized he hated asking as much as I hated agreeing. Well, almost. "You can leave, but it would help us out a lot if you could just stay."

"If only Emily had wanted me to stick around as much as you do," I said grimly. I didn't want to ruin the show for them. I took my socks out of the side pocket and shoved them back into the drawer. "All right." I decided to take one for the team. "Can I at least borrow your phone?"

Brenner breathed a sigh of relief, reached into his pocket, and handed me his cell phone. "Thanks, buddy," he said. "It means a lot, but who are you calling?"

"Home."

"You do realize it's three o'clock in the morning Dallas time?"

"My parents have to know what's going on," I said, taking his cell and disappearing into my room. For the first time in weeks, I knew for sure that no one was listening to me. No one would be monitoring my calls to determine what might make for good television.

"Yeah," my dad answered the phone, his voice thick with sleep.

"Dad?"

"Son, what's going on?" he asked, and I noticed a trace of concern in his sleepy voice.

"I'm going home," I said. "And I've had my heart broken." Suddenly, it was just me, my mom, and my dad—separated by more than two thousand miles. It took them a few seconds to process what I was saying.

"Oh, Sean . . . I know you've never experienced this before," my mom said gently. "But you're gonna get through it."

"We just want to get you home and love on you," said my dad. "Come on back."

"I can't even do that," I said, explaining the situation as my dad listened attentively.

"Okay, then just get through the day. We're going to be waiting for you when you get home."

"Yeah, we're going to have the family over when you get home, just like every Saturday," Mom added. "Shay and Andrew will come over, and they'll bring the kids."

I could tell Mom was trying to remind me of real life, to tell me life could get back to normal, to emphasize that everything could be the same.

"The last time I was at your house, Emily was there," I said. The yard, the house, my life would feel dingier in her absence.

"Yeah, I know. I know," she said. To her credit, Mom didn't try to reason with me. Instead, she simply commiserated. "It'll be okay."

I hung on to that promise as I spent the next several days in what could've been a fun, relaxing resort. Taking one for the team, in the *Bachelorette* world, was not so bad. They got me a two-story, picturesque townhouse on the ocean, which I barely even noticed. In my head, I relived every moment between Emily and me a million times. *Should I have said this? Should I not have said this? Should I have done this differently?*

"You've got a week on the ocean," Brenner said. "Wanna get your scuba license?"

I had to hand it to Brenner. He knew I wanted to become scuba certified, and he was by my side the whole time encouraging me to appreciate the moment. But I never took him up on any of his suggestions. I was devastated, because I had been certain Emily would be my wife.

One day, we went down the street to eat some sushi, and my twisted sense of humor got the best of me. "Brenner, do you know what would make me feel better?"

"What, buddy?" he asked. This was the first time I even indicated a possibility of happiness, and he was eager to do whatever would help.

"If you ate that," I said as I pointed to the golf ball–size glob of wasabi next to my sushi.

"That?" He looked at the mound of wasabi, also known as Japanese horseradish. "The whole thing?"

I nodded.

To my surprise, Brenner popped the whole ball in his mouth. His eyes started watering, and he began coughing. If we'd been in a cartoon, smoke would've come out of his ears. I started laughing, and—once he stopped choking—Brenner started laughing too. It was the first moment my thoughts weren't consumed by Emily since I'd been sent packing.

"Thanks, man," I said when I finally regained my composure. "You're a real friend."

Since this was our favorite sushi place, we went there the following night. "Wanna make me happy again?" I asked, probably taking advantage of Brenner's good nature and eagerness to cheer me up. "It would really make me laugh if you drank the water out of that vase," I said, pointing to the flower vase that was sitting on our table.

Without a thought, he picked it up and took a swig. I was so surprised that he'd done it, I started laughing and couldn't stop. That's the amazing kind of guy Brenner is—he was a great friend during a tough and terrible time.

One night, after Brenner had gone to his place, my mind raced. As I got ready for bed, I picked up the phone and dialed my hometown friends Laura and Stephanie. It had been a long time since they'd helped me make my audition video for the show.

Understandably, the producers requested secrecy and warned me not to tell people of the results. However, they're also reasonable people who knew there was no way to keep the results a secret from everyone, especially those closest to me. Since I trusted Laura and Stephanie implicitly—and they'd been with me all along this journey—I just had to hear their voices.

"It's Sean," I said, knowing I was calling from an unfamiliar number. I got emotional as I told them all the details.

"We love you and can't wait for you to get home," Stephanie told me.

"I just know Emily made a mistake," I said. "Nothing adds up."

"I'm sorry," said Laura.

"I can't stop thinking about all the things she told me," I said. "All the reassuring things she told me and how our faith aligned. Nothing makes sense."

"You're not thinking of . . ." Stephanie began.

"But she's made a mistake," I said. "I feel like I need to talk to her."

"No!" they both said in unison before I could finish my thought. "Don't do it!"

"As loyal *Bachelorette* watchers," Laura said, "you have to listen to us. When people who've been sent home show back up to plead their case, it never ends well."

"Yeah," agreed Stephanie. "Don't do it. Don't be *that* guy."

I decided to listen to their advice, because I knew they had my best interests at heart. Knowing they were right didn't stop me from tossing and turning in my bed, though. I stared at the ceiling, counted sheep, and prayed. Despite how tired I was, thoughts of Emily pushed any possibility of sleep far from me. I couldn't make sense of it all. *If she thought I was "the one" when we arrived on this island, what possibly could've happened to change her mind? And what about all her winks, knowing glances, and secrets?* My mind raced. Was it possible that all this was a misunderstanding? I couldn't imagine her in a relationship with Arie or Jef. After a couple of hours, I slipped out of bed, out the door, and into the streets of Curaçao.

I started walking down the road toward Emily's hotel. Streets that looked quaint and welcoming in the day looked ominous under the cover of darkness. We'd been warned not to walk around the city at night because of the crime. But when your heart's broken, you think—and do—crazy things.

Not that I was doing anything more than walking. I didn't actually have a plan.

Maybe I'll see her somehow, I thought. *It's late at night, so maybe I'll run into her.*

As I walked farther from my resort, the streets got seedier, and I became more aware that I—a big, blond American—stuck out like a sore thumb. I had only a vague knowledge of where Emily's hotel was, so I walked in that general direction for over a mile, passing guys standing in packs on the street corners and lone women standing in alleys.

I finally found her resort, next to the ocean. The glowing lights from the windows looked welcoming and cozy.

Now what? I was the dog who caught the car. *What do I do next?*

I just stood there, looking at her hotel, and imagining where she was in it. Asleep? Thinking of me? With Arie or Jef?

Pain washed over me anew. Finally, after standing there for far too long, I figured there was nothing I could do, turned around, and walked back to my room.

Alone.

———————

"What are we going to do when we see you kissing?" Stephanie asked, making the whole room groan.

I stuffed a fistful of popcorn in my mouth and settled in to the couch. I didn't know how I would feel to see myself fall in love—and out of love—on national television. But I knew there was no other place I'd want to be than at Stephanie's house with my tight-knit group of five or six friends.

"Tonight, Emily meets twenty-five of America's most eligible bachelors. And then, the party gets started and the romance begins. It's all coming up tonight on the exciting season premiere of *The Bachelorette.*"

As Chris Harrison's familiar voice came through the television, my throat tightened. I'd never been on television before, so I was excited to see how I looked and what the producers selected to broadcast, and—mainly—how I would react when I saw Emily interacting with the other guys in ways I didn't see while going through it. Before this moment, Chris Harrison had only existed within the context of my relationship with Emily. Now I was sitting in Dallas with my friends, watching him appear on Stephanie's television screen. It felt odd and jarring, like a kid running into his teacher at the grocery store.

"There you are," Laura said the first time I appeared on-screen as the room erupted with laughter and cheers.

"He's as red as a beet," Stephanie said.

"Look at how you strutted up the stairs," Murrey said.

"Emily looks amaaazzzing," they agreed.

During the moment, I had felt like I had blacked out—I didn't remember one syllable of our introduction. It was like an out-of-body experience to watch myself do something I barely remembered.

As soon as that scene ended, the room erupted and my phone lit up with texts.

I just saw you on The Bachelorette!

Was that you on The Bachelorette?

I just saw a guy who looked just like you on The Bachelorette!

Most people had no idea that I went on the show, and I got a kick out of all the shocked messages.

During the commercial breaks, my friends peppered me with questions.

What is Chris Harrison like?

Was the guy holding the egg actually nuts?

Could you tell who Emily liked?

It was such a relief to be home and felt so good to be around people I loved, but I couldn't shake the feeling Emily had made a grave mistake.

※

After the first episode aired, I received an e-mail from Jeremy Anderson, a Texas attorney who had appeared on *The Bachelorette* season 4, starring DeAnna Pappas. He had made it all the way to the third position before being unceremoniously sent packing, making him one of the few people on the planet who could empathize with my situation.

"If you just want to talk about things and grab a beer," he wrote after getting my information through mutual friends, "I'd love to talk to you."

I was glad I took him up on it. We had a lot in common, and it felt good to talk to someone who knew what I'd been through.

"I actually met Emily once at a charity event," he said, sipping his beer. "I can see why you'd fall so hard for her."

"You did?" It seemed so odd to meet someone who knew her in the real world.

"Do you have her phone number?" I blurted out.

In normal relationships, the first way you connect with a person is to exchange phone numbers and e-mail addresses. But in the context-free world of *The Bachelorette*, you can propose to a woman without ever knowing her number or address.

"Actually," he said, scrolling through his phone contacts, "I think I did get it."

He wrote it on a piece of paper and slipped it across the table. Taking it felt like some sort of treasonous act. Because only one episode had aired, I had no idea if she ended up with Jef, Arie, or neither. In my heart, I assumed she ended up alone. It was inconceivable to me that either Jef or Arie would've been her soul mate.

I put her phone number in my wallet, right behind my credit card, and tried not to think of it. For about five or six days, I successfully fought the temptation to call. I couldn't stop wondering how she was doing and whether she was happily engaged.

Finally, I couldn't take it anymore. I drove to my apartment, shut the door, and sat on my couch with nothing but my phone and that slip of paper.

If she didn't answer and didn't call me back, I'd know she had gotten engaged and wanted me to leave her alone. I wasn't going to be the crazy person who calls repeatedly.

I promised myself I'd make one call.

If she called me back, fine. If not, I'd throw away her number forever.

My heart raced as I pressed her number into my phone and lifted it to my face.

One ring. Two. Three. Voice mail.

"Emily, this is Sean," I said, wishing I'd planned the voice-mail message a bit more. "The show was very rough for me. I don't know how it was for you, but I was just hoping to catch up with you for a second."

When I hung up, I felt some sort of release. At least I'd tried. If she

Shay and I, Christmas 1984

My first snow in Dallas (age two)

1987 (age three)

Shay and I, Christmas 1988

Cruising my bike in some sweet overalls (age four)

1989 (age five)

Looking super dorky in kindergarten in 1989

My first-grade school play in 1990

In my grandparents' bed pretending to be Granddaddy in 1991

My second-grade class picture

Family Vacation to Colorado in 1991

My third-grade class picture

Playing football for the Bulldogs in 1993 (age ten)

My fifth-grade class picture

*My sophomore year of
high school in 2000*

*My football picture when I was a
junior in high school (age sixteen)*

My senior class picture (age seventeen)

With Shay at my high school graduation

With Mom and Dad at high school graduation

My high school graduation in 2002

*On the field my freshman year of college
at Kansas State University in 2002*

Vegas with Shay and Andrew in 2006

Celebrating my cousin Brandon's wedding in 2007

At the park with my dad and our dogs in 2007

My first day with Ellie in 2006

Playing with Kensington in 2009

Holding Kensington after church in 2008

Holding Smith in hospital in 2010

Easter 2014

Waiting for my beautiful bride to walk down the aisle—
having my dad officiate made it all the more special

Catherine and I dancing our first
dance as husband and wife to
Randy Rogers's "One Woman"

My grandfather Papa saying grace
at our wedding reception

Credit: Caroline Jurgensen Photography

Catherine and I dancing at our good friend Laura's wedding, summer 2014

My girls waiting for me to come home from the gym in front of our house

During my and Catherine's hometown date in Seattle on The Bachelor

Catherine and I getting ready to skydive in 2014

wanted to contact me, she now had my phone number. I put the phone on my coffee table and wondered if she was listening to my message.

My phone never rang.

———

Absent any communication with her, I still had the chance to see her every Monday night. The episodes turned out to be very therapeutic. As I watched our lives unfold on-screen, I got to see her interact with the other guys. When I watched her have one-on-one dates with Jef and Arie, in particular, it eased my heartbreak. It was obvious they had a connection. Oddly, seeing her become so infatuated with those guys helped me heal faster, because it became clear she hadn't made a mistake. She simply liked the other guys better. Every Monday night, we met at Stephanie's, passed out the pizza, and watched—literally—an episode of my life pass before my eyes.

With each passing week, I got more airtime, and I couldn't wait until someone in public recognized me. It took three weeks. After the third episode, I was at a restaurant when someone came up to me and said, "Are you the guy from the show? Sean?"

It gave me such a jolt.

Plus, this was when I got introduced to the wonderful world of Twitter. Because I'd never tweeted, I set up my own account and decided to participate in the fun. This was technically against the show's rules, but I noticed a lot of the other guys were tweeting. Bachelor Nation is a vibrant online community that loves to interact with the people on the shows. After I sent out my first tweet, my feed went nuts. While Twitter is sometimes a horrifyingly brutal place, most tweets were positive and affirming, and it was exhilarating to read all the comments people were sending. Within minutes, my phone rang.

"Sean, this is Jonah," I heard on the other end. "You gotta stop tweeting."

"Why?" I asked. "Other guys are doing it."

"Other guys didn't get to the final three," he said. "You gotta stop. You might accidentally give something away."

And so I was no longer able to send out tweets, but I was able to search my name on Twitter—a fascinating and bizarre phenomenon because it allowed me to get real-time feedback from people all over the nation.

@EmilyMaynard, pick the hottie @SeanLowe09! #TheBachelorette

That Sean guy's a tool with no personality #TheBachelorette

I don't care who Emily picks, as long as #SeanLowe takes his shirt off again.

I found myself staying up until two in the morning, reading tweets from random people. During *The Bachelorette*, I gained twenty thousand followers every Monday night, which might translate into half a million tweets. My name trended nationally on Twitter. There I was, a normal guy sitting at home alone in my apartment, reading all this chatter about me. I also Googled my name and found many blog posts.

What is going on? I wondered. I wasn't prepared for the celebrity that came along with the show. *Celebrity* isn't the right word, because I certainly am not one. To me, a celebrity is someone like Brad Pitt (a guy with immense acting ability), Kevin Durant (a guy with dazzling athletic skill), or John Mayer (a guy with a smooth voice). Yet, every Monday, people loved live-tweeting *The Bachelorette*—even honest-to-goodness celebrities tweeted about my fate. It sucked me in. *Whoa, this celebrity knows my name. What?*

With each passing episode, I started getting more and more recognition.

"Hey, that's Sean from *The Bachelorette*," I began to hear in hushed tones when I was at a restaurant or the post office. It was all new, fascinating, and bizarre. I had no idea what I was stepping into.

It was just a taste of what was to come.

* — ᴇᴇᴇ — *

Halfway through *The Bachelorette* season, I got a call from one of *The Bachelor's* executive producers, Travis Wunderli, who's married to Mary Kate, the producer assigned to Emily.

"Did you see someone on the Internet has already spoiled the fact that Roberto is the next *Bachelor?*"

"I saw someone wrote on a blog that Roberto's contracts were already signed," I said.

"Well, those are just rumors," said Travis. "What do you think about being *The Bachelor*?"

"Me?"

"Of course you!"

"I don't know," I said. "Let me think about it. Give me a few days."

I didn't want to make a hasty decision, but I was definitely intrigued. Frequently, people leave the show saying, "It's contrived. You can't fall in love on a television show. It's all fake. It's staged."

While I understand their sentiment, I'd pushed my chips into the center of the table. I was all in.

Can you fall in love on a reality TV show?

I did. And so did Arie and Jef.

Even though it seemed incredibly unlikely that the producers of *The Bachelor* could somehow put my future wife into the mix of potential mates, I still knew the possibility of love existed.

"Travis just asked me to be the next *Bachelor*, and I don't know yet," I told my parents.

To be honest, I felt bad for putting Mom and Dad through this wild-goose chase. When Shay and Andrew originally signed me up to go on the show, I never once considered I'd end up with a broken heart. My family had been supportive, kind, and encouraging, even through the worst moments.

But I assumed they looked back at the show as a generally negative experience. I'd tried to hold the snake by the tail and I'd gotten bitten. Because of what I'd put them through, I was hesitant even to bring it up. I valued their advice, though, so I braced myself for their reactions.

"You'd be crazy not to do it," my dad said.

"Aren't you skeptical?" I asked. "After the way everything unfolded?"

"This door has been opened for you, son," my dad said. "Maybe you should walk through it."

Even my mom—the original *Bachelorette* skeptic—was onboard. "You have to do it," she said.

It seemed like an amazing opportunity, and I was honored that the producers would even consider me. I called Travis back at the end of the week. "I'll do it."

⊱───⋆⋅⋅⋆───⊰

This was yet another secret I had to keep while watching the show with my friends. With each passing week, things intensified on the show, and I was dreading the episode in which I snuck out of our hotel in Prague and secretly went looking for Emily after her date with John Wolfner. He was one of my closest friends on the show. I felt guilty I sabotaged his one-on-one date with Emily with an impromptu date of my own. The week our secret excursion was going to be broadcast on television, I called him.

"Wolf, don't be mad at me, but I have something to tell you," I said before explaining the whole story.

"I don't care," Wolf said in his typical easygoing way. "I didn't like her anyway!"

This was no surprise. Throughout the show, it was obvious who was falling for Emily and who wasn't. It wasn't that some guys were inauthentic in their interactions with her. It was just that some people connected and others didn't. Just like in real life.

As we watched that episode later that night, my friends were supportive, but they also gave me a hard time.

"You're running through the streets of Prague screaming her name?" Stephanie asked.

"Did you think the producers didn't know where she was?" Murrey asked.

Anytime I did or said something weird on the show, my friends quickly pointed it out and laughed. Even worse, everyone groaned when they saw me kissing Emily on-screen. There is nothing more peculiar than seeing yourself kiss another person—especially in the close-up way *The Bachelorette* films it. I knew my friends' teasing came from a place of deep love, so I laughed along with them. As the weeks progressed, my relationship with

Emily got more serious on the screen, even as the stranglehold of sadness loosened its grip on my heart.

When the episode aired during which I got the boot, the room was stone silent.

"Are you okay?" one asked, giving me a hug. My phone lit up with concerned texts and calls. All my friends wanted to express kindness to me, which I so appreciated. What most people failed to understand was that my heart had been broken months prior to airing. By the time she sent me home on television, I'd finally gotten over Emily.

In fact, after seeing how everything ended up for her, I was sort of relieved she'd sent me home. Though I think I could've made her happy as a husband, I saw that she was attracted to a very different type of guy. It was all for the best, and I was thrilled when I finally realized that.

My newfound peace of mind didn't stop me from enjoying all the love my friends and supporters sent my way. It felt good to be loved on.

After the season was over, I saw that Emily had ended up with Jef—an all-around great guy. Something about seeing them get engaged and the show wrapping up gave me a gigantic sense of relief. I'd heard so many horror stories about how producers in reality TV have such power over how people are portrayed. By taking clips out of context and using selective quotes, they could make a perfectly reasonable person look like a lunatic. Perhaps that's true on some reality TV shows, but I found that I was portrayed on the show exactly how I am in real life. In general, people who end up as reality TV villains usually are jerks in real life. The ones who seem like nice folks usually are. My theory is that the camera doesn't really lie—at least, not on *The Bachelorette*. Because they film for many consecutive weeks, what you see is usually what you get because it's hard to maintain a fake personality for that long.

I flew to Los Angeles to meet the producers of *The Bachelor* and to solidify my standing as the next Bachelor. Also, there were other fun activities I got to participate in as a member of the cast of *The Bachelorette*.

For example, Cole Hamels—a pitcher for the Phillies and apparently a *Bachelorette* fan—invited some of us to his event for the Hamels Foundation, a charity supporting Philadelphia inner-city schools and a school in Malawi.

When I arrived at the event, I grabbed a drink and looked around the room to see if I could find any other *Bachelorette* alumni. That's when I saw her.

Brooke.

Now married to a Phillies baseball player, we somehow ended up at the same party on the other side of the country. There were a lot of people at this charity event, and I wondered if I should pretend I hadn't seen her. As I was standing there gawking, I caught her eye. She looked momentarily surprised but smiled back. It was going to be weird to say hello to her and her new husband, but I figured it would've been weirder not to.

"Brooke?" I said, walking up to them. She looked radiant.

"Hey, how you doing?" I introduced myself to her husband, who was well aware of our previous relationship. "Great to see you."

"How are the dogs?" she asked.

As we exchanged awkward chitchat, I wasn't sure if I'd made the right decision. After a few minutes of stunted conversation, I excused myself.

As I walked away from them, I realized how much I missed her. I was thrilled she was happily married, but seeing her reminded me that she'd moved on and our friendship was—necessarily—over. An hour or so later, I ran into her again, but this time she was alone.

"I watched the show," she said. "When you talked about us, you didn't really tell the whole story."

"I know," I said. On television, I explained I'd had a three-year relationship with someone who simply wasn't the one for me. I'd left out the part about me going back to Brooke and asking her to take me back. "I had to paint a picture without going into exhausting detail about any former relationships."

Her face fell a bit.

"I'm sorry," I said with a pang in my stomach.

Later, I saw Brooke and her husband from afar at a church in Dallas. I watched the two of them with their hands in the air, worshipping together, and it brought me so much peace. I left church with a huge smile on my face, a strong sense of satisfaction, and not a trace of jealousy.

I was so happy she ended up with such a great guy and an amazing marriage.

I wondered if I'd ever find that for myself.

ten

THE DRIVER'S SEAT

"God, lead me. You're in control of this," I prayed while waiting for the women to arrive for my season of *The Bachelor*. (I had expected twenty-five women, but later learned there would be an extra woman that season, making a total of twenty-six.) The mansion was on Canaan Road in Agora Hills, just north of Los Angeles and east of Malibu. Tucked in the hills among other beautiful mansions and scenic wineries, the girls' house was about a mile down the road from the amazing multimillion-dollar home at which I'd be staying. The home was set on a cliff, and almost every wall was floor-to-ceiling windows. It had a home gym and an awesome pool.

"I could get used to this," I told Mary Kate. I'd arrived a week earlier to start shooting for the show and teamed back up with the army of producers. It was a little strange to see Mary Kate because of her friendship with Emily during *The Bachelorette*.

"So, how is Emily?" I asked her between takes while we filmed the B-roll footage. They filmed me in a Jeep driving down the Pacific Coast Highway, working out, jogging, and generally getting ready for the girls to arrive.

"Well, she got your message," she said. I looked at Mary Kate to make sure I'd heard her correctly. Until that moment, I doubted whether I'd called the right number after I'd just arrived back in Dallas. Because I promised myself not to call twice, I wasn't sure whether Emily knew

I'd tried to reach her. "Emily told me you called, and she wrestled with whether to call you back."

"She didn't," I said, perhaps too abruptly. "I wouldn't have called her had I known she was engaged to Jef."

Mary Kate nodded. "You okay now?"

"I can now say it was for the best," I said. "I was never completely comfortable with her. She was very sweet, nurturing, and loving, and I could see myself marrying her. But I never showed her the goofy side of me."

In fact, when my name was being thrown around as the next Bachelor, people in the press and social media said I was too serious and boring to carry an entire season.

"Now's your chance to change that," she said.

The week of preparation came down to this moment. Since I'd been standing in front of the girls' mansion for so long—"hurry up and wait" is *The Bachelor* filming philosophy—the anticipation kept building. My nerves were getting the best of me, so I shut my eyes and asked God to lead me in the right direction. The cameras caught this moment, and the producers decided to air it. I don't think anyone realized I was praying.

"Look, he's so nervous!" a girl in the approaching limo screamed as they drove up.

Hearing the squeals from the arriving limos was—I had to admit—pretty nice. It felt different being the star of the show. Now, instead of being one of dozens of people trying to make it from week to week, I was the one who would decide who was staying or going. It felt good to be more in control of my situation. Plus, I had an army of people waiting on me hand and foot. Being the central figure of a television show, if only temporarily, felt really empowering. I don't think it went to my head, but it allowed me to be a lot more comfortable and natural than I had been on *The Bachelorette*.

Did I believe this was the best way to meet women? No.

I never anticipated falling in love on *The Bachelorette*. But my cynicism quickly evaporated when I fell in love with Emily and was convinced I'd spend the rest of my life loving her and her daughter. After the heartbreak of losing her, I came to realize that while my feelings for Emily were real, she wasn't the one for me.

So there I was, standing in a suit hoping that my future wife would step out of one of the five limos lining the driveway. Would this work out? Doubtful. I've always been selective in whom I date. (Even as I write that, I hear Emily's words echo in my ears: "No, you're picky.") There was a really good chance I could meet all twenty-six girls and not have a connection with any of them, no matter how excited they were when they drove up in front of the mansion. Their giggling and squeals may have given me a big head momentarily, but it gave me enough confidence to get through the introductions.

I was eager to meet the women. *Will I feel a connection with anyone? Am I going to meet my future wife tonight? Can I really carry on twenty-six different conversations with twenty-six different women? Am I going to make it out alive?*

Those questions, concerns, and fears were all put to rest as soon as the first person stepped out of the limo. The women amazed me. They seemed sweet, funny, and gorgeous! Any nerves I had going into the first night were calmed by the unusual and very funny antics of a few women, who—of course—tried to pull some stunts in order to stand out among the crowd.

A woman named Robyn attempted a back handspring—in her formal dress, no less—and landed on her head. While I hated that it happened, I have to admit, it really broke the ice. I love a girl who doesn't take herself too seriously. A woman named Lesley definitely scored points with me when she pulled out a football. But the woman who made the biggest entrance of the night had to be a woman named Lindsay. The girl showed up in a wedding dress! Was she crazy? Probably, but I definitely wouldn't forget her.

There were other antics. One brought pennies to toss into the fountain, one left a lipstick imprint on my face, and one did a *Fifty Shades of Grey* thing. Though I hadn't read the books, when she pulled a tie out of her cleavage and wrapped it around me, I got the message.

The woman who made the best impression on me was Tierra. Her piercing eyes and beautiful smile stopped me in my tracks. I knew right then and there that I wanted to give her a rose. The producers had told me, "If you see a girl outside after she gets out of the limo and you want to give a first impression rose to her, then go ahead and hand it out." Handing out more than one rose—and right there on the spot—had never been done before on the show. I didn't stop to think that by giving her a rose so quickly I might be putting a target on her back. All I knew was that I wanted to spend more time with this woman with the big, welcoming smile.

"Stand here and wait for me just a second," I said. It was a little awkward to leave her standing there in the middle of the driveway, but I didn't actually *have* a rose.

"I'm gonna give a rose to Tierra," I said to a producer, who had been hiding around corners so he wouldn't be seen on camera.

"Okay, we have to get Harrison in place."

Chris Harrison is a real guy's guy who loves to talk about sports. Even if he's in the middle of a crass joke, he can flip a switch and suddenly become insta-host. Once he was in place, I walked into the boardroom as if he'd been there all along.

"Oh, hey, Chris," I said. "I want to hand out a rose."

Chris switched from his casual, hanging-out self into his serious *Bachelor*-hosting self and said, "Okay, Sean, if you're sure."

When I gave Tierra the rose, she lit up. I knew I'd made the right decision.

A girl named Catherine got out of the limo wearing a sparkly navy dress and said, "Wow, you're such a hunk." There was something quirky and funny about her, which I also liked. I wanted everyone to be more authentic this time around, and it looked as though we'd have no problem with that.

After meeting all the women, I was finally able to go inside and hang out with them all. I'd never been so overwhelmed in my life!

"I want you guys to be comfortable around me because I wasn't always a hundred percent comfortable with Emily," I said. "We're never going to figure out if we're meant to be together if we're not real. If you're feeling nervous at all, just be yourself."

After my speech, I sat down and talked to each woman on an individual basis—at least, once the initial shock of being in a room full of beautiful women wore off. As soon as I got into my conversations, it was clear they were smart and accomplished too. I've always said there's nothing sexier than a woman's intellect—and I was certainly not disappointed by this group.

Honestly, it was exhausting. I wanted to be attentive so I really focused on each woman, but it wore me out. Everything takes so much longer than you can imagine. The hours ticked by on the grandfather clock in the mansion as the cameras were being set up for the rose ceremony. There came a point during the evening when I had to get away for a few minutes by myself to eat and decompress. Even though time passed, the wine and champagne never stopped flowing. That's why viewers at home might have seen some of the women drink a bit too much. Lindsay, in her wedding dress, was a little tipsy by the time I made my way over to her during the cocktail party. She invited me to dance—without music—and even asked me to kiss her.

"How about I kiss you on the cheek?" I offered.

"Are you one of those *traditional* people?"

"Maybe a little more than you are." I laughed.

I didn't fault her for having one too many drinks because I'm sure she didn't anticipate the party lasting so long—it didn't wind down until seven o'clock the next morning. I only drank Red Bull because I wasn't going to be the guy who casually sipped on a drink all night and ended up with a lampshade on my head.

The night was both invigorating and exhausting because I had to stay focused when having conversations with so many women—making eye contact, keeping facts about them straight, and remembering their hometowns—even though I could tell immediately that some of them were not going to work out. Thankfully, Brenner, assigned to be my handler again, ushered me from one girl to another and helpfully reminded me of the pertinent details.

When I made my way over to talk to Catherine, she pulled out a tray of ice cream with four bowls.

"Which type of ice cream would you choose?" she asked, pointing to the chocolate, vanilla, cookies and cream, and mint chocolate chip servings.

"I guess cookies and cream," I said.

"Good choice!" she said, indicating it was some sort of "manly flavor." I'm not sure the science behind her ice cream test was rock-solid, but I knew from the beginning I liked hanging out with her. Was there a romantic connection? Not really. However, I tried to remember the words of wisdom Mary Kate gave me before the show started.

"You're going to do yourself a great disservice if you pick out your final four on the very first night," she'd said to me. "Stay open-minded."

And so I stayed open to all the ladies, handing out roses to the ones I liked and wanted to get to know more. I thought handing out roses left and right would make the actual ceremony easier. But when it came time to stand in front of the ladies during the ceremony, I realized it made it more challenging. I looked at the tray, and there were so few roses left. But in front of me, there were still so many great women.

There were only seven roses to give, which meant several women would have to go home that night. I felt bad about doing it, because I know there's a certain level of disappointment that comes with being sent home on the first night.

I'd have to get used to making tough decisions.

＊———&&&———＊

After getting the first night out of the way, I was excited to get to know the women better. However, I was nervous about the dynamic of the group date because group dates with Emily had been so uncomfortable. No one really acted like himself in our group dates because it's awkward to share time with the same person. As the Bachelor, I wanted to set the tone and try to treat everyone equally. I knew this was a virtual impossibility, especially when I found out we were all having a "Harlequin date" and had to act out romance novels. Because romance novels are full of, well, romance, things got uncomfortable pretty quickly. Soon, I was kissing one of the girls while the other women looked on. Don't get me wrong, I really enjoyed kissing. But I didn't enjoy kissing in front of a room full of people whom the PDA is actually hurting.

I could tell Tierra was visibly upset.

"What's going on?" I asked when I could pull her away. She'd definitely won me over on the first night, and I wanted her to be happy—even if the circumstances were a bit odd.

"I'm here for you," she said. "But I don't want to make friends with the other women."

This is a long ride, I thought. *Don't isolate yourself too much because you might be living with these girls for the next ten weeks.* However, I could tell she was uneasy about the idea of vying for attention in a larger group. I understood that.

As awkward as the group date was, I had a good moment with Catherine. She slipped me a note that read, "I'm vegan but I love the beef."

Of course, this was implying that I'm a beefcake, which I loved. I'd known Catherine was beautiful, but only on our group date did I begin to see that she also had a great sense of humor. As a steak-loving Texan, I'd never dated a vegan. Regardless, I definitely wanted to spend more time with this girl from Seattle.

The one-on-one dates gave me a chance to really get to know the women. My first of the week was with a woman named Desiree, someone with whom I'd gotten along so well the first night. Talking to Des by the fire at the bachelor pad was everything I hoped it would be. She was witty, sarcastic, intelligent, loving, and caring, and our morals seemed to line up. Did I mention she's beautiful? This girl had it all, and I could feel myself really starting to fall for her. We ended the night with a romantic dip in the hot tub. She left the date with a rose, and I left it thinking Des might just be the one for me.

Of course, there was never any time to sit around and dream of one person.

During the next few weeks, we had one-on-one dates, two-on-one dates, and group dates. Some dates were better than others. One good group date was when we got together on the beach for a volleyball match. Apparently, none of these ladies had ever played volleyball, but we had a great time playing around, tossing the football, and throwing the Frisbee. Catherine got on my back to see if I could do push-ups with her added weight—which, of course, I could. I felt comfortable around her, and she seemed to make the most of every situation. This was a good trait to have, because the next group date—at a roller derby—was pretty disastrous.

At first, I thought it would be fun to see who would compete and embrace the physicality of the sport. But as soon as the girls put on their skates, I knew it was not practical to ask the women to skate on an embanked track while hitting one another. Everyone was having a tough time during practice, and then one of the girls—Amanda—fell and busted her chin.

"Let's do an old-school free skate instead," I suggested. I was there to spend time with the women, not to watch them hurt one another.

While some of the girls didn't want to skate—understandably fearing they'd get hurt—Catherine was game for anything and had a fun time.

Wow, she's really enjoying this, I thought. *Even though this date is awkward, she's just enjoying the day.*

After the roller derby, the girls got dressed to get ready for the night portion. We went to the Roosevelt, a cool Hollywood hotel, where a beautiful rooftop party had been set up for us. On the group dates, the night always ended going from girl to girl to girl, getting to know them better. The only problem was logistics. No matter where I was, I was inside with the girls most of the time.

"Mary Kate, can you put me somewhere with Catherine where we can be alone?" I asked off camera. I'd had so much fun with her, I wondered if it was the right time to see if there was also a romantic spark.

Mary Kate put us in a private area where there were curtains, so nobody could see in. Well, nobody except the millions of people watching from home. My main goal was not to be insensitive to the other women.

While we were chatting, I put my hand on her knee to send a message: *I'm interested in you.* However, she didn't reciprocate. She acted nervous and—to be honest—kind of weird. *Does this girl even like me?* I wondered.

Since she'd given me a note during a previous date, I handed her a little note of my own, which read, "I really like your nose crinkles." When she smiled, her nose crinkled up in the most adorable way. When I handed the note to her, I thought, *If that doesn't do it, nothing's going to do it.*

It didn't do it.

And so, even though the setting was perfect and private, I didn't swoop in for a kiss. The moment had passed. When we wrapped up our conversation, I was kind of bummed. I couldn't read her at that moment. *Was she nervous? Giddy because of the odd situation? Maybe she just wasn't feeling me.* Catherine was really hard to read, which left me with a lot of questions.

—◦—

The Bachelor has to have a nice ride, and the show always made sure I got the best cars.

That week, I picked up my one-on-one date, Leslie Hughes, in an Aston Martin. During our *Pretty Woman*–themed date, I took her to Rodeo Drive, where she got to pick out a dress, purse, and shoes from Badgley Mischka.

"I'm a tan Julia Roberts!" Leslie (who's African American) laughed.

She looked even more stunning when Neil Lane let her wear a 120-carat diamond necklace.

Leslie was friendly, kind, and down-to-earth. I think she said "Holy moly" at least a dozen times because of the extravagance of the date. I could tell she was grateful to be on the date with me, and I was thankful to spend it with her.

We had dinner at an old building in downtown Los Angeles, but I was distracted the whole time. Even though she was beautiful, elegant, and charming, I didn't feel a connection with her. At the end of the date, I had a choice to make—to hand out the rose or not. If I didn't feel a romantic connection, it meant I had to send her home at the end of the date. My stomach churned along with every sip of wine and every turn of the conversation.

Mary Kate pulled me aside for my ITM interview.

"Sean, how do you feel your date is going?" she asked.

"Leslie's gorgeous and our conversation flows effortlessly," I said. "I can't put my finger on it, but the connection isn't there."

When I went back to the dinner table, we were supposed to talk for a few more minutes. The producers were standing inconspicuously in the background. While we were chatting, I had an eye on the producers in my peripheral vision as I watched for their "wrap it up" sign. When I saw it, I moved the conversation to a close so we could move into the part I was dreading most.

Whether or not I handed out a rose, the producers wanted me to pick up the rose before I explained my decision. That night, I picked up the rose. Leslie smiled. My heart sank. I explained that I regrettably didn't see a future for us.

"You don't see any romantic connection?" she asked, caught completely off guard.

Sending her home was one of the more difficult things I had to do all season because she didn't see it coming. I admired and respected Leslie for so many reasons, but I knew she wasn't the one for me.

I escorted her outside, and we began saying our awkward good-byes.

A producer, who had been lurking in the background, pulled me aside to deliver urgent information. "You have to take that necklace off before she gets in the car," she said.

"What?" I couldn't believe my ears.

"It's worth over one hundred fifty thousand dollars," she whispered.

"No," I said flatly. "I'm not going to do it."

I felt awful about sending Leslie home. Asking her to hold on while I took the necklace off her felt like putting salt in the wound. I continued with our good-bye conversation when a lower-level staff member showed up.

"I'm sorry, but you have to do it," the staffer said.

This time, Leslie overheard the conversation, and I was furious.

"No, it's okay," she said graciously.

I quickly unlatched the necklace, tossed the $150,000 necklace to the producer, and stormed back inside.

Leigh Anne, the executive producer, met me as soon as I stepped inside.

"I'm so sorry," she said. "We didn't mean to surprise you like that."

"It was such bad form," I said. "Not only did I send her home, but I had to snatch the necklace off her neck?"

James Taylor's son Ben was scheduled to perform for us that night, and the show went on as planned. I listened to him sing a song undoubtedly selected anticipating this would be some sort of romantic moment. My mind raced as I leaned against a railing, holding the rose I didn't give to Leslie.

eleven

MOVING OUT OF
THE FRIEND ZONE

The next pre–rose ceremony cocktail party seemed to go on and on. I had to make my rounds to talk to every girl. A palpable sense of desperation hung in the room as each woman made a last-ditch effort at proving she deserved to stay another week. When my time to talk to Catherine came, the producers put us in the mezzanine area above the pool.

"I was really hoping to kiss you tonight, but unfortunately the other girls can see," Catherine said, handing me a card with her lipstick imprint.

I'd thought Catherine had put me squarely in the friend zone by not seeming interested on the last group date. This card filled me with confidence. "You know, I'm the Bachelor. I can go anywhere I want."

It was a totally arrogant statement, but I wasn't going to let anything stand in the way of our first kiss. I grabbed her hand and walked to the front of the mansion, around the house, and through the gate. When we got to the front driveway, I put my hands around her waist. Because she's so much shorter than I am, her face only came up to my chest.

So there we were.

She'd told me she wanted to kiss, and I definitely wanted to kiss. Catherine, however, wouldn't look up at me. She later told me she was nervous because she knew looking up would mean I'd lay one on her. After a few seconds of her giggling, making awkward small talk, and avoiding my eyes, I finally took matters into my own hands.

"You can look up whenever you want to," I said.

When she lifted her chin, I leaned down, put my lips near hers, and—finally—kissed her.

The kiss was short and sweet, but it apparently made all her nervousness go away. Catherine suddenly got excited and giddy.

"I just want to frolic," she exclaimed.

Frolic? I thought. *Who uses a word like that?* What I was beginning to appreciate about Catherine was her willingness to show her emotion. It might be the Italian in her—but when she's happy, she just can't hold it back. When a girl needs to frolic, a girl should be able to frolic.

"Okay," I said. "Let's go frolic."

We grabbed hands, skipped around the front driveway, and acted absolutely goofy.

She was on top of the world and so was I. And so we danced around the front yard, high on emotion and our budding romance.

Of course, our time together couldn't last forever. Pretty soon, producers whisked me away for another tough rose ceremony. I was exhausted from the day-in, day-out emotional roller coaster by the time I went back into the girls' mansion to do my ITMs. It was four o'clock in the morning, and I could barely think straight.

I shook my head a bit to wake myself up before Mary Kate went through her list asking me about every girl. She—and the rest of the producers—wore earpieces that allowed them to hear everything that was going on. Whether I was on a date, at a rose ceremony, or frolicking in the driveway, the producers heard every word. Even though Mary Kate was always out of sight of the cameras, she was taking notes that she used during the ITM interviews. She might ask, "Tierra told you this tonight. What did you think about that?" Or "How did you feel when Catherine said this about this?" What the girls didn't know was that I filmed these interviews inside the mansion while they were upstairs sleeping.

After I wrapped up my interview, I shuffled through the mansion, my head down as I thought about my head hitting my pillow. Tired, exhausted, and hungry, I was getting weary of the eighteen-hour days. Just then, I saw Catherine at the top of the staircase. Her face was cleanly scrubbed, and she had her toothbrush in her hand.

"Sean." She paused. "What are you doing here?"

"Catherine, no!" her house producers said as they realized we'd seen each other and practically threw their bodies between us. Their ironclad rule is this: no interaction off camera. If something is said off camera that changes the direction of the relationship, it's hard to convey that on film. (This recently happened on Juan Pablo's season, when he uttered something profane to one of the last two remaining girls in a helicopter, causing the show to awkwardly try to convey what we'd missed and why the woman was so angry.) "No!"

As they tried to hold her back, Catherine fought through them, ran up to me, and gave me the biggest hug. It was such a special moment. As I went back to my place, my mind swirled with thoughts of Catherine.

✦ ⸺ ⸺ ✦

My time in Los Angeles was amazing, but I was excited to get away from California for a change of scenery. Our next stop was Whitefish, Montana, one of the coolest towns I have ever visited. The mountains, trees, and rivers made this the perfect destination for romance. I'm an outdoorsy guy, so I knew I would really connect with the women who shared a similar appreciation for nature.

My first date with Lindsay couldn't have gone better. We felt so comfortable around each other, and being together felt right. We took the helicopter to the stunning mountaintop of Glacier National Park and set up our picnic. You'll notice picnics are a staple of most dates on *The Bachelor* because they give couples a picturesque moment to chat.

I liked Lindsay from the moment she stepped out of the limo in her wedding dress. Well, maybe a few minutes later, when I finally realized she wasn't crazy. On our one-on-one date, however, I began to connect with her in a real way. She told me she wrestled in high school, which, of course, meant I had to challenge her to a match. Believe it or not, she took me down. I loved seeing Lindsay's playful and fun spirit, and I felt like I had accomplished my goal for my season—to let the fun and goofiness of my personality (and the girls') shine through.

Lindsay also had a serious side. She opened up about her fear when her dad was deployed to Iraq and how her mother held the family together during his absence. This was when I realized where Lindsay's supportive and caring nature came from. Every other girl would hound me about getting a one-on-one date, but Lindsay never brought it up. Instead, she always reminded me she wasn't going anywhere. She once mentioned she thought it was good for me to get to know everyone else so that I would eventually learn she's the one for me.

That's confidence, and I liked it.

We ended the night dancing in the town square. It was one of the most memorable nights of my life.

Could Lindsay, I wondered, *one day be my wife?*

Honestly, I could see it.

<hr />

The group date in Montana was, suitably, called the "lumberjack challenge." The girls had to saw wood, carry hay bales, and canoe—a nice change of pace from the normal bungee cord jumping or Beverly Hills–type dates common to the show. Definitely safer than roller derby. Before the date started, I walked through the downtown Whitefish restaurant with the director, who pointed out all the spots I could sit with the girls.

"Here's a spot right here," she said, pointing to a table. "Or you could also sit here," she said, pointing to an area they'd set up in the corner. The producers thought carefully about where we could sit and talk so they'd be camera-ready when the time came.

The evening portion of the date was going well, and I was dutifully taking each woman to the predetermined, candlelit spots. Halfway through the evening, Catherine grabbed my hand.

"Let's go outside!" she said. Judging from the way the cameramen scurried to follow us, the producers apparently didn't know this was coming. When something unexpected happened on the show, they didn't try to stop it from unfolding. Rather, they did the best they could to capture it on film—which is why close observers of the show sometimes see cameramen running in the background. Usually, that's when something good is about to happen!

We walked out the back door and went back behind the restaurant/bar into their parking lot holding hands, laughing, giggling, and having a good time. There were a couple of guys out in the back who weren't impressed by our giddy lovefest.

"Get out of Whitefish," one of the guys slurred. "We don't need you here!"

"Why don't you shut up and go back inside the bar?" I said.

It was a funny backdrop for what was supposed to be a romantic conversation. *Maybe that's why the producers set everything up in advance*, I thought. The drunk guys' disapproval didn't matter to us. Catherine and I sat on a bench and chatted away excitedly.

While the group date was pleasant, the pre–rose ceremony cocktail party that week was a disaster. Tension among the girls bubbled right under the surface, and apparently the drama surrounded Tierra. I was beginning to sense a pattern. I heard rumblings that she was different around me than she was around the girls, but I hated taking secondhand information. I wanted to judge someone based on what I'd seen—not what I'd heard. Tierra was kind and nice to me at all times, so I pushed any criticism I heard about it out of my head. But I couldn't ignore the snippy fighting I heard all night. During the party, there was an epic battle raging from room to room, focusing on Tierra and putting everyone on edge.

When I finally had a chance to sit down with Harrison before the rose ceremony, I was fed up.

"I feel like I've wasted everyone's time," I told him. "Including my own."

"What's going on?" he asked me.

"I've had a good time, but I am so sick of the drama. I can't imagine my wife is in this bunch."

Harrison, to his credit, didn't push me too hard. He just listened and nodded, and assured me he'd seen much worse. "Listen, Sean, I know it seems overwhelming right now, but this, too, will pass."

I listened to his counsel, sent someone home, and went back to my place.

I couldn't shake the feeling.

This just didn't feel like the right way to meet a wife.

⊷——ᚖᚖᚖ——⊶

Though Whitefish was beautiful, I was glad to pack my bags for Canada. Our next destination was the Fairmont Chateau, nestled on the shore of Lake Louise in the Canadian Rockies, which had—over the years—hosted many kings and queens. Surrounded by enormous mountain peaks, the jaw-dropping Victoria Glacier, and a vibrant teal-blue lake, it was the most majestic area I'd ever seen.

The date card that week read, "Let's find our fairy-tale ending" and went to Catherine. I was over the drama, over the women talking about the drama, and ready to find a partner I could see myself with for a lifetime. Could Catherine be that person? I doubted it but was excited about exploring the opportunity.

Everything was working against us on our date. I arrived early because they had to teach me how to drive a gigantic bus that would take us on an excursion to a glacier in Jasper National Park. However, blizzard-like conditions crept up on us as we prepared.

"You ready?" Mary Kate asked, standing next to the enormous vehicle. "It looks like there's a storm coming that we didn't anticipate."

"Ya think?" Pellets of ice stung my face, causing welts to form.

After a quick tutorial, I drove up to where the producers had dropped off Catherine, who wasn't dressed for a snowstorm. The wind blew around her, the temperature had dropped well below freezing, and she looked like a Popsicle.

When I opened the door, her face lit up. "What are you doing? I didn't realize you were driving this thing!"

I walked down the stairs, gave her a snowsuit to put on, and told her about our date. The wind kicked up the snow around us so that we couldn't see very far in front of our faces. Even though the producers had left us sleds, there were no real hills, and the snow beneath our feet had solidified into ice.

What could've been a disastrous date, however, turned into a blast. Catherine joked around the whole time, jumped on the sled, did cartwheels in the snow, and made snow angels. But by the time we spread out our picnic blanket, I couldn't feel my feet. The storm had started to move in even closer, and we were getting slapped in the face with snow. She laughed because my hair was white like Jack Frost but my face was as red as a tomato. We were freezing our butts off, but we still tried to cuddle up on a little picnic blanket and have hot chocolate. Catherine, as a vegan, didn't normally drink hot chocolate. Since it was the only thing standing between her and hypothermia, she made an exception.

"All right, guys, we've got to get out of here," the crew said as they packed up their equipment. "We're not going to get off the mountain."

Since our date was cut short, Catherine and I prepared to go back to the hotel to rest before the evening portion of the date. During this off-camera time, Catherine and I were supposed to travel in different vehicles since every interaction needed to be caught on camera. I was having so much fun with her, however, I asked Mary Kate for a favor.

"Can she please drive back with us?" I asked, feeling like a high school kid without his driver's license asking his mom for a favor. "Can she please?"

"Absolutely not," Mary Kate said, frowning.

"I promise not to do anything interesting that you wish you would've caught on camera," I said.

"Sean," she said. "I want to help out, but you know the rules: no off-camera interaction."

"But I'm having such a good time," I said. "Come on, you guys almost froze us to death on that date. Don't you owe us?"

Mary Kate looked around, as if to see if anyone was listening. "Promise me you won't talk about anything important?"

"I promise," I said. "I just want to be with her."

Catherine, Mary Kate, Brenner, and I piled into the car and asked the driver to turn up the radio—a novelty, since we hadn't heard it in such a long time. We were casually singing along to songs we knew and laughing.

When a song by Erykah Badu called "Tyrone" came on the radio, Catherine came alive. The song is a soulful lament that the singer's boyfriend never buys her anything and always calls his friends instead of being content to hang out with her.

She sang along with every word. But she wasn't just singing; she somehow had morphed into a soulful hip-hop artist. "Why can't we be by ourselves sometimes?" she sang along with the song.[6]

She looked straight at me when she said those words and laughed.

Mary Kate, Brenner, and I watched in amazement as this Filipino-American-Italian girl gave us a soulful rendition I definitely wish we'd caught on film.

"I'm so impressed right now," Brenner said, watching her belt out this song without missing a syllable.

The drive took about an hour and a half, and our giddiness over being together gradually gave way to the exhaustion of having been in a snowstorm all day. When the hum of the engine began casting its spell on us, Catherine put her head in my lap and dozed off.

A couple of hours later, I was standing in the lobby of the hotel, having showered, freshened up, and gotten a bite to eat. As I stood there waiting for Catherine to emerge from her hotel room for the evening portion of our date, I was excited. The sight of her walking down the stairs at the beautiful Fairmont took my breath away. Then a horse-drawn carriage took us to an ice castle built just for us.

Yes, an ice castle.

They put a fire pit inside and blankets on top of the ice bench, but the walls and seats were made of solid ice. We cuddled up once again, which—of course—I loved. We talked all night. It was picturesque, with the snow falling and the moon shining—though at one point the wind changed direction and the smoke from the fire almost suffocated us.

During the date, the producers took us out separately for the ITMs.

"So it looks like you and Catherine really have something cool going here," said Mary Kate, who always had a great sense of how things were going. She had listened to every conversation and knew me extremely well by this point. "Now it's time to give her the rose." As mentioned earlier, normally during the ITMs, I decided whether to give my date a rose. This time, however, there was no doubt.

When I gave the rose to Catherine, she was so excited. We went out to the grassy field on which the ice castle was built and danced under the moonlight with light snow falling around us. It was a perfect moment.

"We're not gonna use this anymore," the producers said as they wrapped up filming for the night. "You guys can destroy the ice castle if you want."

"Really?" I saw a gleam in Catherine's eyes.

We took chisels and started tearing the ice castle apart. I made a luge out of the ice castle and tried to pour champagne through it. It didn't work out well, but we had a blast. I hadn't shared that type of fun with anyone else besides her. It wasn't televised, but it gave me another memorable moment with Catherine.

Of course, I had been collecting these really memorable moments—and they weren't all with Catherine. I'd go on an awesome date, have the time of my life, then wake up the next day and have another amazing date with a totally different woman.

She might be the one, I'd think.

Then the next date, I'd think, *No*, she *might be the one*.

When I was talking to the producer early on, I described my dream girl as "someone who shares my faith, someone funny and easygoing." In the beginning, just like in everyday life, you're drawn to some. But if someone had asked me who would be my top four, I would've been wrong. As time went by, I realized that first impressions were not always the right impressions. Over the course of several weeks, I started to mentally rearrange that top four. But I could feel confusion settle over my heart, with so many legitimately wonderful—and different—women vying for my attention.

We packed our bags, said good-bye to snowy Canada, and headed for St. Croix, the largest of the US Virgin Islands. Though I loved the ice castle, the snow bus, and the glacier lakes, a warmer climate appealed to me.

It was October, so it felt like we were getting away with something going to a tropical setting in the fall. Plus, Shay's birthday was coming up, and I hadn't seen her in so long.

"I think it would be so cool to do something with my sister," I suggested to one of the producers, "since she's a *Bachelor* nut and is actually the reason I'm here."

The producers had enjoyed meeting Shay when they visited Texas and met my family during Emily's season. They thought it was a great idea. When she heard she could travel to beautiful St. Croix, Shay was thrilled.

Again, the ironclad rule the producers enforced was always the same: no off-camera interaction. This applied to Shay too. The producers created an entire scene for her arrival. I stood on the beach, where the show had set up tables for us. I hadn't seen her in a couple of months, so it was really good to see her running through the sand with her sandals in her hands.

"I have to let two girls go home tonight that I really care about," I said after Shay and I sat down at the table.

"Is there anyone you can see yourself marrying?"

"Almost all of them," I said. "Honestly, none of them stick out as being 'the one.'"

"Well, our biggest fear as a family is that you pick a girl who isn't as committed as you are," Shay said. "I don't want to watch it unfold on television and say, 'No, don't pick that one!' Because sometimes the Bachelor ends up with 'that one.'"

I totally understood what she was saying. I distinctly remember watching one of the guys on Emily's season, thinking, *There's no way she is falling for this jerk.*

"I have a pretty good feeling for all of the girls, but the only one I could question is Tierra," I said. "People have told me there is a different side to her that I haven't seen. I've heard she doesn't hang out with the other girls and isn't a nice person."

I could tell Shay didn't like what she was hearing.

"I don't want to be the guy who keeps the girl that no one likes, but I enjoy being with her."

"Have you liked her from the start?" Shay asked.

"Well, I gave her a first impression rose because she seemed fun, warm, and outgoing." Then I explained the various things that had happened that gave me pause. Even though our relationship had grown to the point that she'd reached the final six, it had not been uneventful: she fell down the stairs under curious circumstances back at the mansion, causing the EMTs to wonder if she had a concussion. In Canada, we took a polar bear plunge into a frigid, glacier-fed lake. Admittedly, it took forever—with the preparations and the interviews. We probably stood in thirty-two-degree weather for two and a half hours before we jumped in. I remember that I couldn't feel my feet—I've never felt colder in my life. However, most of us ran into the water, dunked ourselves, and ran out screaming and laughing. But Tierra suddenly started gasping for breath, clawing at her chest, and shaking uncontrollably. Once again, she was hauled off by the EMTs.

I paused for a moment in my story, thankful to have Shay there to help me figure this out. Was it possible that Tierra had done all that for attention? She seemed sincere to me, but it was an awful lot of trouble surrounding one person.

"I like her, but the other girls really don't seem to care for her." My sister is a great judge of character, and she knows me better than anyone else. Her advice to me before I left Dallas was simple: avoid the girl surrounded by drama. After hearing bad reports about Tierra, I thought it would be a good idea to have my sister sit down and visit with Tierra so I could get her opinion. "Stay here and I'll run and get her."

At least that was the plan. Tierra was in her hotel room, just a golf cart ride way. As soon as I walked through the door of the hotel, I sensed there was something amiss. The girls were quiet. Apparently, an enormous fight had erupted between Tierra and the other girls. I knew Tierra was having a hard time being on the show. I sympathized with her a great deal because I freaked out when I'd heard Emily had kissed Arie. Her discomfort was understandable, and I was looking forward to working through it with her.

When I walked in, no one explained what was going on. Though the house producer was aware of the argument, my producers were also caught off guard by the chill in the room.

When Tierra saw me, her face fell as though she'd seen the grim reaper. I sat down and put my arm around her, preparing to invite her to meet my sister. Because I never went to the girls' home unexpectedly—the only other time I'd shown up was to send another girl home—Tierra feared the worst. Her shock turned into sorrow, and she started bawling.

"Tierra," I said. "What's wrong?"

"I can't do this anymore. I can't do it," she said. "I like you so much, but I can't do this."

Though I really liked Tierra in the beginning, I knew there was something seriously wrong.

"Please tell me what's going on," I said, though she could barely speak. Instead of taking Tierra down to meet my sister, I figured that we might need a change of plans. "I'll be right back," I told her.

I walked outside and sighed.

All the producers were outside, looking surprised at how our plans to introduce Shay to Tierra had gone awry.

"Jonah, I've got to send her home now," I said. "She's miserable." Of course, he'd heard our entire conversation, so he agreed.

"That might be the right move," he said, running his hand through his wild hair. Sending someone home, of course, is a big production. I stood out there for probably twenty minutes while they got the cameras ready. I'm sure Tierra was wondering what on earth was going on, because I'd told her that I'd return in just a second. (Not to mention Shay, who was still sitting at the table, waiting for my return.)

"Okay, we're ready," the producers said. "Tell her she doesn't have to pack her bags. We'll do all that for her."

"You don't want her to grab anything?"

"No," he said. "We'll get the shot of you putting her in the van after you walk Tierra out the front door."

Most of the girls were in the living room by the front door, which gave me pause. I knew it would've made great television to see the shocked reactions of the girls who already disliked Tierra as she was escorted away from the show. *Yes, the show*, I reminded myself. We were making a television show, no matter how high emotions ran.

"I think you should go home," I said. She sobbed even more and tried to pack her stuff.

"No," I said. "The show will get your things for you. Let me just walk you out."

She immediately started walking toward the back, but I stopped her. "Hey, let's walk out the front door."

Even in her sorrow, she knew this didn't make sense. She stopped dead in her tracks. "Why?"

"You're right," I said. "Let's go out the back door." I realized that it wasn't kind to parade her in front of the other girls, and I knew the producers would rather me be considerate than dramatic. I couldn't do that to the poor girl.

After we walked out the back door, she stopped crying and suddenly looked furious.

"Are you going to be okay?" I asked. This was probably the worst question I could've posed.

"No," she tersely responded and then got in the van.

As I watched the van drive away, I heard her scream and cry as it disappeared into the distance.

In a state of disbelief over what had just happened, I walked back to my sister, who'd been waiting on the beach. It was nice to be able to talk through these issues with her and also to show her this crazy life I was now living. When we were growing up, fighting over what television show to watch, I never thought we'd one day be sitting in a tropical location on an actual television show.

I was so glad to have my sister there. What woman—especially a mother of young children—wouldn't want to fly to a tropical location, get a free hotel room, and enjoy nice spa treatments? Plus, she loved seeing the behind-the-scenes details unfold during filming. One of the best parts was that she got to hang out with me and Harrison in my room as we got ready for the upcoming rose ceremony.

While we put on our suits, the producers walked in and out to tell us about the details of the night. She was really surprised when Harrison came out singing "Happy Birthday" to her with a cake we'd made just for her.

Plus, it was good to have my sister there during what was probably the most controversial episode of the season. After the show, people asked me about Tierra more than anything else.

"How could you keep her as long as you did?"

"Did you not see how crazy she was?"

To be perfectly honest, I didn't see what everyone at home saw—not even close.

At the beginning of my *Bachelor* journey, I told the girls, "I'm going to create my own opinion, and I'm not really going to listen to the others." Knowing human nature, I knew girls would inevitably start talking about other girls. "I'm going to base my opinion on what I've seen, not what I've heard." Perhaps I relied so much on my direct experiences that I blocked out some of the bad things I heard regarding Tierra.

I realize now I should've listened to what the others were saying.

To put it simply, I liked her. When I was with her, she was nice, kind, and fun to be with. Because *The Bachelor* is not the most natural dating situation, it's totally understandable to flake out under the pressure. I sympathized—and even empathized—with it. Because I never saw her mistreating the other girls or being mean to the others, I let her stay so I could get to know her better.

Tierra always said, "I'm here for love, not to make friends." It seems in every season, one person carries that banner. What they don't realize is that they'll be spending a whole lot more time hanging around the mansion with the others than on actual dates. Obviously, no one has to make best buddies for life, but friendships sure make the experience a lot more enjoyable.

I can speak from experience. I'll be friends with guys from Emily's season for the rest of my life. I loved getting to know Jef, Arie, Charlie, John,

Alejandro, and Travis. To be honest, the rose ceremonies were sad for me, even when she sent the other guys home. Though I should've been relieved that I'd survived on the show another week, I was always disappointed because I'd miss seeing the guys around the house.

Regrettably, none of the girls seemed sad to see Tierra go.

At the end of that crazy week, I was left with four amazing women and a lot of questions swirling around in my mind.

Hopefully, it was nothing a few hometown visits couldn't cure.

twelve

ONE STEP AT A TIME

Family is very important to me, so I knew the hometown dates of the four remaining women—AshLee, Lindsay, Catherine, and Desiree—were going to be critical. I couldn't believe I'd already gotten to this point in my journey. I knew each of the four remaining women would make a wonderful wife, but none stood out above the others. I decided I was going to focus on each relationship, without comparing them or muddling them together in my mind. I decided to try this approach: when I was with AshLee, I would focus on AshLee—without thinking of the other girls. Then, when I was with Lindsay, I'd try to think of her exclusively. I hoped their families would give me insight and information on each of them that would help me make good decisions. All four of them were evenly ranked in my mind going into that hometown week, and I desperately needed to find clarity for the upcoming days of decision.

A lump formed in my throat as I packed my bag for Houston. I couldn't believe I would be possibly engaged to one of these women. I tried to push this thought out of my mind. At this point, I couldn't think about the finish line. Not everyone on the show proposed at the end of it, and I didn't have to either. After all, who actually finds a spouse on reality TV? Never before in the history of the franchise had the Bachelor proposed to someone on the show and ended up at the altar with the same person. I didn't have to be the first one. I placed my T-shirts into the suitcase and zipped it shut, willing myself not to think too far ahead.

One step at a time.

AshLee was first up. She'd been a front-runner from the beginning, because she was the type of woman I was looking for: loving, compassionate, sweet, and nurturing. Though I loved how we seemed to share the same values, I never saw her having fun or being goofy. She was serious and sober-minded. Knowing her story, I saw that her serious nature made sense. She'd been through a great deal. Her childhood had been less than ideal. In fact, it sounded more like a nightmare than a typical childhood. She told me she spent time in the foster-care system before finally being adopted when she was six years old.

Though I knew she'd make an excellent wife and mother, I couldn't shake the feeling that I couldn't really let loose and have a goofy time with her. I remember when I was in St. Croix, I was telling the producers that I needed to figure out if she could be funny. Jonah, who has a twisted sense of humor, always told me jokes. One of his favorites was this:

A horse walks into a bar.

The bartender says, "Why the long face?"

And the horse says, "My wife just died."

Jonah and I laughed at that forever. The joke, of course, was that the horse really *was* sad. In St. Croix, I decided to test this out on AshLee. I've been known to tell a few off-color jokes—I got that from my dad and Mimi—and I thought her response would tell me all I needed to know about her sense of humor. When I tried it out on AshLee, she looked at me blankly. Of course, it's a terrible joke.

Maybe it was to her credit she didn't laugh.

But when I got to Houston—and met AshLee along with her fluffy dog, Bailey—I was determined to figure out if we could have fun together.

"My parents aren't your typical pastor's family," she told me as we talked about meeting her family. "My dad's into motorcycles and he's extremely outdoorsy."

Because my dad is also an ordained minister, I knew our families would share the same values. I wasn't even nervous to meet them—I normally do pretty well meeting parents and talking to families.

Immediately, I hit it off with her parents. I could tell her dad was a man of deep faith, and I enjoyed talking to him about his life and ministry. Her mom was great, too, and really opened up to me. She confided in me a pertinent detail about AshLee's life: the year prior to her adoption, AshLee had been in *five* foster homes.

That hit me hard. I've always thought I'd one day want to adopt and really value people who invest so heavily in children in need. When her dad told me about meeting AshLee as a little girl, it really touched me.

"She walked in and right away I looked at her, and I looked at the social worker, and I said 'This one's going to be really hard to give back,'" he said, with the practiced cadence that indicated this was a story he loved to tell. "The moment I saw her, I fell in love with her. So whatever man takes her for the rest of her life is going to have to fall in love with her like that."

It made me appreciate AshLee even more.

After meeting her parents, I could see where her big heart came from. Her mom and dad were both kind and loving, and I could tell they genuinely wanted their daughter to be happy. It was easy to imagine myself being part of her family. Even though she wasn't as carefree as the other women, her past made her serious nature more understandable. Though I'd been nervous about the potentially awkward hometown dates, the first one was so amazing I was ready to face them all.

＊—⠢⠶⠶⠶—＊

When I arrived at Seattle's Pike Place Market, a historic farmers' market built on the Elliott Bay waterfront, I was excited to see Catherine. We began our date in a fish market, where we tossed fish with their crew of fishmongers. I had an advantage over Catherine because of my football experience, but she definitely held her own. (Plus, she actually was on a football team as a kid, until her mom made her quit to be a cheerleader!)

Anytime we went to a market or strolled around a city, staffers always came over and put a bunch of cash in my pocket. That way, on television it would seem like I had money instead of being a bum without cash. Anyway, after visiting a doughnut stand, I put my arm around Catherine and jammed a powdered doughnut in her ear. In turn, she smashed a chocolate doughnut on my face. We were having so much fun together, like two kids.

Then we came upon a gum wall, which is exactly what it sounds like: a wall with millions of pieces of gum stuck to it. The tradition is that people write notes, fold them up, and use gum like glue to hold them to the wall. Ever since the beginning of the show, Catherine had been sending me silly notes—"I like it that you don't have arm hair" was the most recent one. So we wrote notes to each other and stuck them to the wall. I felt a certain joy when I was with her, but everything changed when we got to her home.

Everything there felt different. Catherine was from a Filipino culture, she lived a couple of blocks from her mom, and her grandma and cousins lived in the house next door. While AshLee's mom was a typical Southern mom—"Come on in. Let me get you some iced tea"—Catherine's mom was warm but much more skeptical.

Catherine had prepared me in advance that there was a culturally sensitive way to approach "Lola," the Filipino word for *grandmother*. When I walked in, Lola offered me her hand. I took it and pressed it to my forehead, which Catherine had explained was a gesture used as a sign of respect to older people. As I was doing this, I halfway wondered if this was some sort of joke and if everyone would suddenly break out into laughter. It wasn't, and my attempt pleased her grandmother.

"Handsome," she said approvingly. "I'm going to get him." Catherine's grandmother was one of the funniest women I'd ever met. She seemed like a movie character. Her husband had died thirty-six years earlier, so Lola teased, "I'm single, but I'm still hunting."

I felt like I'd won over Catherine's grandmother, but I got the very real feeling that her mom and sisters were unsure a reality TV romance could work. In other words, they were reasonable folks.

Catherine's mom and I had a chance to chat in her kitchen as we rolled *lumpia*—Filipino pastries, sort of like spring rolls. She was welcoming and kind, but I could only get so deep while wearing a frilly apron. We chatted in her living room, Catherine sat on my back while I did push-ups, and we laughed.

I knew before I arrived that I wouldn't be meeting Catherine's dad during this hometown date. When we were in St. Croix, Catherine told me a harrowing story about how he had battled depression when she was a kid. When she was fourteen, he tried to commit suicide in front of her and her sisters and was immediately taken away. He recently moved back to the states from Taiwan and had been doing much better.

I could tell that Catherine's sisters were a little upset that Catherine had told me about his situation on national television. Even Catherine felt like she may have told something to the world that shouldn't have been shared. She definitely didn't want to hurt her dad and always spoke of him with honor and respect. I think this reveals the authenticity of the show. People understand that reality TV can be scripted. But *The Bachelor* is much more authentic than people think. In normal relationships, people have tough conversations. On *The Bachelor*, they just happen to occur on camera.

When I talked to Catherine's sisters, Monica and India, I liked the way they were both protective and honest about their sister.

"Do you think she's ready to settle down?" I asked. Honestly, I thought this was a slow ball question. The sort of thing you toss out there to get a conversation going.

Monica paused for a long time, then smiled. "I can't see her having kids right away. She goes in 100 percent with guys and makes things really fun. But when the fun wears off . . ."

I swallowed hard. One of the main reasons I liked being with Catherine was her silly sensibility the other girls lacked. Was her sister saying this was a temporary phase that would soon wear off?

"She wants to be with someone who supports all of her dreams. If you don't support her dreams, she'll leave," she said.

"Her dreams?" I asked.

"Well, she has a strong desire to pursue a career as a graphic designer and live in New York."

Odd, I thought. *Catherine never mentioned that to me.* I'd love to have a wife with a career and dreams, but I found it interesting that Catherine had not—at least not yet—mentioned her aspirations to me. It was also the first time I'd heard that she planned on living in New York. I'd always expected us to live back in Dallas.

"Plus, every guy she's dated has been too easy on her," Monica said. "She needs a guy who can call her out."

I laughed, a little nervously. "What kinds of things does she need to be called out on?"

"She's messy," India said. "I mean, she's not dirty, but she has clothes strewn around. Everywhere."

I couldn't decide if her sisters were being too hard on Catherine or if they were just skeptical of, well, everything.

"Plus, she needs someone who can handle her moods. She's either very happy or very focused. Some guys get a little nervous about that."

The conversation unnerved me. When I went to the kitchen to talk to her mom, I had no idea what to expect. I could tell everyone was surprised with how quickly things had progressed. And I understood. Catherine had gone off to do this show as a fun adventure. They didn't anticipate that she'd show up with her heart fully invested in some stranger.

"So how are you feeling about things?" I asked her mom.

"This is an adventure. This is very unique. Will it work? I don't know," she said, standing next to the sink. We were in the same kitchen where I was wearing a floral apron just hours before, but the mood had sobered. "I don't want anybody to get hurt. I don't want my daughter to get hurt. You don't want to lead her on because we don't want that. She shouldn't lead you on because you wouldn't want that. Do you have any other questions for me?"

Well, there is this one little thing, I thought.

"I obviously don't know where this relationship is going," I said. "But I wouldn't want it to get to a place where I knew I wanted to spend the rest of my life with your daughter and not have your blessing."

Of course, this process is so awkward. It makes complete sense for a parent to withhold his or her blessing in this rather unusual romantic circumstance. However, I had to ask. I wouldn't want to propose to someone whose family was opposed to our marriage. This was my last chance to spend time with Catherine's mom before I had to make some very serious choices.

"Well, you have to leave, you have three other ladies, and you have to mull it over," her mom said. "We'll see what happens."

In other words, I asked her for her blessing, and she didn't give it.

At the end of the day, I was disappointed and frustrated. Her family's skepticism—though understandable—made me uneasy with my relationship with Catherine. Plus, her sisters brought up things about Catherine that gave me doubts.

⊶ ·ɯɯ· ⊷

"How should I address your dad when I meet him?" I asked Lindsay during my next stop in Fort Leonard Wood, Missouri. "Mister or General?"

Lindsay's dad was the head of a post that contained the Military Police School, the Army Engineer School, and the Chemical, Biological, Radiological and Nuclear School. He'd recently done a duty in Afghanistan, where he commanded the Corps of Engineers operations. Though I wasn't nervous to meet the man, I wanted to show him the proper respect.

"I don't know." Lindsay laughed. "I think maybe just avoid saying it."

When I met him, however, I went with what felt natural. "Hey, Mr. Yenter, nice to meet you."

Turned out, he was an amazingly nice guy. I highly respect people who serve in the military, and I could see how her father's values and courage helped shape Lindsay's life. But I was also eager to meet her mom. Lindsay's strength, stability, and supportive nature, I suspected, came from her. When I met her in person, I knew my suspicion was right on target. She was so warm and welcoming, and I loved getting to know the woman who had kept the family together throughout all the uncertainty of military life.

My favorite member of Lindsay's family might have been her brother, Marcus. I sat down with him and talked to him about video games and comic books, which I know very little about. He was the sweetest kid I've ever met, and we really hit it off.

Her family was just like my family. They loved to watch *Seinfeld*, her mom talked about their Christian faith, and they seemed comfortable around one another and me. I laughed that the girl in the wedding dress was turning out to be the one who most closely shared my values.

When it came time to talk to her dad about the possibility of marrying Lindsay, however, my heart raced. This was where things had gone bad at Catherine's house, and I was hoping my talk with Mr. Yenter would go more smoothly.

"Being a paratrooper is all about managing risk," her dad said. "If you guys figure out that's what you want to do, you have to have—as we say in the army—the authority to make the decision. So you have my blessing." I was so relieved—and then he added, "As long as Lindsay says yes. If she doesn't say yes, you no longer have it."

I was so touched by the visit. It felt like her father accepted me and even thought I was worthy to be with his daughter. It made Lindsay even more attractive to me.

Before I left, her dad gave a speech about how it had been an honor to have me in their home. In the middle of it, Marcus interrupted and said, "I want you to be in our family."

Though I couldn't say anything, I thought, *Marcus, the feeling is mutual.*

The last hometown date was the most dramatic. Yes, that word might get overused when describing *The Bachelor* episodes, but it is the right word to describe what happened in Los Angeles when I met Desiree's family.

I noticed that every time Des spoke of her family, she got very emotional.

It was easy to see how much she loved them and how badly she wanted the kind of lifelong love that her parents share.

When I finally got to meet them, I understood her affection for them. Her parents could best be described as salt of the earth. They were kind, encouraging, and accepting of my relationship with their daughter. Her brother, Nate, was great too.

"I was planning on giving you a hard time," he said. "But there's nothing wrong with you." We seemed to share the same faith, and he even told me he was thinking of becoming a missionary.

My night is done, I thought. *I've won everyone over.*

During dinner, we told her family about all our adventures. I was always aware of how the parents might perceive our relationship. The dates were short, so parents tended to notice every detail of the day and draw conclusions. While we ate, I wondered if Des might have been showing me more affection than I was showing her. She was touching my arm, laughing, and putting her arm around me. It sounds sort of self-conscious to be thinking of these things, but I didn't want her parents to think I wasn't interested in Des. I put my arm around her and told them some of the funny adventures we'd had. Everyone laughed. I loved her family.

Suddenly, however, her brother told the producers he needed to talk to me again.

Okay, I thought. *Maybe he forgot to tell me something.* We went outside and began a conversation that I thought would be a continuation of the nice, affable chat we'd shared earlier. But when he began to talk, it was as though I were talking to a different guy.

"I believe she's really into you, but you're not into her," he challenged me. "If you're feeling that way, you can't ask her to marry you."

"I don't see where you got that," I said, though I wondered if he noticed I wasn't as affectionate to Des as she was to me. Was he picking up on something even I didn't see? "I'm crazy about your sister," I said.

"You're crazy about a lot of girls," he sneered.

"Of course, I have three other great girls."

"You don't know who you'll choose?"

"I hope when the time comes," I said, "I'll know."

The silence that followed was suffocating.

"Did that put your mind at ease a bit?" I asked, in an effort to at least wrap up the strange conversation.

"Not at all," he said. "You're just a playboy. You're just having fun with the circumstances."

I had been wondering if he had some sort of sense I should pay attention to. Now I knew he was off base. My integrity was very important to me, and the way he was so dismissive of me—when he'd previously been so affirming—was bizarre.

"I'm sorry I gave you that opinion," I said, trying to control my anger. "But that's not me."

"I'm not buying it," he responded quickly.

He didn't know me, and he sure couldn't speak to my integrity. As badly as I wanted to confront him, I held back. I didn't want to cause a huge scene and embarrass Des and her parents even more than they already were.

Though my interaction with her brother didn't affect the way I looked at Des, it made me wonder.

Could I choose to be in the same family with a guy who seems to hate me?

Normally in the "rose rooms," there are lots of cameras carefully arranged to capture every moment of the rose ceremony.

First, I'd pick the bachelorettes I was going to send home, then the producers would tell me the order to call out the names of the remaining girls. That way all the cameras would be positioned just right to catch the reactions of each girl.

But that night I couldn't think straight.

"Listen," I told the producers, who were patiently waiting for me to tell them who was going home so they could position the cameras and stay on schedule. "I just don't know."

That was the first—and only—time I couldn't tell them.

"It's okay," the cameraman said. "Take your time. We'll do the best we can with the cameras and everything."

Two producers, Scott and Jonah, had been with me every step of the way, but hadn't yet given me any type of advice. I was standing in *The Bachelor* mansion upstairs before the girls arrived, out on the balcony.

"I don't know what I'm going to do," I told them. "It's between Des and Catherine."

"Well," Jonah said. "I think Des makes more sense for you."

"You might match up better with Des," Scott agreed.

"Maybe you're right," I said.

By the time I talked to Harrison, I was still uneasy about making a decision.

"Are all four women on the chopping block tonight?" Harrison asked me as I tried to sort out my feelings. I could tell everyone was worried about me. They had never seen me suffer from indecision.

"No," I told him. I could picture myself with Lindsay. I could picture myself with AshLee. But when I closed my eyes and tried to imagine being the husband of Des or Catherine, I couldn't conjure those scenes. "It's Des or Catherine."

I couldn't get my conversation with Desiree's brother out of my head. Was it odd that I had to think consciously about putting my arm around Des instead of it being a natural expression of my feelings? As odd as her brother's behavior seemed at the time, could he have put his finger on at least one real issue? Plus, I knew Des loved and respected her brother. If she valued his opinion, what would his input do to our relationship?

Though I had fun with Catherine, I didn't see us lining up as a couple. What was she, deep down? What did she believe in? What made her tick? I wanted kids—not necessarily right away, of course. But I wanted to have biological children and maybe even adopt. I'd love to support her career, but would she view kids as an impediment to her life?

I didn't know who would go home that night.

"Well, take a moment, think about what you want to do," Harrison said. "We'll see you out there."

I stood before the four ladies with three roses to hand out.

"I want to thank you all for having me in your hometowns this week. I was amazed at how warm your families were," I said. I could tell the girls were nervous. I felt like my heart was being ripped in two. "As I stand here, I still don't know who's going home. I'm afraid I'm going to regret my decision tomorrow morning. But with each rose I pick up, I'll give it to a person I can imagine spending the rest of my life with."

I picked up a rose and held it. I didn't know to whom I should give the first rose.

"Sean," Des said, breaking the silence. It's very unusual to interrupt a rose ceremony, so my pulse quickened. "May I speak to you for a moment?"

We went into a different room as the cameramen jostled to record what was about to happen.

"I wanted to apologize for last night," she whispered. A boom mic floated above our heads, trying to get the hushed exchange. Des was upset about how things had turned out with her family.

"It weighs heavy on my heart," she whispered. "I don't want you to let my brother affect us."

When we got back to the ceremony, tensions were high. I could see on Catherine's face that she wondered if the last-minute conversation with Des would end up sending her home.

I gave the first rose to Lindsay and the second to AshLee.

The last rose stuck to my hands. I wanted to give it to Catherine, but it didn't really make sense. Of the four remaining girls, Catherine and I were the most different. And I definitely had a connection with Des.

Instead of giving out the final rose, I left. I simply couldn't decide, and it wasn't helping that the two people I was thinking of sending home were staring at me with big, teary eyes.

"What's going on?" Harrison asked.

"I don't have clarity."

Harrison was kind as he listened. "Get this right," he finally said. "Take your time."

Everyone made sense on paper—AshLee, Lindsay, and Des all seemed to line up with my values. I really liked Catherine, but she was a Birkenstock-wearing, vegan food blogger from Seattle. I was a meat eater who'd worked in the oil and gas industry. She came from a Filipino culture. My family was a bunch of Texans. How could that possibly work out?

Reluctantly, I went back out to the ceremony, picked up the rose, and paused. On the show, it looks as though the ceremonies happen pretty quickly, but it takes a long time between the moments when the roses are handed out. Before I handed out the rose, I stood there awkwardly. As I waited, I could hear the earpieces of all the producers, the director talking, and the cameras being positioned. I stared at the ground, because I didn't want to make eye contact with the woman I was about to send home. Plus, I confess I have a nervous habit that drives people crazy. When someone is angry at me, if I'm anxious, or in trouble, my involuntary response is laughter. It made all the rose ceremonies absolutely terrible, because I was always on the verge of looking like the most insensitive man on the planet. If I looked up and saw the girls, I might get a smirk on my face. Which, of course, didn't make sense in the circumstances. So I'd look back down at my shoes and think, *Don't laugh. Don't laugh. Don't laugh.* Of course, when you're not supposed to laugh, the whole world seems like a punch line.

This rose ceremony, however, I didn't have the luxury of waiting and talking myself out of nervous laughter. My mind was racing as I tried desperately to make a decision. That's when it hit me.

I could see myself saying good-bye to Des, but I was not ready to say good-bye to Catherine.

"Catherine," I said. "Will you accept this rose?"

Des was devastated.

"I know you have every quality that I'm looking for in a wife," I told Des as I was walking her to the vehicle.

I wasn't ready to see her go, but I knew if I kept her I'd have to send someone else home in her place. I wasn't prepared to do that. It was an excruciating, confusing, and emotional night.

"I really think you're making a mistake," she cried. "I really do."

As I watched her drive off, I was starting to believe her.

thirteen

WARNING SIGNALS

It was going to be a tough week.

With three women left, I knew whoever was sent home next was going to be as devastated as I was during Emily's season when I was rejected so close to the finish line. There's something that happens after the home-town dates—everything gets more emotional and challenging. Most people watching from home assumed I had a secret favorite, a front-runner about whom I harbored marital hopes. Even I figured if I was just a week away from proposing to someone, surely I'd know who'd be receiving the ring.

And my heart.

Surely the indecision, people asked me, was just to keep the show interesting—to make people watch until the end. But it was real. Somehow, the final three bachelorettes were all on a level playing field as we went into the week that would result in the final rose ceremony.

I smiled when I saw AshLee, taken aback by how much I'd missed her over the past ten days since Houston. If I wrote down everything I wanted in a woman, AshLee would have met all of the requirements. Well, almost all of them. At the top of my list was faith. I needed someone who would challenge me in my spiritual walk. AshLee professed Christianity, was from an amazingly loving family, and seemed to be ready to settle down. The only thing she lacked was a sense of fun. It bothered me that I didn't laugh as much with AshLee as I did with Lindsay and Catherine, but her other qualities made her intensity easy to overlook.

Our date—as always—was amazing. We got on a boat and sailed between Thailand's huge rock formations—maybe two hundred feet tall—that jutted out of the water. Eventually, we got to a gigantic rock formation with a dark cave. The producers gave us a life raft with a camera mounted on it.

"Swim into that black hole and find your way to the light," Mary Kate told me. "Just hold on to this while you swim so we can film it."

I swam with that raft out in front of me while AshLee was on my back. While it may have looked romantic when it aired, I struggled so hard to stay above water in that pitch-black cave. I couldn't find my way around. Finally, well after I wanted to give up, the producers started helping me out a bit. "This way," they would tell me. "Now go here." When we finally got out of the terrible darkness, we emerged into the middle of a rock formation where the rocks encircled our own private beach. I'd never seen anything like it.

Could I marry this woman? I asked myself throughout the date.

As I looked into her eyes, the answer was always the same.

Yes.

We finished the date with dinner by the ocean in the most picturesque setting imaginable. Something, however, loomed over us.

"Look what I have," I said as I picked up the envelope the producers had left us.

"Sean and AshLee, welcome to the magical country of Thailand," she read after opening the envelope. "Should you choose to forego your personal rooms, please use this key to enjoy your time in the fantasy suite."

I learned a great deal from how Emily had handled the fantasy suite issue, and I wanted to do things differently. The bottom line was that I wasn't going to have sex with any of the remaining three women that week. I'd already lived my life in a selfish, self-gratifying way. Now that I'd recommitted my life to Christ, I was going to live by the sexual standards I knew were right. Plus, why would any woman have sex with a guy who was also presumably going to hook up with two others the very same week? There's no way I was going to put women I cared about in that position.

However, I had only ten weeks to find a wife, so every second counted. I decided not to make a big deal out of saying no to the fantasy suite. To do that felt like moral posturing. Instead, I wanted to use that night, alone, without any distractions, to really connect with the women. Plus, I wanted to know how they'd act when the cameras weren't rolling.

"Before you tell me what you think," I said after AshLee read the card, "it's important for you to know my intentions. I want to use this time to be alone, no distractions, just you and me, so we can talk."

When she heard the word *talk*, she smiled in relief.

"Obviously, I agree the time is important. I worry this will come across that I'm crossing a boundary. I know where you stand, and you know where I stand. I completely trust you."

It was obvious she and I shared the same outlook on the overnight dates. We went to the fantasy suite and spent the rest of the evening talking about the future. Though I could envision my life with AshLee, I recall her saying something that caught me off guard when we were—finally—alone.

"I have an idea!" I remember her saying.

"Lay it on me."

"After we get engaged, we should do a newlywed show," she said.

"*Another* show?" I asked.

"Yeah, that way it'll take pressure off of us."

"You think a reality show would take pressure *off* of us?" I laughed. *Surely, she's joking*, I thought. But she wasn't joking.

Of course, I shouldn't have been surprised. After all, we met on a reality TV show, and we were having the conversation in the context of a reality TV show. However, it caused a red flag to go up in my heart. One of the biggest fears I had was that I'd fall for someone who was addicted to fame. Usually you can spot them from day one. They show up with a guitar and a song they wrote "just for you." It's obvious they're trying to parlay the notoriety of the show into some longer-lasting fame. I thought I'd already sent all those women home. But during this off-camera conversation, I wondered if maybe I had let one of them slip through.

As a comparison, Lindsay also accepted my talk-through-the-night invitation to the fantasy suite. While we were there, the talk invariably went to hypothetical wedding scenarios.

"If this works out," I asked, "would you want to have a televised wedding?"

"Nope," she said emphatically. "I don't want to be on camera anymore. My parents have property in Nevada with a barn on it. I want to get married in that barn away from everybody. Just you and me and the people we love."

I really appreciated her authenticity.

When I met Catherine on the beach for our date, I realized I'd missed her so much. Although I'd almost sent her home after the hometown dates, I found myself thinking so much about her. Every week, Mary Kate asked me the same question: "Who are you most looking forward to seeing?" When she asked me this week, I was surprised to find myself thinking of Catherine.

Our date consisted of sailing on a junk boat, which is an ancient Chinese sailing vessel still used today. Ours was flat bottomed, lined with teak, with big red sails. As the overcast day turned sunny, we kicked back and talked on the ship's deck. There was a lot to talk about. I left the hometown date wondering if we had the same life goals and if we wanted to live our lives the same way. Of the three remaining girls, Catherine's life seemed the most different from mine. It wasn't a deal breaker, but I needed to know if she was serious about this whole thing.

"Do you think you could live in Dallas?" I asked. "The reason I ask is because in this environment, it's so easy to get swept away. We're having so much fun now."

She looked at me with her big, brown eyes. I wanted to believe all would be well, but I needed to get answers. "When all the cameras go away, it's just going to be you and me. Can we make it work?"

She told me that she hadn't been ready to settle down in the past, but she was now.

"What makes it different?" I asked.

"It's you," she said simply. "I'm myself around you . . . and you aren't freaked out about it."

Her response was interesting. When I became the Bachelor, that was my main goal: to be real and to encourage the girls to be real. Catherine had obviously taken that to heart. It made me feel more relaxed around her and more authentic. I felt I got her and she got me. And I could really see her as a potential wife.

Later, in my ITM interview, I told Mary Kate, "Catherine put my mind at ease about being ready to settle down and maybe have a family."

After swimming and snorkeling, we got back on the boat to head to the hotel and prepare for the evening portion of the date. The sky had grown ominous again, and rain began to fall. Off in the distance, lightning danced in the sky. There, on the boat in the rain, Catherine and I shared the most romantic kiss.

When we went to dinner, the fantasy suite card loomed heavily in the background. Catherine was the first to address the elephant in the room. Before going on the show, she explained, she never thought she'd participate in the overnight dates. "I also didn't even think I'd fall for you." As the time went on, she said, she had developed feelings for me but she still wanted to be considered a lady.

I loved that she said that.

"I realize now the overnight dates are a way to spend time with you," she explained.

"Hopefully, you understand my intentions," I said before offering her the key.

It was wonderful to be able to talk to her that night in the overnight suite. She opened up and became really vulnerable, explaining that she'd been made fun of as a kid. She'd been called chubby, for example. "Not in a mean way," she said. "They thought I could handle the teasing and I couldn't."

I couldn't believe such an attractive person would sit there telling me she was nervous to be in a swimsuit. So I assured her by stating the obvious: "You're smoking hot."

Our time in the fantasy suite allowed us to talk—for the first and only time—without being mic'ed up. It was an important point in our relationship, and I left the date with many fewer questions than I had going into it.

That week at the rose ceremony, I knew what I had to do. It was raining that day, which set an appropriately depressing mood. We were supposed to have the rose ceremony on the beach, but the weather wasn't going to cooperate. The crew had prepared the beachside set all week, so they hoped the dark clouds would roll away in time. As the rain continued to pour, the producers decided to move it into the hotel's lobby. In about an hour the show's art and lighting departments created a set for the ceremony that looked amazing.

I walked out to the ladies, who looked particularly nervous. As always, I had to deliver a speech. In the beginning of the season, Mary Kate helped me organize my thoughts into bullet points. The first was always something like, "I had a wonderful week getting to know you better," the second was usually about something that happened during the week, and so forth.

"The speeches will always end abruptly," she said. "There's not going to be a smooth transition from your speech to the ceremony, but it comes off okay on camera." She was right. Week after week, I made my well-crafted speech, but there was no good transition to, "Okay, now it's time for one of you to leave."

By the middle of the season, I no longer needed help organizing my thoughts for my speeches. Eventually, I ad-libbed them. Though all of my speeches were absolutely from the heart, my speech in Thailand—during the last rose ceremony—was the most agonizing.

"I had the most amazing week this week," I said. *Bullet point number one? Check.* "I feel so blessed to be here in Thailand and see one of the most beautiful parts of the world with three of the most beautiful women I've ever met. This week brings painful memories for me. This was the week Emily sent me home. I was blindsided. I didn't see it coming. My worst fear is that the same is going to happen today. It kills me inside to know I might break your heart. I also hope you realize how much you mean to me, and how hard it was to make this decision."

The producers were standing out of sight of the cameras, nodding. They looked genuinely moved at the heartfelt speech. Catherine looked terrified, as she did in every rose ceremony, because she never felt confident. That night, I remember her face was trembling. Lindsay looked as though she was going to be sick. AshLee, on the other hand, was staring straight through me.

Did she know?

"Lindsay," I said, handing the rose to her. One of the directors had hurt his back traveling to Thailand, so he wasn't in his normal spot off in the background holding a rolled-up piece of paper to indicate when I should call the next name. No one gave me a signal, so I must've stood there for several minutes until someone stepped in and waved his or her arms at me. Now that we were so close to the end, the next rose was the last rose.

"Catherine," I said.

Of course, anytime you give out that last rose, everyone is thinking about the person who *didn't* get it. Catherine came up and hugged me, but I was looking over her shoulder to see AshLee's reaction.

Ever heard that saying, "Hell hath no fury like a woman scorned"?

Instead of saying the customary good-byes to the other ladies and to me, she made a beeline for the van.

"AshLee," I said, following after her. "Can I talk to you?"

"No," she said. "Stay there!"

"Just let me explain," I said. When Emily sent me home, she never told me why. She simply said I was "perfect" and that she thought I had been the one. While that was moderately flattering, it didn't give me closure. Plus, I realized later that it wasn't true. Her inability to tell me honestly that she loved the other guys made me wonder for months if Emily had made a terribly wrong decision. I wanted to talk to AshLee honestly, to give her a little closure during what I knew would be a hard time.

"If you're going to tell me something," she said, swirling around, "tell me."

"Okay," I said, taken aback by her severity. "I just didn't feel like we shared that element of fun. It's important I have that, and I just couldn't find it with you."

She turned around and tried to get in the van. Regrettably, she tried to get in on the same side where the camera guy was sitting.

"No, you've got to get in on this side," I said, reaching for the door. That only infuriated her more.

As she drove off into the sunset, her livid response chilled me to the bone. It also made me realize I'd made the right decision.

———

It had been three months since I'd last seen my parents.

For the last week, the producers set me up in a gorgeous house on private property. It was owned by an extremely wealthy man who had a hundred staffers. The house staff was there to wait on me hand and foot—they served me food, made my bed, and got me anything I needed. It was the perfect place to host my family.

I was thrilled to see them and loved that they were able to be at least a small part of this adventure. Here I was, facing the most difficult decisions of my life. Even though I hated to admit it, I definitely didn't want to go through this alone.

"I'm falling in love with two women," I told them. "I truly don't know what I'm going to do."

"Well, if you don't know which way to go," Mom said, "there's no way you can propose at the end of this." Of course, that made sense. I liked Lindsay for a long list of reasons, and I liked Catherine for a long list of different reasons. It sounds odd, but I never compared the two or pitted them against each other in my head. I simply knew I really liked both girls and had no idea what to do next.

"Well, logically," I said, a little upset at her certainty, "I can see how you'd say that. But I've really fallen for two girls at once."

Mom paused and smiled, ever a polite and encouraging lady. "Okay." She nodded. "It just makes us all the more excited to meet *both* of them."

Lindsay was the first to arrive. I met her outside while my family waited inside the house. Lindsay and I walked in together, and she met the family on camera. Someone suggested we sit down at the lunch table, but almost immediately a producer said, "Lindsay, why don't you go talk to Sean's dad? Sean, you go talk to your mom."

It was filmed to look like a relaxed afternoon, but it was orchestrated to squeeze in as many important conversations as possible. Lindsay felt comfortable around my parents and had a youthful energy about her that everyone loved.

Plus, she said things like, "I feel very blessed to be here."

Blessed is one of those evangelical code words. It was obvious that Lindsay shared our Christian faith, which put everyone at ease. My family instantly fell in love with her. And Lindsay was so impressed by my family's warmth and laughter that she wanted to be a part of it as well.

It seemed like an open-and-shut case.

———

The next day, when Catherine arrived, they began to see how complicated this was. It was raining, so I met her with an umbrella at the producers' van.

"Do I call your parents by their first names?" she asked nervously as we walked to the house.

"Listen," I assured her. "They are going to love you. Just be yourself."

As we sat down to eat, my prediction came true. Quickly, it was apparent that everyone enjoyed Catherine as we exchanged casual conversation about the show, her past, and Seattle. When Mom took her off to have a personal chat with her, I knew she'd come back with a helpful opinion about Catherine—and she did. Mom told me that she wished we could have more time together before I popped the question. However, she confided, she could totally see Catherine as her daughter-in-law.

"She's lovely," she said.

When Catherine talked to my dad, they had a touching, poignant conversation.

"When Shay married Andrew," my dad told her, "he became my best friend. And I love him. If you and Sean marry, you'll never have a bigger fan than me. That's the truth."

Catherine's eyes filled with tears. Even though she loved her dad, he hadn't always been able to be a great support system because he was living halfway around the world.

"I'll love you like my daughter," he said. "I just met you, but sometimes you just know."

When Catherine left that day, there was no doubt she would make a great addition to the Lowe family. I could totally see her fitting in at my parents' house in Dallas on a lazy Saturday afternoon. She'd be tossing a salad while the big game was on. My niece and nephew would be underfoot, and the dogs would be asleep at the foot of the couch.

As much as I dreamed about that, I knew—if pressed—my family would've probably chosen Lindsay. I could tell they latched on to her evangelical key words as they tried—in a very short amount of time—to pick up on any clues that might help them determine which woman would be a good match for me. We talked about everyone's opinion of the women. Then my dad diplomatically added, "It's a win/win, because they both will fit in just perfectly."

"You've got forty-eight hours," said Andrew. "You better start figuring this out."

I could tell Mom wasn't happy. She didn't understand how I could still be thinking of proposing without a clear front-runner.

"You don't want to propose to anyone if it feels like pressure," she said.

"Hopefully, you can see the dilemma I'm in," I said.

"Yes, but you don't have much time to decide," she said, pointing out the obvious.

"I don't need the added pressure," I responded, maybe too tersely. In fact, I felt the time coming down on me with every passing minute.

"If you don't know," she said, "you don't need to be proposing to either one of them."

I understood where Mom was coming from. I didn't know if I was going to propose, because I really didn't know which girl was right for me—if either of them were right for me. I tried to justify my indecision, but Mom's opposition rubbed me the wrong way.

"You've only seen a few minutes of this," I said. Of course, that wasn't fair. That was all the time she'd been given in this artificially accelerated time frame. "I want your perspective and opinion, but more than anything I want your support."

When I said that, my mom started to cry.

It killed me.

She's the most loving mom in the world and only wants the best for me. The gravity of the situation weighed heavily on her. The fact that I needed to make such a big decision in such a short amount of time stressed her out. Plus, I'd been a little short with her.

"I don't want you to succumb to the pressure of doing something you don't want to do just because it's on TV," she said. "And because the people associated with the show want you to do it."

"It won't end badly," I told her, much more gently.

"Yes, and you don't have to choose either," she added helpfully—in case I'd missed it the first hundred times.

Before my family left, I grabbed my mom and whispered in her ear, "I promise I won't propose if I'm not sure."

In the end, my family didn't provide me the clarity I was looking for, but I knew I had their support no matter what happened.

That was just as valuable to me.

fourteen

THE DECISION

"Can I please have my iPad?" I asked Mary Kate. At no time was I allowed to get on the computer, check my e-mail, or—heaven forbid—Google anything. The producers wisely didn't want me to be swayed by some random blog post about the girls that might or might not be true.

"No way," she said.

"Come on. I just want to listen to my music."

"Okay, but no Internet," she said, handing it to me.

"How can I get on iTunes without an Internet connection?" She looked at me skeptically and then broke into a smile.

"All right," she said. "But behave."

As soon as she was out of sight, I got on FaceTime with Laura and Steph.

"What's going on?" they squealed.

Quickly, I gave them a rundown of the two remaining women. "I don't know. I've got equally great girls left."

They were excited to hear from me and relieved I wasn't calling them completely devastated as I did during Emily's season.

After I hung up, my curiosity got the best of me. I got on ABC's website and looked at the profiles of the girls. Catherine's profile had the usual information—name, age, and hometown. But the random questions, like "What's on your bucket list?", intrigued me. Believe it or not, one of the dreams she listed was to ride elephants in Thailand. (And she had filled out that form months before we knew we'd end up there.)

When Mary Kate came back into the room carrying a clipboard with information, I put down my iPad somewhat guiltily.

"Okay, we've got a date where you're going to ride elephants and another date where you're going to take a little boat down a river," she said. "You can choose which girl goes on which."

I was amazed. Elephants! Catherine would be so surprised.

"Catherine has to go on the elephant date," I said.

"Why?"

"Because it was on her online profile."

She looked up from her clipboard and opened her mouth before deciding to let it pass.

"Never mind. Okay, so get some sleep, because the elephant date starts bright and early."

I had forty-eight hours, two dates, and a lot to think about.

* —— *

The next day, I was so happy to see Catherine I could barely stand it.

"You're not going to believe it, but I saw an elephant at the hotel," she said after we hugged.

"No way," I said. "They don't have elephants just roaming around the hotel."

She was getting frustrated because I wouldn't believe her.

"No, I promise!" She was facing me, and meanwhile I could hear the elephant in the background making its way up the hill. When she turned around and saw it, she squealed with delight.

We had an amazing day riding this gigantic elephant up a hill where they'd set up a cabana filled with food and champagne. The view was enchanting and a half dozen elephants stood right next to us as we chatted. It felt like we were part of a fairy tale. The producers noticed how amazing the scene was too.

"Would you guys mind kissing right here?" Mary Kate asked. "The shot is just beautiful."

"Heck no," I said. "I don't mind kissing her."

We started kissing, but it was all a ploy. The producers had planned that the elephants would blow water out of their trunks on us. We got doused, which was so funny. It was a great day.

That night, Catherine invited me back into her room for one last chance to talk. This was the last time I was going to get to talk to her before the proposal—or non-proposal, as the case may be.

I could tell she was nervous, but we had a good conversation.

She hadn't told me she loved me. Lindsay had, Tierra had, and many of the other girls had professed their love. However, Catherine—to whom I was thinking of proposing—hadn't come out and said it. I knew it was a hard thing for her to say, so I didn't press.

I also had never said to her, "You're the one." Mainly, because I wasn't sure she was. More than anything, I was confused. Our conversation was intense but—at some point—the producers had enough. "Okay, we've got to wrap it up."

Catherine's lip jutted out. She wasn't ready for me to leave. When I hugged her good-bye, she knew it was her last chance before the proposal. She whispered in my ear, "Sean, I love you."

It was a moment of vulnerability. Catherine finally admitted her true feelings.

The only problem? I didn't hear it. She was so nervous to say it that it was barely audible. The producers didn't hear it in their earpieces either. Apparently, one of the sound techs—whose job it is to listen to everything—was the only other person on earth who'd heard Catherine's sweet proclamation.

After she said it, I hugged her. "Thanks for today," I said before walking out the door.

Of course, I had no idea I'd just devastated her. Outside her room, I walked up about five stairs to the landing where the producers wanted to film my ITM. I was about ten feet from her door. She was inside crying while I was outside obliviously chatting about what a great day we'd had. During my ITM, Catherine came outside and was shocked to see me still there.

"Hey, what's going on?" I asked. I could sense she was sad, but I chalked it up to pre–proposal day jitters.

"I'm scared," she said. "I've never been this vulnerable before."

I still didn't quite get it. She was referring to the fact that she'd opened up to me about her feelings and I'd casually walked out the door. I'd never seen her cry before, and it split me wide open.

"It's going to be okay," I said, and I gave her a hug.

But in my mind, I wasn't so sure.

<hr />

The following day, I had my final date with Lindsay. It began with drifting down the Mekong River on a Thai boat and ended with releasing paper lanterns into the night sky.

During the date, I started to understand my feelings for the two women. I had a long list of reasons why Lindsay was wonderful and a long list of the reasons why Catherine was. But when Mary Kate conducted the ITM interviews, I found myself repeatedly saying, "I just don't know if I can ever say good-bye to Catherine."

We wrapped up the day portion of the date, and I felt like my mental anguish over the decision meant I hadn't been as attentive to Lindsay as normal. When it was time to get dressed for the evening portion, I pulled Mary Kate aside.

"I think I've decided."

"Decided what?"

"That I want to marry Catherine." There was just something about her that I couldn't bear to be without. I think that's what it came down to. There was nothing about Lindsay that I disliked or made us incompatible, which is why I'd struggled so much to come to this decision. But when I thought about sending Catherine home, it tore me up.

"Are you sure?"

"Just about," I said. "I know I can't hurt Lindsay. I might need to send her home right now."

But I wasn't certain.

For the next two hours, I wrangled with my thoughts on the matter. Didn't Lindsay deserve to have those last few hours? After all, it would give her the chance to tell me anything she needed to tell me before I made my decision. Finally, I decided it was best to give her that time and try to stay open-minded for the rest of the date. I really wished I could call my friends to talk through the decision with them. Trying to figure it out alone made it that much harder.

At the end of the date, time had officially run out. The next day, I would propose to someone.

Maybe.

That night, I prayed continuously.

"Lead me, God," I said. "Guide me. Don't let me make a mistake. I love you, Lord, and if you want me to walk away from all this just tell me."

I prayed everything I could think of, but I was still a wreck. I loved Lindsay, much like I loved Brooke. Though I loved Catherine, I still had big questions about her faith. Before I started the show, I had made a list of all the nonnegotiables I needed in a wife. *Being a Christian* was at the top of my list.

What did I really know about Catherine's faith?

When I was in Seattle for the hometown visit, I had noticed a cross hanging on the wall of their small home. During our overnight date, she told me she had been raised Catholic. She used to go to church with her mom and grandma every Sunday. So she was generally friendly to faith and to God. However, I sensed there was a gap between her church attendance back in the day and her commitment now.

Was she a Christian? Was she serious about faith?

Though the Bible doesn't talk a lot about how to date, there are scriptures that indicate single Christians should marry "only if he [or she] loves the Lord" and warn, "Do not be unequally yoked with unbelievers" (1 Cor. 7:39; 2 Cor. 6:14 ESV). Marrying a non-Christian is unwise for the Christian and unfair to the non-Christian. I didn't want to begin a marriage with such an obvious gap between us.

I'd never been so torn in my life. I decided there was no possible way for me to propose to Catherine without knowing—really knowing—where she was spiritually.

"I need more time with Catherine off camera," I told Mary Kate. It was past midnight. By this time, everyone was busily preparing for the next day.

"You know, Sean," she said firmly, "we don't do *anything* off camera."

"I need it," I said.

"After ten weeks of protecting the show from leaks, unexpected turns of events, and old girlfriends, do you think in a million years that I'd let you talk to Catherine off camera *on the night before you propose?*"

"That's just it," I said. "I can't propose yet."

"Why?"

"I need . . ." I paused. "More information."

She was frustrated but relayed my request to Ronald, the head executive producer who's always behind the scenes but never interacts with the people on the show. A few minutes later, I got a knock on my door.

"Okay, let's talk this out," he said in his German accent. "What's going on?"

"I need to make sure Catherine and I are on the same page on . . . some things."

"Like what?"

I realized how absurd this conversation was. How could I possibly explain to the executive producer of *The Bachelor* that I needed to know if Catherine and I were going to believe in Jesus in the same way? I wasn't aware of anyone on the show saying he or she was Christian. Though everyone was nice to me, I got the feeling that most of them either overlooked my Christianity or thought it was quaint and old-fashioned, like a rotary phone.

"Well, my faith is the center of my life, and I want to make sure it is—or can be—the center of her life too."

"Didn't you talk about that in the fantasy suite?" Ronald asked. It was well known that the fantasy suites were backdrops for all-night conversations.

"Yes, we did, but I need more," I said. "I need more information and more time."

Ronald was in my room for forty-five minutes, which was really awkward and strange since I was wrangling with the toughest decision of my life with a man I'd only seen occasionally, and time was of the essence. He went through the decision rationally with me step-by-step.

"Okay, I've been married for years, and marriage is bliss," he said. "But I can tell you this . . ." He proceeded to give me a lot of very good advice. He asked me questions, and I answered as honestly as I could.

"I think it's safe to say from what you've told me and what I've heard tonight, we can put Lindsay aside," he said. "Right?"

As hard as it was for me to admit, I nodded.

"Okay, then," he said. "It's time to let go of Lindsay."

"Right." I swallowed hard. "I can do that."

"Now let's talk about Catherine," he said. "So you're falling in love with her?"

"Without a doubt."

"But you still have questions."

"Right," I said. "I need to talk to her."

"Okay, so here are your options," he began. I've never had anyone lay out my relationship options in quite this way. I had a feeling Ronald would be happy in a boardroom with a dry-erase marker, mapping out my future.

"Number one, you can leave here tomorrow without anyone. Brad Womack did that." He saw my face fall. "I know what you're thinking. Everyone hated Brad when he failed to choose someone. But don't let that affect your decision-making process. I think our viewers will know who you are and will trust your decision."

"Okay, but I don't want that," I said. "I'm falling in love with Catherine."

"Option number two," he continued, "you can decide not to ask Catherine to marry you, but instead ask if she wants to continue in this relationship with you outside of the show."

"Got it." I said, trying to be logical. It was hard because confusion settled on me like a heavy weight.

He continued, "You can ask her to stay in the relationship with you so you can answer whatever questions are still apparently lingering in your heart. Then six months or a year down the road, you can propose on your own."

"Okay," I said. "That might be the smartest decision."

"But let me add," he said, "this is your one and only chance to give her the proposal few people on earth get to have."

I couldn't tell how much of this was sincere advice and how much of this was just spin from a producer who wanted to make a great television show. Those two things don't always go hand in hand, and—though I was confused—I was fully aware of the fact that he had ulterior motives. He also made some very valid points.

He stood up, ran his hands over the creases in his pants, and sighed. I could tell he had said everything he needed to say to me and was trying to keep the desperation out of his voice. He had a ton resting on my decision. Not only did a multimillion-dollar television show hinge on the proposal, but there were practical concerns. The show had spent a couple of weeks building a proposal set on the property of the wealthy man who'd let us use his home. They had planned a gorgeous setting, including a bridge and a pond they dug just for the occasion.

"I just want to know where you're at so I can make sure everyone's prepared tomorrow." I knew, even at that hour, that there were hundreds of people busily preparing for the next day's production. "Everyone needs to know what they're doing tomorrow."

"I think I'm going to propose to Catherine," I said.

"You think or you know?"

"I know." I said it emphatically, hoping it would stamp out any lingering fears.

It didn't.

When he walked out of the room, I had determined the following: I was in love with Catherine; I could see spending the rest of my life with her; I had the chance to give her the proposal of a lifetime.

When Ronald left my room at two in the morning, my mind raced out of control. There was no way on earth that Ronald—a nonbeliever—could understand why I had reservations about Catherine. I knew for a fact that Lindsay shared my faith. Her family shared my faith. It would be the easiest thing in the world to seamlessly incorporate my life with hers.

But Catherine? It wasn't enough for me to be with someone who generally believed that there was a God.

"I still need time alone with Catherine," I told Mary Kate, who was still outside my room preparing for the next day.

"What?" She looked genuinely surprised. "Ronald just told me you guys had settled this."

"Please," I said. "I just have some lingering issues." Mary Kate disappeared. I sat on my bed with my head in my hands, trying to control my emotions. Five minutes later, I heard a knock on the door, immediately followed by Ronald barging back into my room.

"I thought we went over all this," he said.

"I know," I said apologetically. "I just need fifteen minutes."

"You mean to tell me that your deep, dark worries can be solved in fifteen minutes?" He looked skeptical but eventually relented. He knew this was a hard decision that would affect the rest of my life. Even though he was potentially putting millions of dollars of investment at risk, his face softened. "If that's what you really need to put all your worries to rest," he said softly, "I'll give it to you."

Then he looked me straight in the eye. "But you must promise me— and I mean *promise* me—that you will not give her the impression that you're proposing tomorrow. I have hundreds of people making the perfect spot to dazzle her for a moment she'll never forget . . . for a moment millions of viewers will never forget. We must catch her actual response on camera. If you ruin that in your fifteen minutes . . ."

He didn't finish the sentence, but I was so overwhelmed with gratitude, I wanted to hug this man's neck.

"I promise," I said.

"No, I want you to *swear* to me that you won't say anything about tomorrow," he said.

"I swear."

"You will not give it away?"

"I won't give it away."

"Sean," he said. "I am serious. There's a lot riding on this. I'm an idiot for letting this happen."

"I promise you," I said. "I want her to be surprised in the moment as much as you do."

I slipped on my shoes and headed to Catherine's resort. The producers had already relayed the information that I was coming to see her. Scott made sure she was awake, first of all. Turns out, she was so nervous about the next day she was unable to sleep. When he checked on her, she had just gotten out of the shower.

"Okay," he said. "You can go in."

I knocked on the door a couple of times before poking my head in. "Hello?"

She was dumbfounded that I was there. "Everything okay?" she asked. Her hair was wet and she had no makeup on. I couldn't help but notice how naturally pretty she was.

"Yes, but I'm kind of freaking out."

"Why?"

"Tomorrow's such a huge day and there are things that have gone unsaid."

She nodded slowly, though I'm certain she was not tracking.

"I just want to make sure about your faith," I said. "I want someone who's going to challenge me spiritually. My faith is the most important thing in my life. I want someone who will love Jesus as much as I do. Someone to help me raise my kids in the Christian faith. Someone who won't mind getting up on Sunday mornings and going to church." I was rambling, because I wasn't sure how to explain it. I simply needed to do something that was quite impossible: to look into her heart. "I need to know that you're that person."

Her eyes were wide as I spoke. One second she had been brushing her teeth, the next I was in her room babbling about kids we didn't even have yet and a faith I don't think she was certain about. She swallowed hard and smiled at me.

"I want to be that woman in your life."

We talked quickly for about ten more minutes, in a rapid-fire conversation about Jesus and faith.

Eventually, Scott popped his head in the door. "Okay, we gotta get you out of here. I promised Ronald I'd only let you stay for a few minutes, and he'll kill me if I let you stay."

"Thank you," I said. "I needed to ask these questions so I could sort out my feelings about tomorrow." I hugged her without giving anything away about my intentions. Catherine's confidence was boosted because of this late-night visit, but I'm sure she was also a little confused as to why I decided to come to her room at two in the morning.

I went to sleep that night confident. I knew she loved God. Maybe she didn't understand theology the way I did, but her heart was bent toward Jesus. Even though Catherine hadn't yet given her life completely to Christ, it was almost as if God allowed me to see her as the woman she was becoming. I knew beyond a shadow of a doubt that God had called her, and that he allowed me—in some mysterious way—to make the decision to propose.

As I put my head on the pillow, all I could think was this: *I'm going to propose to a Seattle, vegan, food blogger, and I've never been happier.*

fifteen

DOWN ON
ONE KNEE

"What's going through your head as you approach this day?" an executive producer named Leigh Anne asked me on the morning of the proposal. Normally, Mary Kate did my ITMs, but for whatever reason Leigh Anne—a mother of two—filled in for Mary Kate that morning. She had a kind, conscientious manner. If I'd met her on the street, I never would've guessed she was a big-shot Hollywood producer. The gentle way she asked the question unleashed a flood of emotion.

In all that had happened over the past ten weeks—in all the conversations and heartbreak—I hadn't shed one tear. That day I started crying, and Leigh Anne's eyes also filled with tears. We sat there, knee to knee, with a cameraman to her side. She gave me a few seconds to compose myself, then—in a sweet voice—asked, "You want to explain it to me?"

She said it in such a gentle way, it caused me to burst into tears again.

"I'm about to break the heart of a girl I love," I cried. "Lindsay is so sweet. She doesn't deserve this. She thinks we're getting married and I feel awful," I said before correcting myself with a more accurate word. "Make that guilty. Tremendously guilty."

If I let my mind go to her family—her brave dad, her caring mom, and her awesome brother—I was overwhelmed with sadness. Plus, I knew she and Catherine had each been preparing for this moment by selecting a special dress with the help of a stylist. This was the only time in the show that the girls had assistance in getting dressed, and I knew they'd both look dazzling. Just thinking of the preparations choked me up.

Then Leigh Anne flipped the script. "Okay, why don't you tell me about Catherine?" I think she thought—hoped—this would stop the crying. Instead, it caused me to cry even more. I was about to propose to a woman with whom I'd fallen madly in love and could not compose myself. The film crew showed up to get some B-roll footage, which consisted of shots of me getting ready, walking around, putting on my suit, and fixing my hair in the mirror. Thankfully, those shots didn't require talking, except one important scene.

One of the major advantages to being on the show is that they provide an amazing diamond ring by prominent jeweler Neil Lane. He showed me several jaw-dropping rings. I'd never held anything so small with so much value. In the end, I selected what Neil described as a "cushion-cut diamond, filled with diamonds everywhere."

"This is it," I said, marveling at the ring.

"It's called micropave," he said. "That just means it has really tiny diamond work and detail. It's very classically made."

On a day of big decisions, I prayed continuously, "Lord, I know your hand is in this. I just pray that if this is not the direction you want me to go, let me know now." Normally, I don't put a time restriction on God, but this was coming down to the wire. "Lord, let me know right now."

Then time ran out.

———✦——✦———

"Okay, Sean," Mary Kate said. "We need to walk you into position." It was ninety degrees, and the humidity was suffocating. I was wearing a full suit and had already sweated right through it. Even though I was uncomfortable and looked as though I'd taken a shower in my clothes, I wasn't thinking of any of that. Above everything else, I was terrified of what was about to happen to Lindsay.

Obviously, she was up first.

The production crew had built a wooden square over the pond they'd dug just for this moment. Lindsay's limo pulled up a pretty far distance away from where I was standing. Chris Harrison met her and escorted her all the way to the bridge. It was a really long walk, and my heart raced as I saw her walking toward me.

"Sean is waiting for you up the path," Harrison told her. The road was a winding gravel path that meandered all the way down to me. As she started over the bridge, camera crews followed her every move. A huge camera on a crane swept in around her to record every painful detail.

Of course, she had no idea there'd be pain involved. I could tell from her face that she knew—without a doubt—that she was about to have the most romantic proposal imaginable. I was about to ask the question. She was about to say yes. Everyone watched her as she made her way to me.

It felt like an eternity.

While she was walking, I planned out my response to her. I didn't want to give her false hope. But when she finally arrived—and I saw her looking so beautiful—I couldn't help but smile. I was always so happy to see her, but that joy soon evaporated when I remembered why we were there. I grabbed her hands and pulled her up on the wooden platform. The producers had given me very specific instructions on how to handle this moment.

"After you tell her she's going home, she's not gonna hear a word you say," they advised. "Make sure the first words you say to her are the words you really want her to hear and remember."

I didn't want to build up to a climax before I lowered the boom. Rather, I wanted to make sure she knew how much I cared about her.

"You have been such a surprise. I didn't see our relationship coming. I knew from the start that I loved hanging out and being around you, but I didn't know the depth I'd find. Every time I'm with you I am so amazed. At your strength, courage, love, and generosity. You blow me away."

Finally, the "but" had to come.

"I want to give you my heart, but my heart is leading me somewhere else."

When she realized I was not proposing, I recognized the look that came over her face. It was the same look of dejection that had been on my face when I realized I was being sent home. Her shock gave way to sadness. She tried to compose herself while I was talking. Then, to her credit, she mustered up the courage and held back the tears long enough to say, "I'm happy for you and Catherine. She's a great girl."

It was hard enough for me already. But Lindsay's kind, gracious response was a punch to the gut.

I walked her back to the bridge where Harrison dropped her off. It seemed like it took forever because she didn't say anything. I cried the whole way.

"Why did you let me go through all of this?" she finally asked. It was a fair question that implied so much more. Why did I sit in her kitchen with her family and drink a beer with her dad? Why did I let her select that stunning dress with the help of a stylist? Why did I let her make that long walk, with a camera on a crane following her?

The fact of the matter was this: I hadn't decided until the night before, when I wanted to send her home quietly. The producers had talked me into giving her one more chance. They said it'd be better for her to go through that last night as an opportunity for her to share any last things with me. They thought it might be unfair to deny her that chance.

Had I made the wrong decision? I gave Lindsay a final hug good-bye and shuddered at the thought.

As she drove away, the sadness clung to me like the hot, humid air.

＊━━━＊

"How did you feel when Lindsay said she was happy for you and Catherine?" Mary Kate asked in my ITM between Lindsay's departure and Catherine's arrival. The camera was rolling. I opened my mouth to speak, but I stopped myself. Anytime I mentioned the name "Lindsay," I started crying all over again.

I had heard from previous Bachelorettes and Bachelors that they knew who "the one" was well in advance. I doubt any of them had been more invested in the final two than I had been. I'm not sure what questions

Mary Kate asked me, but I kept saying the same responses over and over—between heavily flowing tears.

"She's so sweet."

"She didn't deserve that."

"I'm so sorry I hurt her."

"It's time to get you into position," Mary Kate said. It had been about thirty minutes since I'd watched Lindsay get into the limo with a broken heart.

How could I emotionally switch from gut-wrenching rejection to a marriage proposal? I had a pang of excitement, followed by a wave of agony as I thought about the two women and all the emotion this day held.

I dutifully followed Mary Kate's instructions and climbed onto the same platform. The sun beat down and the humidity wrapped around me like a wet blanket. Production assistants gave me water. Another held an umbrella over me. Someone gave me cold towels to cool my face and neck.

I'm about to propose to the woman I hope will spend the rest of my life with me, I thought. It was almost unfathomable.

I felt vaguely like I was not actually a part of the moment. Instead of me making things happen, I felt like things were happening around me and to me. Cameras shifted around me, people dabbed my face, and I couldn't get deep breaths in the tailor-made suit that suddenly seemed too tight around my neck.

When Chris Harrison appeared and handed me a letter, I was taken off guard.

"Catherine gave me something she wanted you to see," he said, handing me the letter and disappearing off the platform.

I was expecting to see Catherine—not a letter. My hands trembled as I opened it. Had she gotten cold feet?

Sean,

This journey has already been the most memorable experience of my life. Coming into this, I had little expectation. I was skeptical. I knew great things about you, but since the first day you have never ceased to surprise me. I knew you were a man of God, that your family was very important to you, and that you were deeply attractive. Meeting your family gave me a great perspective of the type of life we could—and will—have.

Your family has shown me so much how our family can be . . . full of happiness, support, and unconditional love. I'm so excited to build our own family together. There will be hard times, no doubt. Neither one of us is perfect, but I truly believe we are perfect for each other. I was always nervous about being a wife. But after getting to know you, I can't imagine being anything but your wife. All I want to do is to move to Dallas, become a part of your family, and build our own family together. I will love you forever, if you let me. You have my heart.

Always,
Catherine

Then I saw her.

Up in the distance, Catherine was walking toward me on that winding pebble path. She wore a mesmerizing gold dress. I suddenly realized, *That beautiful woman followed by cameras and producers and staffers is about to become my wife.*

She came on the platform, and I started the speech that had been swirling around in my head.

"This has been such a crazy journey. There have been so many unexpected, wonderful moments with you. I knew from the beginning that you were someone I wanted to be around," I said. "I had no idea my feelings were going to turn into what they have turned into. You never cease to amaze me. You never do. I miss you every time we have to say good-bye. I don't want to say good-bye anymore."

That's when I got down on one knee, opened the Neil Lane box, and showed her the ring. "Catherine, will you marry me?"

Her reaction was priceless. She gasped and started waving her hands. I thought she was going to pass out. The producers were on their walkie-talkies saying, "Medic, stand by. Possible fainting." She looked as though she'd lost control of her body.

Then I heard the word I'd been waiting so long to hear.

"Yes!"

She trembled as I hugged her.

"Are you serious?" she asked. "Are you serious?"

"Did you even see the ring?" I prompted. It was just like Catherine not to even look at her finger.

"It's gorgeous," she said, but I could tell she didn't realize her hand was seventy-five thousand dollars heavier. She would've been just as happy with a piece of yarn wrapped around her finger.

As I hugged her, she kept saying, "Is this for real?"

It was an interesting question. If anyone had asked me when I first decided to be on a reality TV show if there was anything "real" about it, I would've laughed. It's hard to take seriously the whole show, filled with glamorous dresses, heavy-handed rose symbolism, constantly flowing champagne, fake eyelashes, and strained dating situations. However, as I stood in Thailand, looking at the woman who would become my future wife and the mother of my children, I knew—definitively—the answer to that question.

"This is real," I said. "I'll love you for the rest of your life."

sixteen

TRYING TO DANCE
WITH THE STARS

"One more thing," Mary Kate said after the dramatic proposal.

Emotions were high, Catherine and I were exhausted, and my mind swirled with the possibilities of our new life together.

"We've arranged for you to ride an elephant into the sunset," said Mary Kate. I soon saw that everyone was excited about that, except the elephant. Maybe he wasn't a romantic at heart, but—for whatever reason—the elephant wasn't cooperating that day. He would get down for a second, and then he'd stand back up. As Catherine was trying to get on, she made it on top of the four-step platform. The elephant started getting up while she had one leg out. She lost her balance and jumped off the platform, which was about four feet above the ground, and landed on her feet somehow. Oh yeah, she was wearing heels.

"That's my future wife," I said proudly.

———

The next three days were incredible, even though we were in lockdown mode. Now more than ever, we had to be careful not to let anyone see Catherine and me together. Since the show hadn't aired yet, most people wouldn't have taken notice of us at all. However, there were show stalkers and paparazzi who could've ruined the entire season with a single photo.

Catherine, Mary Kate, her husband, Travis, and I all hunkered down in the amazing house for a few days—though it was hardly a sacrifice. We were served delicious food while we hung out on the property. Travis and I got along as though we'd known each other forever, and we quickly devised a game that involved throwing tennis balls at big flowerpots. We spent the days hanging out, laughing, eating, and having fun. At some point during our time there, we wanted to use the home's awesome movie theater.

"What should we watch?" Mary Kate asked, flipping through a stack of DVDs and calling out the names of them.

"No," Catherine said emphatically after she read out the name of a popular romantic comedy. "I hate chick flicks."

It took me aback. After our rather whirlwind—and unconventional—romance, I realized I had no idea how Catherine drank her coffee, what she liked to eat, or what kinds of movies she liked.

"How can you hate chick flicks?" I asked. "I thought that was a prerequisite for being selected to go on *The Bachelor*." We all laughed, but it hit me with a thud: I knew very little about my fiancée.

When we left Thailand, we went our separate ways. I hated to say goodbye to Mary Kate and Travis because I'd grown so close to them. Plus, this marked the end of a very special time of our lives. Even worse, it meant I'd have to stay away from Catherine and keep our relationship secret until after the show aired.

"I'll see you soon," I said to Catherine, kissing her before being taken in a different car to the airport. I landed in Dallas two days before Thanksgiving. Since the show wouldn't air until early January, we had to keep our engagement secret for several months. Obviously, the producers had to balance their need for complete secrecy with the reality that it was important for Catherine and me to see each other. After all, we'd only spent ten weeks together before our engagement. A long separation after the proposal didn't seem like a recipe for continued relationship success. To allow us to secretly see each other, they set up homes in Los Angeles, which they called "Happy Couple." Every two weeks, we'd both fly to LA under aliases: she was Bonnie, and I was Clyde. The limo driver always held a sign that read "Clyde Mankoff," borrowing from the executive producer Ronald Mankoff's last name. With my alias, they figured I would be able to get though LAX without tipping off the paparazzi.

Believe it or not, it worked.

The first time we conducted this undercover operation, a driver picked me up at the airport and took me to a secret house. Brenner was already there, preparing for our arrival.

"We've come a long way since Emily dumped me in Curaçao and you ate wasabi to cheer me up," I said.

"If you want wasabi"—he laughed—"just let me know. But hopefully, you won't be a blubbering mess this time around."

"I think we're safe on that."

"I'll be getting your groceries and any movies you may want to see," he said. "You guys *have* to stay in this house. You can't venture out."

When I saw Catherine again, I couldn't believe how much I'd missed her. Just a few months before, I was a happy single guy who liked my space. Now I felt a little weird when she wasn't with me. We ate tons of food. We pigged out on those weekends, and I tried a lot of her vegan food (which I have to say wasn't all that bad). We discovered that we were both movie buffs, so we whiled away the hours watching movies—no chick flicks allowed.

We also had a chance to talk about our faith—without members of the production staff waiting outside the door. As she had explained the night before the proposal, her mother was Catholic, and her dad had been practicing Buddhism over the last several years. Though she went to Mass every Sunday with her mom and grandmother, she didn't feel like she really knew God. Plus, there were many things she didn't understand. For example, in Christianity, God is described as being the Father, the Son, and the Holy

Spirit. Commonly referred to as the "Trinity," it's one of those foundational teachings of the Christian faith.

"I just don't get that," she said. "I've always grown up thinking of God and Jesus as two different beings."

"Try to think of God as three-in-one," I said. "Every part has different roles."

"Okaaay . . . ," she said hesitantly. "Like what?"

"Well, the Holy Spirit does a lot of things—comforts you when you're sad, gives you strength. But the Spirit also opens your eyes to your need of God."

She didn't say anything, so I went on. "Once the Spirit draws you, that's when you encounter God the Father. He loves us so much that he sent his Son to pay the penalty for our sins."

I could tell this was hard for her to really comprehend since she'd spent her whole life thinking differently. I let it drop. I knew God was working on her heart, and I didn't want to get in the way. If Catherine came to faith, it would be on her own time, in her own way. I was thankful to see her wrestling with Christianity and also thankful to have the time to sit around and talk about these issues without having to worry about cameras or deadlines.

We had four or five "Happy Couple" visits but were forbidden to see each other anywhere other than this hypercontrolled, secure location. It got old. One day when I missed Catherine so much, I texted her: *Let's sneak you down to Dallas.*

Really? she immediately texted back.

It was a few weeks before the show aired, so no one would be able to identify Catherine. I figured it was worth the risk.

"What the producers don't know won't hurt them!" she said. That's what I love about Catherine—she is always game for everything.

Catherine flew down to Dallas, and I didn't even go inside the airport to greet her. When she got her luggage, she met me outside the airport, where I whisked her away to meet my friends. Laura, Stephanie, Austin, Jeremy, and Kevin all loved her. And I got the feeling she loved them as well. The next day I took her to my parents' house, where we got to hang out with family. My fiancée fit in very well, and I loved introducing her to the people I love.

"I have some news," she said during this trip. "I went to church!"

"You did?" I asked. "All alone?"

"No, my friend Crista went with me," she said. "It's a nondenominational church in Seattle."

"What was it like?" I asked, hoping it was a good experience.

"It was contemporary," she said. "Very different than the services I used to attend. The pastor even wore jeans!"

Though Catherine still hadn't committed her life to Christ, I was happy to see that she had made it to a church service. I so wanted to take her to my church, Fellowship Church, in downtown Dallas. I knew she'd love my pastor Ed Young, the cool vibe of the church, and—of course—the message of hope and truth. However, there was no way we could risk being seen in public together, so I'd have to wait to introduce her to that very important part of my life.

All in all, Catherine's trip to Dallas was a success. Mostly because the producers never found out about our secret rendezvous. (Until now, I guess. Sorry, Mary Kate!) After she went back to Seattle, we texted, FaceTimed, e-mailed, and called. Being apart was tough, but it was the price we had to pay for meeting on the most popular dating show of all time.

One day, however, my phone rang. I answered it, wondering about the unfamiliar number. It definitely wasn't Catherine.

"Sean?" asked a sweet voice. "This is Lindsay."

"Lindsay who?" I asked. I wasn't expecting this call, though I should've been.

"Lindsay *Yenter*," she said. I stood there in the health-food store, completely immobilized.

"Oooh," I said. "Listen, I'm getting some groceries. Let me call you back in five minutes." I bought my groceries—and a little time to collect myself. When I got back out to the car, I took a deep breath and dialed her number.

"Hey, what's up?" I said, trying to sound casual.

"I just wanted to call you, because . . ." She paused. "I'm still in love with you, and I still pray over us. I think it's important that you know that."

I was so sympathetic—empathetic, really. I'll never forget picking up my phone a thousand times considering whether to dial Emily's number. As kindly as I could, I said, "I didn't really give you closure, so I hope I can give you closure now. I've fallen in love with Catherine."

The call lasted fifteen minutes, and she handled it very graciously. I left that conversation convinced Lindsay really was a class act.

※

"Sean, you'll need to fly to Los Angeles to do some pickups," Mary Kate said.

"I don't do pickups anymore," I said. "I'm engaged, in case you didn't notice."

Mary Kate didn't laugh at my joke. Even though this was a downtime for Catherine and me, the producers at *The Bachelor* were frantically trying to make all that footage into an actual story. The story producer had taken notes throughout the season, just like the producer, and was now busy formulating everything that happened during the season into a narrative.

Now that the season was over, I had to fly to LA, where I discovered they had my entire wardrobe from the season all neatly arranged—down to the belts and socks. When I'd been a contestant on *The Bachelorette*, I had to bring my own clothes. But one of the perks about being *The Bachelor* was the wardrobe they provided.

"How did you do all this?" I asked.

"Remember when Brenner took photos of you before each date?" Mary Kate asked. "Well, that wasn't for Facebook. He was documenting exactly what you were wearing on each date so we could replicate the outfit down to the detail."

"Why?"

"Put on week-one clothes to find out," she said before leaving the room. "Actually, you only have to put on the top half. Here's the Polaroid for reference."

There, laid out perfectly, was the suit I wore with Des on our first one-on-one date.

After I put on the top half, the producers came back in with a cameraman, and I'd say things like, "I'm having a blast with Des tonight, and I can't wait to see what the future holds." It wasn't disingenuous, because I expressed what my true feelings were at the time. Mainly, it was boring. I did pickups for countless hours over probably four days. Even though I'm pretty good at public speaking, I was surprised at how hard it was to remember six sequential sentences of pickups.

When I went back to Dallas, the producers contacted me again, saying they needed a bit more.

"This time, we need audio to play over the footage of your date," Travis e-mailed. "You can do it on your iPad." What he didn't know was that I lived in a loft with concrete floors and a good amount of open space. The only place I could get decent audio was in my closet.

"I don't think the girls like Tierra," I said into my iPad, crouching in my closet weeks after the actual date had occurred.

Although they were able to clean up the audio a little bit, I laughed when I watched the show and heard the substandard quality. No one would've guessed I recorded that while in my closet in Dallas, weeks after the fact.

While watching the show, I told my friends these behind-the-scenes details that made it interesting. Plus, it was enjoyable to relive that fun season of life. As I watched the show in Dallas, however, I worried how Catherine would react to seeing all this footage of me kissing other girls—in some cases, girls who ended up being her dear friends.

This, of course, is the inherent problem of the show: relationships solidified in the final days of the show are immediately put at risk when the newly engaged person watches ten weeks of his or her future spouse making out with other people. Emily Maynard, after she got engaged to Brad Womack on the show, said she turned into a ball of anxiety and self-doubt every Monday night when she tuned in to see the show. This ultimately contributed to the demise of their already shaky relationship.

Would Catherine and I be able to withstand it?

Since she was watching two thousand miles away, I had no idea how she was feeling.

"How's it going?" I asked her during the first episode.

"I can't believe the show has started!"

"I know," I said. "But how do you think you'll feel while watching it from week to week?"

"Sean, I understand everything you did on the show ultimately led you to me," she said. "It's all a part of it. We're good."

And that was that. Even as the show progressed, she never gave me grief over anything that happened.

⁂

"Guess what," Catherine casually said one day. "Crista accepted Jesus into her heart."

"Really?" I couldn't believe my ears.

"Yes, we met with the pastor," she said.

"The one who wears jeans?"

"Yes, that one," she said. "And she decided she believed."

I was thrilled to hear Crista's news, but noted that Catherine herself hadn't taken the plunge. It might seem like Catherine is the type of girl who makes decisions quickly—if based alone on the fact that she accepted my marriage proposal! However, she is normally a very deliberate, careful person. I knew she wasn't going to jump into anything without counting the cost.

⁂

As the episodes were aired, the ratings climbed. The first episode's ratings were so-so, because it debuted on the same night as the college football national championship game. (I confess—even I flipped back and forth.)

However, every week the ratings increased. Very consistently, we gained audience members every week until we reached between ten and twelve million. *People* magazine came out with a special *Bachelor* issue, which detailed America's "favorite bachelors." I was pleased I handily won—with 68 percent of the vote.

When I saw that magazine article, I thought back to those days when I was in the insurance office with Andrew, and we were nervous as to whether I would make it on the show. My biggest fear was that I didn't want to go home the first night. It was amazing how far I'd come.

With my newfound notoriety, I began getting opportunities to be on other television shows. This gave me financial opportunities that dwarfed those in insurance sales. With a soon-to-be-wife and—hopefully—family, I needed seriously to consider each opportunity. However, I was mindful that I didn't want to get into the reality TV rut, which would propel me into a series of diminishing opportunities—each show being less prominent than the last. I didn't want to take every opportunity that came along.

"Your phone is about to start ringing," Mary Kate said after seeing our amazing ratings. "You should only take big opportunities."

When I proposed to Catherine in the finale, everyone was so supportive. Suddenly, we were able to be seen together in public, and—best of all—she could wear her ring. We immediately were plunged into the post-*Bachelor* media circuit. I can't remember when it first happened, but some reporter— out of all the reporters I talked to—asked me an obvious question.

"So are you and Catherine waiting until marriage for sex?"

The reporter knew I was a Christian. Though it was hardly mentioned on the show—only vague references to faith—people knew that my faith had caused me to conduct myself differently on the show. In an interview even before my season started, Chris Harrison told *US Weekly* that I was looking for "a lady: someone who respects herself and her family. It's not a crazy, 'let's get drunk, let's get naked' type of season because that's not Sean."[7] In other words, the reporter knew the answer before he asked, but wanted to grab headlines with *Sex. Sex. Sex!*

Maybe I should've dodged the question. After all, it was personal. I think people would've understood had I told him it was none of his business. Because I'm not ashamed of my faith, I answered honestly, and everything changed. My original goal was to downplay sex in our relationship—to put it in its appropriate place: marriage. This one question, however, had the opposite effect. Now every reporter in every conversation—television or print—brought it up. In every interview, I knew it was coming up.

Originally, it was: "Are you going to wait until marriage to have sex?"

Do we have to talk about this again? I would think. *You've already heard my answer from a million other sources. Why are you asking me again?*

After weeks of repeatedly being asked that question, even the reporters couldn't pretend not to know the answer. Then savvy reporters asked a mutation of that question: "Why have you made that decision?" When that got old, it was, "What do you think about how reporters constantly ask you about your decision not to have sex until marriage?"

There was no way to escape it.

Suddenly, I was on multiple magazine covers. Even actual celebrities couldn't match the number of times I was on tabloids at the grocery store. When I was on the cover of *US Weekly*, it was the best-selling edition in a fifteen-week period. But the magazine Catherine and I were most excited about was *People*. When they invited us to have our own cover story celebrating our engagement, it was like our engagement announcement to the world—the first inside look at our lives together. We had a blast doing a photo shoot dedicated to the cover.

The big, bold headline superimposed over our photograph, however, was a little jarring: "Waiting for Our Wedding Night: No Sex Until 'I Do.'"

I hated that everyone wanted to talk about how I was the "born-again virgin bachelor," a phrase I never had used before in my life. First of all, I'd already made the mistake and had been sexually active. But I'd learned from my mistakes. I'm a Christian. Because of my faith, I no longer lived selfishly and didn't do many things that might tempt me—I wouldn't rob a bank if I lacked money. I wouldn't murder someone if I got angry. Not having sex until marriage was not the defining aspect of my life or personality. Rather, it simply was the one that garnered the most headlines.

One day, I got a call from my manager, Matt. "I've got bad news."

"What is it?" I asked. I definitely didn't want any bad news. Everything had been going so well, other than having to deal with the sex-obsessed media attention.

"You're gonna have to learn how to dance."

"You mean for the wedding?"

"No," he said. "You've just been asked to be on *Dancing with the Stars*!"

This was one of the shows Mary Kate had indicated would be "big" enough to justify my participation. As Matt explained the structure of the contract and the pay, which involved a base pay with incentives each week I survived the vote, I was so excited. Matt also explained the show would provide a furnished LA apartment that allowed dogs—and a rental car. Plus, they offered to get Catherine an apartment so we wouldn't have to be separated.

"I think it's a great opportunity," I told Catherine. "I mean, some people make enough money on the show to buy a house."

"If you think so . . . ," Catherine said, but I could tell she was skeptical.

"It's just a great chance to capitalize a little on *The Bachelor* popularity," I said. "We're in the spotlight now anyway. We might as well make a little money and then settle down."

"Hm," she said. "I think I could pass on the added spotlight."

"It's not the money or the spotlight," I said. "It's an amazing experience . . . an experience of a lifetime, really."

She nodded, seeing my excitement.

"Plus, wouldn't it be fun to start out our lives together in a place neither of us calls home?" I said, wrapping my arms around her. "It will just be you and me, starting out together in a new place."

"I'm not sure how it will work out logistically," she said. "But yeah! I can see it."

"We can handle it." I smiled. "We just need to figure out a plan."

Our strategy was that I'd move to Los Angeles and begin rehearsals. Catherine would wrap up her job in Seattle and relocate to Los Angeles so we could spend as much time together as possible.

My involvement with the show was all very hush-hush, because they weren't ready to reveal my participation in the show quite yet.

When I moved to Los Angeles, I was assigned Peta Murgatroyd as my professional dance partner. Raised in Australia, she was easy to be around, and I could tell that she would be patient with me as I tried to learn the dances. Peta and I met in studios all over Los Angeles to keep the paparazzi off our trail.

What I didn't know—but quickly figured out—was that dancing is hard. Our first dance was the fox-trot, and Peta taught me how to move my hips in a figure-eight pattern. Or at least she tried. The whole thing felt odd to me.

"Now hold your arm up, but slightly bent," she said. It was awkward at first. There was so much to remember that it made those six sentences of pickups pale in comparison. I practiced eight to ten hours a day and talked to Catherine every night.

One evening, I was exhausted—but I noticed Catherine wasn't very talkative.

"Everything okay?" I asked. At the time, I was still learning about Catherine—how she handled conflict, how she expressed concern, or how she dealt with problems. Since we had met in a controlled environment, there were many things about her I didn't know.

I was about to have a crash course.

"Aren't you spending *a lot* of time learning these steps?"

"Of course I am. I want to do well."

"Listen, this is just par for the course," I said. "Everyone is struggling to learn their steps. It's all so new!"

"I understand," she said, with a forced cheerfulness. "I hope Peta can teach you some good moves. I'm sure you can do it."

Catherine's efforts to be supportive were both sweet and unconvincing. I promised myself to do well. I had to make this financially worth it after disrupting our new relationship with yet another television show. *Dancing With the Stars* announced me as a last-minute contestant two weeks after they announced the original cast, which included Olympic skater Dorothy Hamill, country singer Wynona Judd, reality TV star Lisa Vanderpump, comedian Andy Dick, NFL wide receiver Jacoby Jones, professional boxer Victor Ortiz, Olympic gymnast Alexandra Raisman, Disney star Zendaya, soap opera star Ingo Rademacher, comedian D. L. Hughley, and country singer Kellie Pickler.

When Catherine arrived, I hoped spending time together would give her more confidence in our relationship. During every ounce of my free time, we hung out and enjoyed getting to know each other. Yes, it was still under unusual circumstances, but at least we didn't have to keep our love a secret anymore.

I made it through the first week of the show, and then the second. Thankfully, my amazing fans from Bachelor Nation kept pulling me through, even though I could tell the other contestants were better dancers. The third week, something happened that would change our lives forever.

Shortly before our move to Los Angeles, Catherine's friend Crista gave her life to Jesus. Catherine was certainly entertaining the idea, but she's definitely one to think long and hard about something before making a decision. One night after a late dance rehearsal, I went to her place and noticed she had a joyful look on her face.

"I have good news," she said. Ever since our stolen conversation in Thailand, we had talked about faith and God. Catherine seemed to be leaning toward belief in God, though she didn't really have a personal faith of her own. For some reason, I had a peace about her. On the night before I proposed, I knew—without a doubt—that Catherine was on a journey. But not the overused, stereotypical "journey" of *The Bachelor*. Rather, I knew she was making her way toward Christ—the ultimate journey anyone can take.

"I understand now what you've been saying," she said, holding up her new Bible. "I accepted Jesus into my heart!"

I hugged her as she told me how she came to that decision. It wasn't rash, it wasn't rushed, and she didn't do it for me. Catherine is someone who thinks for herself, and she was on cloud nine after telling me. After that night, she couldn't get enough of church and Jesus. She's been that way ever since.

—————

We had so much fun during this time on *DWTS*. During my very little time off, we managed to explore the city together. We would go to Runyon Canyon, try different restaurants, take the dogs to the beach, and walk around The Grove. The Grove, an awesome outdoor retail space that's always on television and in the movies, was right across the street from our apartments, so we spent a lot of time there. Not only that, but we created great friendships with the other dancers, including Lisa Vanderpump and her entire family, Victor Ortiz, and Alexandra Raisman. It was wonderful to see Catherine smiling in the audience every week, always cheering more loudly than anyone. She even tried to match her dress with whatever my themed outfit was for the week. Catherine spent the days also studying Scripture and growing in her faith, learning to lean on the Lord.

It was a skill she'd need during the weeks of all those practices and rehearsals. As the weeks went on, the dances got more complicated and the practices got even longer. Thankfully, Peta is a workhorse who wanted to win too. I had to work harder just to stay in the mix, and I know the fact that I was rarely at home began weighing on Catherine. Even though we were making the most of the time there, she was still in an unfamiliar place, alone most of the days.

Want to grab dinner? I texted Catherine on the way out the door of the rehearsal studio. It was close to ten.

I guess, she texted back. *Isn't it a bit late?*

Suddenly, I realized she'd been in her apartment stewing over the fact that I hadn't contacted her. She didn't understand I was spending every free moment I had with her—at dinner, the theater, or just running across the street to the mall. It seemed like no matter how much I tried, my time was never enough for her. In retrospect, I realize that I didn't handle this situation well. I should've been more conscious of the fact that these ten- to twelve-hour practices were going to add too much strain to our relationship. I should've seen this coming and politely declined the opportunity. Of course, hindsight is twenty-twenty, and I was new at being someone's fiancé.

When I arrived, she met me at the door.

"I can't," she said, in tears.

"You can't go out to eat?"

"No," she said. "I can't do this!" She motioned with her arm all around her in the *Dancing with the Stars*–provided apartment.

"What happened?" I asked.

"Nothing ever happens. At least for me. You're gone every day. I never see you."

"I want to spend time with you," I said. "But this is just a hard time of life."

"We just got *out* of a hard time of life," she said. "Remember? *The Bachelor*? That wasn't easy either. We kept saying that once it was over, we could get to live like normal people. Well, this isn't *normal*!"

"Listen to me," I said, in the calmest voice I could muster. "I want to spend time you, but rehearsal is eating up all my time."

Catherine and I never argued on the set of *The Bachelor*. Now that we were in the real world, I was beginning to see a side of her that I'd never known existed. I wasn't sure how to handle it.

"I don't know why I moved down here. I wait around all day just to get five minutes with you I get only your leftover time," she said. Though I appreciated she was trying to be supportive by being in Los Angeles, her unhappiness stressed me out. Sometimes, before I turned the knob to see her after a hard day of practicing, I had to take a deep breath and brace myself for whatever was on the other side of the door. I knew I'd screwed up and overcommitted myself on this show, but I had no way out until the American people wised up and sent me home. With my level of proficiency, I figured, that shouldn't be too much longer.

"I left my career for you," she said. She'd worked her way up at Amazon as a graphic designer but had to quit so we could be together in Los Angeles during filming. Suddenly this self-reliant woman had no income and had to rely on me to pay for everything. I now understand that this was a hard transition for her—not only did she move from Seattle to California, she went from being a professional person to someone's fiancé. She was suddenly supposed to be my main cheerleader in the audience, my main encourager.

However, I didn't feel encouraged. At least not in this moment.

She began sobbing.

"I just feel so lost," she cried.

Every week, Catherine went to the Monday performance and Tuesday results show. She sat in the crowd with my parents and was always there to support and cheer for me. Even though we had troubles, I knew she wanted me to succeed and was doing her best to make this work.

Can this relationship last? Did I jump in too soon? Doubts crept into my mind as I tried to navigate the complicated relationship-conducted-in-reality-TV waters. We had a couple of nights where I thought the neighbors might hear us arguing through the walls. She cried, "I don't know what I'm doing. I've given up my entire life for you."

"Should I quit?" I asked. *Dancing with the Stars* was a huge financial blessing for us. "Should I walk away from the show—and our income—to make sure you have peace of mind? Is it even right for you to ask me to do that?"

"No need for you to quit, because I'm moving back to Seattle," she said. "I can't do this anymore. I'm not going to sit in the front row with your mom and dad, while I watch you out there dancing your heart out. It feels like you've put this show ahead of our relationship, and I just don't want to be a part of it anymore. I can't," she said. "I won't."

I was stuck. And it didn't help that when I finally had the chance to spend time with Catherine, reporters were everywhere.

That's the thing about Los Angeles. No matter where I went, paparazzi showed up. It was amazing how they could find out our location. Had our government hired the Los Angeles paparazzi to find Osama bin Laden, they would've quickly had a multipage spread of candid photos under the headline "Grooming Habits of the World's Most Wanted."

Even though our dance studio had tight security, every single day there were six to eight photographers standing outside all day looking for the shots. That didn't bother me compared to how they hounded me in my off hours. When Catherine and I tried to steal away for dinner, the paparazzi somehow found out and stalked us. Every single time we flew, we were followed by photographers at LAX.

"How do these people know our schedule?" I asked Catherine.

Magazines started publishing those photos, accompanying articles under headlines such as, "Trouble in Paradise?" or, "Are They Gonna Work Out?" Then there was the familiar standby, "Can You Really Find Love on a Reality TV Show?"

When I saw those headlines, I laughed. "Look at this," I said to Catherine, hoping she'd laugh too. In my heart, however, the magazine headlines really bothered me because they touched on a truth I didn't want to admit.

Of course, I never shared any of my hesitation or personal doubt with anybody. When reporters asked me about how things were going, I had the same answer. "Don't believe the rumors. Everything's great with us."

And I hoped one day, this would be true again.

＊———＊

About that time, I was invited to be on *Jimmy Kimmel*. Since I'd been on his show three times, I was excited to be invited again. Jimmy's great, and I love his sense of humor. When I got there, the producers prepped me beforehand.

"Now, Jimmy might bring up the 'virgin bachelor' thing," one producer said. "So be ready."

"Really?" I said. "I figured he might want to talk about *Dancing with the Stars.*"

"We don't know," he said. "Jimmy sometimes goes his own direction. You can't predict what he'll say."

When I went on stage, sex—or lack of it—was the only thing Jimmy wanted to talk about. Since I'd expected a light, fun show, I tried to laugh along with him. In my head, though, I was thinking, *Come on, man, really?*

He didn't relent. Like everyone else, he couldn't believe that we had decided to wait until marriage for sex. But unlike everyone else, he had me on live television grilling me over the topic. Again and again and again.

Catherine smiled from her place in the fifth row, but I wondered how long those fake smiles could last.

I was quiet when I left the show. No one would've made jokes—or even found it noteworthy—had I been some sort of playboy, bedding women left and right. But once I said I wanted to live by basic Christian principles, people thought I was different, weird, and strange.

Matt picked up on my silence really fast. "I'm sorry," he said. "I didn't know he was going to pound you that whole time."

But I wasn't mad at Jimmy. I was mad that no one would give it a rest. Every interview was all about sex, all the time.

＊━━─ɯɯ─━＊

When week 7 of *DWTS* arrived, Peta and I were assigned the rumba, a steamy Cuban dance that demands chemistry. She instructed me, "You have to pretend you're in love with me."

"How can I do that when I don't have romantic feelings toward you?" I asked. My throat tightened. Would this be the week that I'd finally be sent home? It's hard enough when you are doing the fox-trot. I knew the rumba, designed for lovers, would be hard to pull off.

"I have an idea," she said. "Let's get Catherine in here to dance with you. I can watch and see what it looks like when you are dancing with some-one you love. Then, maybe we can fake it onstage when it's you and me."

Every part of me knew this was a bad idea, but I had no other options. Now that Catherine and I were having a few relationship issues ourselves, would she be willing to come in and try to dance with me? I had no other option but to ask, and—to my surprise—she agreed.

When Catherine arrived at the studio, she gave me a kiss. I could tell she was very uncomfortable. Suddenly, she was in a studio surrounded by people she didn't know. I, however, was in my element. I knew the studio, producers, dancers, and sound techs well. This rehearsal was a case of two worlds colliding, and it was hard for everyone.

"Okay, so let me see you two dance," Peta said. There's nothing worse than being told to be romantic on cue—especially with the undercurrent of unhappiness bubbling right under the surface. We made it through the awkward rehearsal.

And honestly, Peta's gimmick to get me to practice with Catherine actually worked. Holding Catherine in my arms made everything feel right in the world. Even though it was a tough time, I knew we were meant to be.

When it came time to perform, I was a ball of nerves. However, I glanced out in the audience. Catherine smiled and waved, trying to be as supportive as possible. When it was all over, the judges said my performance was great, and pointed out—once again—that I'd improved. Though I was up against a lot of naturally athletic people and others involved in show business, I felt like I was holding my own. At least I was out there giving it a try. And so, I lived to dance another day. But at what cost to our fragile, new relationship?

The next week, it felt like the world sat on my shoulders. Not only had my relationship with Catherine strained past the point of comfort, but I also had to learn two dances. I always had trouble remembering all the steps, so we had to practice more than twice as much. By the end of the week, I had every foot placement down pat. I took a deep breath when we went out onto the floor. But when the music started, I simply forgot what I was supposed to be doing. After I messed up our first dance, I was a head case.

"I'm so sorry. I'm so sorry," I said to Peta. "I screwed it up."

"Just forget it," she said. "It'll be okay. We've got another dance to perform."

But my head swirled. I couldn't shake that first dance from my head. It didn't help that I felt like I was disappointing Catherine with every step.

The second dance started with a very basic sequence. The theme was magic, and I was supposed to walk through the middle of the two professional dancers after they raised their hands. I was supposed to push their hands down at the very beginning.

When the music started, I simply walked through them—swatting at one of their hands. What was supposed to look powerful ended up looking as though I had a halfhearted desire to kill a passing fly. I paused, for a fraction of a second, confused at what just happened. Of course, there's no chance to stop the music and start all over. The music kept going, and I kept moving. Inside, I was stunned. One of the judges told me that my performance was "magic" and "tragic"—an insult that definitely seemed preplanned but was pretty accurate.

It was enough to send me home.

When I got booted the following night, I missed out on the fifty-thousand-dollar bonus. However, it was a small price to pay to get our relationship out of the *Dancing with the Stars* pressure cooker.

＊———ℓℓℓℓ———＊

Toward the end of the show, I didn't have time to do anything except dance. I'd wake up, dance, get home, and go to bed—I just danced, danced, danced, with an occasional argument with Catherine squeezed in. Even though I'd been booted off the show, we still had our apartments at the Palazzo and—suddenly—lots of free time. We spent that time enjoying each other, going on dates, and taking the dogs to the park.

On the first Monday after I got eliminated, the last thing I wanted to do was go back to the show.

"Aren't we going to see the episode?" Catherine asked.

"I figured you needed a break," I said.

"No," she said. "I've made friends with those guys. We have to see them."

And so, at Catherine's urging, we were in the audience for the final two episodes.

What you don't see at home is the way the *DWTS* producers insist that the crowd go nuts with applause every five seconds. As we sat in the audience, clapping for our friends, I felt something change. The unbelievable pressure lifted, and everything felt light and carefree. Suddenly, the show—which had felt like such a threat—felt nice. Fun, even. By making it to week 8, I had been able to secure some money to help us get started in our marriage. Also, any fears Catherine had about our relationship seemed to disappear.

Without the added pressure of a television show, Catherine and I began to understand each other and how we handled conflict. For example, I internalized things. When I had a problem, I liked to go away by myself, think about it, and get over it. This, of course, drove Catherine crazy. During a conflict, I'd say, "I'm out of here" and walk down to Starbucks.

Of course, she couldn't imagine why I'd walk away in the middle of conflict, when she wanted to talk it through. It took us a bit to discover that what's healthy for me—walking away for time to think—was not healthy for her. Learning how to resolve conflict together was key to learning about each other. Plus, I realized some of my actions were disrespectful to her even though I didn't intend them to be.

I never quite understood why *DWTS* affected Catherine so much at the time and—like an idiot—I'd always argue with her about the subject. I realized with regret that I should have at least tried to be sympathetic to her. She gave up the life she knew and loved for me, and all I could seem to do was get frustrated with her when she needed me the most.

That summer in California turned out to be an important time for us. Matt got me good-paying gigs that allowed us to stay in Los Angeles and develop a life for ourselves. We'd walk to Starbucks every morning and watch Netflix on the couch in the evenings. Our refreshing summer allowed us to leave everything else behind and grow together as a couple. It was finally just the two of us, instead of the two of us plus several million at-home viewers.

Funny how the removal of cameras caused our relationship to grow in leaps and bounds. During our time in California, we had morning Bible studies together after our Starbucks run. It was a wonderful time of learning about each other. Eventually, however, we had to go back to spend time with family, to look for a place to live after we got married, and to prepare for . . . What was it again? Oh right.

The wedding.

seventeen

THE BIG DAY

It came time for Catherine and me to leave California. Though we were sad to say good-bye to that part of our lives, we were happy to start the next phase: marriage. We figured there was no better way to commemorate the transition than with a good, old-fashioned road trip.

We got in the car with our belongings, a full tank of gas, and lots of wedding details to discuss. During our four-day, fifteen-hundred-mile trip to Texas, we had amazing stops at the Grand Canyon and then Albuquerque. We found the Big Texan Steak Ranch in Amarillo that gave customers a seventy-two-ounce steak if they could eat it within one hour. To my surprise, Catherine pulled that off. Yes, Catherine. You've heard of my vegan fiancée from Seattle? She didn't stay vegan for long after we got together. While I respected her beliefs and wasn't trying to change her, I think eating meat and protein is a much healthier way of life. I introduced her to Sagi, my nutritionist and trainer, who helped her formulate a healthful lifestyle. It included meat, which meant our road trip had many fun adventures and a couple of gigantic steaks.

It was refreshing to be in Texas again. When we got to Dallas, Catherine and her sister moved into a home about a mile and a half away from my loft. She'd live there until the wedding, the theme of which Catherine had decided.

Grown Sexy.

Though I have no idea where she came up with that phrase, it meant she wanted our wedding to be "sophisticated, but with an air of sexiness." Millions of people were about to weigh in on the topic of "Grown Sexy," because we decided to let *The Bachelor* televise our wedding. We didn't decide to broadcast the ceremony for the sake of being on television.

"It's sort of like your series was a good book," Mary Kate said. "Your wedding could be the final chapter."

⊷⸺ⱸⱡⱡⱳ⸺⊶

We were honored ABC wanted to be a part of it. Our relationship began and developed on television. Plus, we loved the people associated with *The Bachelor* and wanted them to be a part of the wedding as well. In fact, we got to work with Ronald again. Every time I saw the executive producer, I smiled. I couldn't help but think back to the night before the proposal, when he gave me advice on women and marriage.

"We want this to be about you and Catherine," he said. "This is your wedding. If there's something that makes you feel uncomfortable, tell us. You give us ideas about how you want the wedding. It's *your* wedding; we just want to capture it."

Chris Harrison, who became an ordained minister when producers Mary Kate and Travis tied the knot, did an amazing job with their wedding. However, there were many ordained ministers in my family who would have to take precedence over Chris. I believe a wedding is a covenant between God and us. Even though it is unusual to make that covenant on national television in front of millions of people watching from home, it seemed like a fitting way to begin our lives together as a married couple. I heard rumors that people were worried that televising our wedding might cheapen the experience—including my dad.

"What do you think Sean's gonna do about the minister?" Dad asked my mom. I'd heard he was concerned about the whole thing. Little did he know we had a surprise for him.

Though my dad is an insurance salesman, he had gotten ordained to perform my cousin's wedding. In my mind, there was never really a question. My dad's dad had married my parents, and I wanted Dad to marry us.

One Monday, I told my parents that the show was going to film at our house, because we wanted to capture the moment when we asked our niece and nephew to be the flower girl and the ring bearer. In reality, we were staging the whole thing to surprise Dad.

"I feel like I know how to be a good husband to Catherine," I said as we sat outside talking to my family. "And that's mainly because of the way you raised me."

"Thanks, Sean," Dad said. "That means a lot. Bringing Catherine into this family has been the easiest thing in the whole wide world. She's so easy to love." Then he turned to Catherine and said, "In fact, we might like you more than we like Sean!"

"We were hoping you would officiate the wedding," I said.

"Seriously?" he asked a few times as my invitation registered in his mind. "I'm very honored. Yes, I would love that. To be on that launchpad is something special. Thank you for asking me. Thank you."

Dad was deeply touched by the invitation. Any fears that this wouldn't be a real wedding were put to rest. "Dad," I said, "I couldn't think of a more godly man to conduct the ceremony. You have had such a powerful and positive influence on my life." Then I added, "But you'll have to hold it together during the ceremony."

"There's no chance of that," Catherine said.

"You guys tell me what you want me to say," he said, "and I'll make sure it's just how you want it."

Catherine quickly stopped that line of thinking. "No, we trust you. We don't have to tell you what to say, because you'll do something wonderful."

"Well, you guys are easy to talk about." Then he choked back tears and said, "It'll mean a lot to me for the rest of my life."

After we got settled in Dallas, I could finally introduce Catherine to my church. My pastor said one time, "The best financial decision you can make for your future is not ever getting divorced." I always have said I'm only getting married once, so his comment—and many other comments about marriage—stuck with me. Catherine and I went through premarital counseling at my church, which allowed us to talk through issues that hadn't come up during our whirlwind, unconventional romance. That's what people don't understand. Though I proposed after only ten weeks, Catherine and I were engaged for fourteen months. During that time, we had a chance to solidify our feelings and prepare well for a lifetime together.

During this time, Catherine decided to be baptized, which is when a believer is submerged in water to symbolize dying to oneself and coming up a new creation. This is a big act—a public declaration of faith—and I was touched that Catherine asked my dad to baptize her. She and Laura were baptized one Sunday, at my home church at Plymouth Park Baptist Church in Irving, Texas. It was a beautiful moment, and I was so glad to see Catherine growing in her faith. In fact, her enthusiasm for faith encouraged me in mine.

I never pressured her into becoming a Christian. She's an independent woman with very strong ideas of her own. I also wasn't heavy handed about the no-sex-until-marriage thing. It was *my* deeply held conviction. Over time, it became Catherine's conviction as well, especially as she dug deeper into God's Word.

I hated that reporters dragged her into conversations about it all the time. For example, about three months after the proposal, Catherine and I were on *Good Morning, America*. The "virgin bachelor" conversation had gone on for months, and I just wasn't in the mood when I was asked about it yet again.

"Why do you think the media has asked so much about your decision to wait until marriage?"

"I guess it's because it's so uncommon these days," I said. "My faith has been the center of my life for a long time, and it's the center of her life as well, and that's no secret. We are proud of that fact. We realize that it's viewed as kind of being weird these days, but we are not going to shy away from it. We are unapologetic."

It's the first time I tried to put a period—even an exclamation mark— at the end of this conversation. This is simply how we felt we should live *our* lives, and we didn't care what anyone else said or did. After I said, "We are unapologetic," the *GMA* reporter moved on, which was a good thing. I was done. I wasn't going to back down from it, but I had—finally—had enough.

I wanted Catherine to be able to sort through her feelings and beliefs without the glare of the spotlight. Sex is not a main aspect of our theology. Christianity is about God's goodness and redemption. The desire of people in the media to focus like a laser onto one aspect was frustrating. I didn't want to be an abstinence spokesperson, because Christianity is about so much more than that. I definitely didn't want to push Catherine into that role. She'd changed a lot since she stepped out of the limo—and not just romantically. It was encouraging to see how Christianity had taken hold of her heart and affected all aspects of her life. I also appreciated how she read the Bible and went to church regularly—even with all the wedding details weighing heavily down on her.

Thankfully, *The Bachelor* provided the best wedding and event planners imaginable. Though I would've been just as happy to go down to the justice of the peace, I knew a big wedding ceremony was one way to commemorate the day's significance. Catherine tried to include me in all the major decisions. She told our invaluable wedding planner, Mindy Weiss, "This is *our* wedding, not just *my* wedding." When she wanted my opinion, I was happy to give it. But mostly, I let her have free rein.

We needed to make sure the people who would be attending in person would put us on their calendars. Instead of going with a traditional save-the-date card, we decided to show our whimsical side by using a photo of us wearing bear heads. Yes, our photographer took a picture of us wearing gigantic bear heads as we rode a tandem bike with a basket full of roses and tin cans trailing behind. None of this had any significance, other than we wanted to be goofy and original.

Our save-the-date card read:

"Lovers, friends, family and Jack Nicholson, please join Catherine Ligaya

Mejia Giudici and Sean Thomas Lowe & Hologram Tupac for the wedding of the century! Our love celebration will take place on the twenty-sixth day of the first month of the two thousand and fourteenth year since we started counting time. Reception to follow, so get ready for major tomfoolery & ballyhoo."

When our friends got that in the mail, they knew they were in for a different type of wedding.

We also needed to figure out where to have the wedding. After considering Dallas and Seattle, we decided on the Four Seasons Resort Biltmore in Santa Barbara—an amazingly beautiful resort right on the Pacific Ocean. Because Santa Barbara has year-round sunny weather, we felt it would be the best option for the outdoor wedding we envisioned. We wanted our friends and family to be surrounded by flowers and the beauty of California. The music, we learned, was going to be provided by 2CELLOS, two famous young cellists whom Elton John described as "astonishing" and "exciting."[8]

Things were falling into place, but the guest list was tricky. Many people wondered whether the show asked us to invite certain people, but they didn't. We were the ones who decided who would celebrate with us in person. Because the ceremony location didn't have a ton of seating, we had to make some hard choices. There were people from my season of *The Bachelorette* whom I wanted to invite and people from *The Bachelor* whom Catherine wanted to include. Of course, we invited *The Bachelor* couples—Jason and Molly, Trista and Ryan, Desiree and Chris—as well as friends from *DWTS*—Andy Dick and Lisa Vanderpump, who brought her dog, Giggy. We invited friends from my hometown church—dear friends who also hosted a wedding shower for us—as well as close friends from Seattle. I laughed at the thought of the Texas evangelicals mingling with the Seattle hipsters mingling with the reality TV glitterati.

This was going to be fun.

＊————＊

There were major advantages to having the wedding with ABC. Catherine's family is far-flung—they live all around the globe. When the show graciously offered to pay for their travel, this enabled everyone to attend. Even Catherine's dad was able to come and walk her down the aisle along with her mother. This was such an amazing development. I'd had the chance to meet him during filming of *DWTS*. He was in the States for a few days, so I flew out to meet him, had breakfast with him, and flew back to Los Angeles. Even though it was a short visit, I immediately loved the guy. Catherine was thrilled for him to be such a big part of the wedding, especially considering the fact that he'd lived so far away from her during her childhood. Plus, she was honored that her mom and sisters were there. Even though they had given me a hard time at the hometown visit, they were now very supportive of us. (When her mom heard I'd proposed, she called me and said, "You've always had my blessing!")

Registering for gifts was a crazy experience, mainly because it seems weird to go through and tell people, "Hey, I want these plates, not those." I guess it's a good way to make sure you don't end up with twenty-seven salad forks, though. It was fun thinking about setting up a home with Catherine. We registered for normal household items—dishes, silverware, pillows, and glasses—and gave people the option of donating to Micaela's Army Foundation. I'm on the board of this organization, which honors the memory of Micaela White, who passed away from childhood leukemia, and promotes awareness of the need for childhood, adolescent, and young adult cancer research funding. I loved using our wedding to shine light on their incredible work.

Catherine asked twelve of her friends to be bridesmaids, which put me in a bind. I could only come up with nine groomsmen, and—I joked—one of them was my mailman! All kidding aside, it was wonderful to share this big day with people who had been with us through thick and thin. Here's how we described them as our party:

The Best Man/Most Likely to End the Night Shirtless: Clay Silver
The Matron of Honor/Most Likely to Become "Cat Lady": Crista Osher
Most Likely to Leave the Party by 10 p.m.: Brandon Higginbotham
Biggest Flirt: Monica Teal Giudici

Most Talkative: Jeremy Anderson

Biggest Bada—: India Giudici

Most Likely to Become a Billionaire: Kevin Tinkle

The Hostess with the Mostest: Shay Shull

Best Beard: Austin Eudaly

Most Likely to Shed a Tear Listening to Our Vows: Stephanie Nguyen

Tightest Game: Kyle Williams

Most Blunt: Laura Caperton

Biggest Metro: Andrew Shull

The Female MacGyver: Kristen Ramaley

Biggest Scaredy-Cat: Mark Melendez

Everyone's Best Bud: Lesley Murphy

Best Dance Moves: Cole Reilly

Most Likely to Be Mistaken for a Mademoiselle: Corina Rochex

The Most 'Hood: Anna Micklin

Most Likely to Need Extra Pages for Her Passport: Rosa Hensley

Biggest Smile: Anna Sabey

The most delicious details, of course, were the wedding cakes. While the bride's cake was a traditional layered cake, Charm City Cakes made my groom's cakes look just like my dogs. Yes, I had two cakes that looked like a boxer and a chocolate lab, because Lola and Ellie have been so important to me. I thought it was a fun way to work in the dogs without having them be part of the ceremony—though it was a little weird to stick a fork in Lola and take a bite.

Catherine didn't let me know anything about her wedding dress and made an effort not to speak about the dress in my presence. I picked out the wedding bands. During the show, I had selected a platinum engagement ring for Catherine. When it came time to pick wedding bands, we decided to do something a little different. Instead of going with the platinum bands, we got unconventional rose-gold bands. Neil Lane again did an awesome job. Though mine was plain, Catherine's had 114 round-cut small diamonds. For the wedding, Neil also let Catherine wear twenty-carat diamond earrings and a fifty-carat bracelet. He gave me platinum cufflinks—with ten carats worth of diamonds—to wear on the big day, along with four matching twenty-carat diamond shirt studs. That definitely wouldn't have happened had we had our ceremony back home. This would mark the first time I wore diamonds and probably the last!

It seemed as though there were a million decisions to make. I felt like we'd waited forever for the big day. Then—suddenly—it was time for us to fly to Santa Barbara, check in to the Four Seasons, and do this thing.

We wanted it to be as much like a normal wedding as possible. However, there were telltale signs that this event would be different. Most weddings, for example, don't have social media guidelines. We'd invited the whole nation to join us in this happy moment—and that meant people would tune in on television, comment about us on Facebook and Instagram, and of course, tweet about everything that happened. Bachelor Nation is the best fan base of any television franchise, and I was excited to share this moment with them. Our wedding happened to fall on the same night as the Grammys, and I wondered if Twitter might actually explode from all the excitement.

When our friends and loved ones arrived, they received a packet that included directions on exactly how to tweet. There were considerations, like hashtags (#BachelorWedding), handles (@SeanLowe09, @clmgiudici), and timing (anytime except during the ceremony itself). In normal weddings, it would be considered rude to pull out a phone and record the details for your friends. However, our guests were encouraged to share their experiences, impressions, and comments via social media. And wow—our fans, friends, and haters on Twitter obliged! People gathered for wedding watching parties, complete with cakes and flowers.

Finally, the day arrived.

I turned over in the bed, looked out the window, and saw an overcast day in always-sunny Santa Barbara. I hadn't seen Catherine, and the idea that my life was about to change forever started weighing on me. People swirled around me—planners, photographers, friends, people with clipboards and earpieces talking about how it had started raining. Of course. This area had been in a drought for months, but there's nothing like an outdoor wedding to bring out the rain clouds.

When former Bachelor Jason Mesnick married Molly Malaney, it began to pour about midway through Molly's vows. The producers had given all the guests clear umbrellas, but the bride and groom got drenched. Jason and Molly handled it with good humor and laughter, and it made the event much more memorable.

I'm not sure whether the producers had learned from that experience or not, but no one seemed worried about the dark skies. Notwithstanding Jason and Molly's damp affair, I assumed the producers had contingency plans for the possibility of a true storm. That morning, the rain was light and erratic. It was about fifty-five degrees, but that didn't stop people from jogging along the coast and riding bikes. It hadn't rained in so long, it seemed as if no one took the threat of rain seriously, as if the locals looked up at the skies and thought, *Yeah, I'll believe it when I see it.*

Their skepticism turned out to be warranted. Nothing ever came of the ominous clouds, and whatever rain had fallen soon was soaked into the dry earth. So after my groomsmen and I went to breakfast, we went onto the front lawn of the resort and tossed the football. A couple of those guys had been on my football teams in high school and college. Throwing the football with them was just like the good old days, except this time we had an audience. Paparazzi lined the edges of the lawn, hoping to get a good shot. We had a blast, tossing the football, joking, and laughing while they took photos.

⊶———⊷

When I got back to my room, I had the gradual awareness that I was about to become a husband. All the details of the wedding—the cakes, the floral arrangements on the reception tables, the music—had been taken care of. Honestly, I didn't care much about those things. The detail I still hadn't been able to work out in my mind weighed heavily on me as I sat down at the desk in my room with a pen and paper.

Our vows.

Catherine and I had decided to write our own vows, so we could personalize the ceremony with our deeply felt convictions. However, every time I sat down to capture my love for her, I couldn't quite do it. How do you convey deep feelings without sounding like a Hallmark card? Over the past few weeks, I must've sat down twenty times to write them, but the words never came. That morning, after breakfast and football, it all came together.

"From the moment I met you, I wanted more," I wrote. The words poured out of me until I sat back and smiled. *This is it.*

<hr />

The clouds meandered out of the skies by the afternoon, and everything was dry by the time guests began arriving. It was still a bit cool, so the producers distributed shawls to keep guests warm during the ceremony.

While the guests began mingling outside, we were all together getting dressed. I couldn't help but remember all those times Chris Harrison and I were getting dressed for those infernal rose ceremonies. During filming of *The Bachelor,* I remember putting on my suit while trying to fight that sinking feeling in my stomach as I prepared to send someone home. Tonight, I was going to be sending someone home, all right. After this day, Catherine and I would both be going home together. The thought was almost too much to bear.

"What do you think?" I asked. I had on my tuxedo and my diamond cufflinks.

"At least the mirror didn't break." My friend Clay laughed.

I was ready. Almost. All my groomsmen gathered around me, laid their hands on me, and prayed. "Father God, we thank you for Sean and this day," Andrew said. "It's been a long time coming. We know you've guided his path until now. We ask you, keep your hand in their marriage from the start."

That "long time coming" comment was true. I never moped around wishing I had a soul mate, but when I met Catherine, everything changed. I felt incomplete when I wasn't with her, and the past fourteen months seemed to take forever.

"All right, it's time," Mary Kate said.

I wanted people to know this day wasn't about me, and it wasn't even really about Catherine. Before I went to the spot, took the arm of my mother, or went over my vows again, I pulled out my phone and sent one last tweet as the Bachelor.

"Jesus, may your name be known today."

eighteen

BACHELOR NO MORE

When I saw Catherine at the end of the aisle, the tears began to flow. For months I'd told reporters I was probably going to be the first to cry at the wedding, and I delivered. Though I'm not an emotional person, there's just something about Catherine. She affects me in a deep way that causes me to choke up when I speak about her. When I saw her in that gorgeous dress, I didn't stand a chance. I know every groom is supposed to say his bride is stunning, but I couldn't believe that gorgeous woman was about to become my wife.

At this point, I was expecting to hear the traditional wedding march. But when Catherine started walking, the cellists played their rendition of Michael Jackson's 1982 tune "Human Nature."

People in the audience smiled at the unconventional choice, and I was surprised too. During rehearsal, they'd played this pop song as she walked down the aisle. However, I assumed we'd have a more traditional song during the actual wedding. I guess when 2CELLOS play at your wedding, they choose the song! Thankfully, it was beautiful, both Catherine and I liked it, and we were thankful they didn't select "Thriller."

When Catherine finally got to the end of the aisle, she hugged her parents and turned to me.

My dad began. "I'm so excited to welcome all of you to this beautiful evening to celebrate the marriage between my son and the love of his life," he said. "Sean and Catherine's journey to find love with each other has been an epic fairy tale on display for the whole world to see. It all began with a simple step from a limousine and spanned many cities, states, and countries, to a beautiful proposal in Thailand, and an elephant ride into the sunset."

I felt my lip quiver, but I held my emotions under control. As my friends and family looked on, my dad decided to get personal.

"Sean, as far as I'm concerned, you are the best son a father could have. You have such kindness and honesty, and it's what draws people to you. But most importantly, I have watched you live out your faith in Jesus Christ your whole life—no wavering, no exceptions. And I am so proud of you, son."

Then he turned his attention to Catherine.

"When I look at you, I smile. You incite happiness everywhere you go. That's what I remembered about you the first time we met you. You just giggled all the time. Sherry and I are head over heels in love with you, girl— as well as the whole family. We're blessed that you're a part of our lives and that we're a part of your and your family's lives as well."

Since this was both a live televised event and a wedding, we had to take commercial breaks. When it came time for that, my dad asked those in attendance to silently pray. Everyone bowed their heads and the cellists played while who-knows-what was being broadcast to the at-home viewers. In person, however, it wasn't off-putting. It was just a moment for everyone to catch their breath.

"Sean, will you take Catherine to be your wedded wife and to live according to God's Word in the holy union of marriage? Do you promise to love, comfort her, honor and keep her, in sickness and in health, and to forsake all others as long as you both shall live?"

"I do."

"Catherine, I would say to you too," he continued. "The man you love is about to become your husband. He has shown a willingness to leave his home and make a home with you. His love will be your inspiration, and your prayers will always be his strength.

"Do you take Sean to be your husband and to live according to God's

Word in the holy union of marriage? Do you promise to love, comfort him, honor and keep him, in sickness and in health, and to forsake all others as long as you both shall live?"

"I do," she said.

In addition to these vows, however, Catherine and I had written our own.

"Before I met you, before I even knew you existed, I knew you were coming," Catherine said. This was when her tears threatened to come, but she was able to hold it together. "I was ready to give my whole heart to someone, and now here you are. The first time I saw you, you were like a light to my bug. I had to find you. You mesmerized me with how brightly you shone. Every time I look up at you, my heart fills with love sprinkles. Every time I kiss you, my whole body feels it. Sometimes I feel like I'm going to explode from how much I love you. I am completely consumed by you, and tonight we get to become one. I promise to love you until after my heart bursts. I promise to love you after our children are old and gray. I promise to love you after we can't even remember our own names. I will still know how fully I have loved you. You're my dream and my reality, my future and my present. My whole heart and my best friend. I thank God for bringing me to you, instilling that light so I could find you. I thank God for bringing you to me and igniting that same light. I can't wait to shine together and make everybody completely blind. I love you."

Her vows were loving, a little quirky, and wonderful. And while her words were still circling in my head—*I am like a "light to her bug"?*—my dad asked me to go ahead with the vows I'd written. I took a deep breath and tried to focus.

"From the moment I met you, I wanted more," I said, squeezing her hands. "I wanted more of your infectious smile, I wanted more of your adorable giggle, and I wanted more of your love. You had me hooked from the beginning, and I didn't want to let you go. We met in the strangest way you can possibly meet someone. On *The Bachelor*, with an army of people following us around with cameras, but I know that wasn't by accident."

Even though I'd sat down twenty times to write these lines, I felt like they'd come together perfectly.

"God says that all things work together for the good of those who love him. I know that we met on *The Bachelor* so that I could fall in love with my best friend. Every day I am encouraged by your love and your selflessness, and as your husband, I promise to always put you first. I promise to be the best father I can be to our children, and I promise to always make you laugh with my silly faces and ridiculous voices. So today, in front of my dad, my family, all of our friends, I want to say that I love you and I'm gonna love you for eternity."

Clay, my best man, brought up the rings. Instead of pulling out the Neil Lane rings, he pulled out a ring pop. We laughed and Catherine said, "Hey, I want that! I'm hungry."

After he pulled out the real rings, we slipped them on each other's fingers and each said, "With this ring, I pledge my love and loyalty to you for the rest of my life in the name of the Father, Son, and the Holy Spirit."

I swallowed hard, realizing that the God who brought us together will also keep us together.

"I've got one thing for you to remember for the rest of your life," my dad said. "Love God the most, and you will love each other more. Are you ready? This is about to happen!"

Everyone laughed, and I somehow kept the tears in.

"By the power vested in me as a minister of the gospel of Jesus Christ and the laws of California, I now pronounce you man and wife. You may kiss your bride."

It wasn't the first time we kissed on national television, but it was the first time we kissed as husband and wife.

"It is now my privilege and my honor to introduce to you Mr. and Mrs. Sean Lowe!"

The cameras swooped in, the confetti was thrown, and the ceremony was over.

At that point, I was overcome with emotion. As I made my exit, the cameras caught me crying like a baby.

I was a bachelor no more.

EPILOGUE

In all this, there was one moment I'll never forget.

It was in Thailand, just after the proposal. A few minutes after I got down on one knee, Mary Kate asked Catherine and me to sit down for our ITM.

"Both of us?"

"Yes," she said, motioning to a couple of chairs situated in front of the camera.

We sat down, holding hands, beaming from ear to ear. It was the first time I'd been interviewed by Mary Kate with another person.

"So," Mary Kate said with a smile, "how are you both feeling?"

"We're excited to start our lives together," I said, squeezing Catherine's hand.

"I've never been happier." She giggled.

After Catherine finished talking, I was thinking about how fun it was to be interviewed for the first time with her by my side. I was thinking of all the things we'd eventually do together as a couple—grocery shop, work out, teach our kids how to ride bikes. As my mind wandered, a sound tech came up.

"All right, you can unhook your mics now," he said.

Throughout the entire season—for ten weeks straight—everyone had been mic'ed up. In my case, I wore an elastic belt under my shirt that held the microphone in the back. The sound tech ran the wire up my shirt so the mic was near my mouth. Those little devices picked up everything, so I knew whatever I said could possibly be broadcast to millions of people. For weeks, I lived with that awareness at all times. I worried I would sneeze too loudly and burst some poor technician's eardrums. I worried I'd forget to turn off the mic when I went to the bathroom. I worried I'd say something that would be misconstrued.

After Catherine finished talking, the guy just stood there with his hand opened. He noticed I was standing still, seemingly immobilized by the simple request. "Do you, um . . . need help unhooking it?"

"No," I said, reaching under my shirt and handing him the device.

Wow, I remember thinking as he walked away. *It's over.*

When you are the Bachelor, it's easy to get caught up in the momentum and the glamour of the show. But life isn't normally televised. Conversations aren't evaluated by thousands on Twitter. Decisions aren't questioned by media personalities.

Most of life is lived unhooked. Unplugged. Unnoticed.

But don't be fooled. Everything that's really important happens when no one else is paying attention.

When I was on *The Bachelorette*, Emily often described me as "perfect." But I'm fallen, flawed, and in need of redemption. Thankfully, I had great parents who taught me how to be a good kid and then how to be a man. I'm still learning that.

My on-camera actions were only a reflection of all the years of living "unhooked"—of the moments when my dad pulled me aside as a kid and spanked my backside, when I was building character on the football field in high school, when I was reading my Bible during college, and even when I was learning from embarrassing mistakes after college. That day-in, day-out work of character development is tedious, boring, and just plain hard.

I sometimes failed.

One of the things I've seen throughout this process is this: only after I was faithful in the little things did I have the opportunity to be faithful in bigger things. I didn't show up one day on *The Bachelor* and suddenly have the chance to show America how to navigate the show with purity, honesty, and fairness.

I did my best to practice integrity every day as I went about my daily life. That meant I honored my parents, treated my girlfriends with respect, politely declined alcoholic drinks at parties before I was twenty-one, and worked hard at everything I tried to accomplish. That meant I cold-called potential insurance clients and tried not to be angry when they hung up on me. My life wasn't exciting, but it was training ground for how to make the right decisions—even if the decision was as seemingly insignificant as steeling my nerves and answering the call of disappointed, furious investors after I'd lost all their money.

All of these character-building moments happened when no one was watching. I made mistakes. But I repented and changed.

People often tell you to "live your dream." But I think the better advice is to be faithful. Treat people well, even when you don't feel like it. Tell the truth, even when it's complicated. Admit your mistakes, even when they make you look bad. In other words, don't save your integrity for the big moments. Practice it at all times so you actually have some when the big moments come.

In my case, that big moment was *The Bachelor*, a place where I was able to meet the girl of my dreams. Thankfully, I managed to do it in such a way that allowed both of us to draw closer to God.

Now we're moving back toward the "unplugged" life.

Since the wedding, Catherine and I have bought a house in Dallas, located near our favorite restaurants and within walking distance of many fun activities. The yard is fenced, so Lola and Ellie have a place to run. We're so happy to be in Dallas, though I'm not sure where I'll end up on—I'll go ahead and say it—my journey.

I heard *Bachelor* fans played a drinking game during my season, in which every time I said the word *journey*, people took a drink. They were making fun of the fact that this is the most overused word in the show.

But I know this. I used to pray as I drove to my job to sell insurance: "God, you know I don't want to live a normal life. If this is your will—if you *really* want me to sell insurance—I'll do it. But there has to be more."

This book ultimately showed where this prayer took me. Jeremiah 29:11 says, "'I know the plans I have for you,' says the LORD. 'They are plans for good and not for disaster, to give you a future and a hope.'"

As I look back at my life over the past few years, I'm thankful.

It definitely was a journey worth taking.

ACKNOWLEDGMENTS

Nancy, I couldn't have told my story without you, and for that I am so very grateful.

I'd like to thank Katherine Rowley and Kristen Parrish, whose edits made my story so much better.

I appreciate the hard work of the marketing team: Chad Cannon, Katy Boatman, and Tiffany Sawyer.

Thanks to Kristen Vasgaard for the great cover design.

My agent, Stéphanie Abou, whose charming French accent made all our conference calls much more interesting.

Thanks to Matt Kirschner for always seeing opportunities and believing in my potential. Thank you for orchestrating my life.

Of course, I need to express extreme gratitude to all the wonderful people at *The Bachelor*. You made the process so fun—I loved all the conversations and jokes that happened during the hurry-up-and-wait moments. I count you all as friends.

Specifically, Chris Harrison, you make roses and romance look manly.

Elan, your hair inspires me every day.

Martin, I so appreciated our late-night chat.

Cassie, thanks for your friendship.

Alycia, your kindness and love always showed up when I needed it the most.

Mansfield, you have such a servant's heart.

Bennett, thank you for encouraging me every step of the way.

Mike Fleiss, thanks for taking a chance on me.

Rob Mills, you are the coolest studio exec ever.

And to my family:

Mom, your love has made me the man I am today.

Dad, your pursuit of the Lord inspires me.

Papa, thank you for being the godly patriarch of our family.

Mimi, your humor and love are contagious.

Grandmother, you are the glue that holds our family together.

Shay and Andrew, I'm forever indebted to you.

And, Catherine, thanks for saying yes.

NOTES

1. Douglas S. Looney, "Futility U Kansas State, Winless Since 1986, Has One Claim to Fame: It Is America's Most Hapless Team," *Sports Illustrated*, September 4, 1989, http://sportsillustrated.cnn.com/vault/1989/09/04 /120464/futility-u-kansas-state-winless-since-1986-has-one-claim-to-fame -it-is-americas-most-hapless-team.
2. "The Brady 6," *The Year of the Quarterback*, Vinnie Malhotra, prod., ESPN documentary, aired April 12, 2011.
3. Author's best recollection of news article from that day.
4. Sarah Young, *Jesus Calling* (Nashville: Thomas Nelson, 2004), 14.
5. Sarah Young, *Jesus Calling* (Nashville: Thomas Nelson, 2004), 2.
6. Erykah Badu, "Tyrone," *Live*, Kedar Records/Universal, 1997.
7. Allison Corneau, *US Weekly*, "Chris Harrison: New Bachelor Sean Lowe Is 'So Sincere,'" October 30, 2012, http://www.usmagazine.com/entertainment /news/chris-harrison-new-bachelor-sean-lowe-is-so-sincere-20123010#ixzz 2ApHlZmFU.
8. 2Cellos.com, Biography, accessed July 7, 2014, http://www.2cellos.com/us /biography.

ABOUT THE AUTHORS

Sean Lowe, one of the three finalists on Emily Maynard's popular season of *The Bachelorette*, later starred in the 2013 season of *The Bachelor*. Credited by the New York Times for "reinvigorating the franchise," he has been voted America's favorite Bachelor and is the only one to marry his match from the show. Sean and his bride, Catherine, live in Dallas, Texas, with their two dogs, Ellie and Lola.

Nancy French is a three-time *New York Times* best-selling author who has written books with former Alaska Governor Sarah Palin, Chinese dissident Bob Fu, Iraq war vet and Constitutional lawyer David French, Olympic gold medalist Shawn Johnson, and Bristol Palin. Read about these—and other books—at www.NancyFrench.com and connect with her on Twitter at @NancyAFrench.